FREEDOM, NATURE, AND WORLD

DATE DUE

N

The University of Ottawa Press

Ottawa

LIBRARY AND ARCHIVES CANADA CATALOGUING IN PUBLICATION

Loptson, Peter
Freedom, nature, and world / Peter Loptson.

(Collection Philosophica, ISSN 1480-4670)
Includes bibliographical references and index.
ISBN 978-0-7766-0662-0

1. Philosophy. 2. Naturalism. I. Title. II. Series.

B995.L668F74 2007   191   C2007-906213-X

Published by the University of Ottawa Press, 2007
542 King Edward Avenue
Ottawa, Ontario K1N 6N5
www.uopress.uottawa.ca

The University of Ottawa Press acknowledges with gratitude the support
extended to its publishing list by Heritage Canada through its Book
Publishing Industry Development Program, by the Canada Council for
the Arts, by the Social Sciences and Humanities Research Council,
and by the University of Ottawa. We also gratefully acknowledge the
College of Arts at the University of Guelph whose financial support
has contributed to the publication of this book.

Typeset in 9.5 on 12 Book Antiqua by Brad Horning
Copy-edited by Elizabeth Macfie
Proofread by Sally Grey
Cover designed by Cathy MacLean Design

Printed and bound in Canada

TABLE OF CONTENTS

HISTORY OF PHILOSOPHY

HOMERIC TOPICS

They live and work thousands of kilometres apart.
One is a poet and playwright, another a philosopher,
the third a painter. Each one is a very dear friend,
whose company is a delight. I dedicate this book to them:
Derrek, Julian, and Janet.

INTRODUCTION

The papers in this volume derive from talks and presentations delivered to live audiences of fellow academic philosophers, academic non-philosophers, students, and others. All were given in the period 1998–2004, in settings such as Auckland (New Zealand), Detroit, Las Vegas, Vancouver, Winnipeg, and five cities in Ontario: Guelph, St. Catharines, Toronto, Waterloo, and Windsor. All were presented under the auspices of universities in those cities, even if not always at those universities' campuses.

Typically, presentations at academic conferences or to university audiences are intended to be way stations on the path to appearance in learned journals or as chapters of single-theme academic books, within a year or two of the presentation. The papers collected in this book, on the other hand, were more informal, or occasion-specific, or unconnected (at least in ways I grasped) to larger, focused topics. In one case — an earlier version of the paper on race in Hume and Kant — I did submit the piece for consideration for publication with a journal. While I received praising comments for style and scholarship, the paper wasn't accepted, primarily on the ground that the topic of Hume and race had been so definitively treated by Robert Palter in "Hume and Prejudice," published in *Hume Studies*, vol. xxi, no. 1, April 1995. As I have fairly recently become one of the editors of *Hume Studies*, I take this retrospectively both as praise and as a particularly stinging (if unintended) variety of rebuke. I entirely agree with the esteem in which Palter's paper is held. I hope, nonetheless, that the reader may find some novel features of merit (or demerit) in my own contribution to this complex issue. The two papers on naturalism included here are linked to a projected independent monograph on that theme, but each of them was written for an audience primarily of non-philosophers, and intended in a more general or diffuse way to make the topic intelligible and accessible and to try to show why a philosopher would see it as mattering.

In a rather obvious way, these 15 papers divide into a philosophy group and a classics group. Two of the essays concerned with topics in ancient Greek epic have also at least modest philosophical content, and seek to make philosophical argument. The third of the Homeric papers, with which the volume concludes, is a rather unremittingly pure classics piece, much of it quite speculative; it tends also to presuppose a greater familiarity with, and interest in, arcana posed by the early Greek epic. The more purely philosophical reader might well prefer to skip that essay. It is included as a kind of companion piece to the two other Homeric essays, the second of which also explores the speculative territory of where the puzzlingly complex and detailed early Greek mythical and legendary material comes from. In preparing these essays for this collection, I considered trying to make the last Homeric one more general, if not philosophical, in its message. I also considered whether to omit it altogether from the volume. The first course proved beyond me; I have allowed myself the indulgence of not surrendering to the probably wiser second option. I hope that some readers, addicted as so many are to interest in these wayward issues, may find something to please, instruct, or detain them in a positive way in its pages.

Apart, possibly, from the last piece, the volume has, I would contend, a comprehensive unity that will not be evident from first perusal. I will not exaggerate that unity; but the collection as a whole stems from a centredness in an enterprise of culture and reflection on nature and our place in it that began in the glorious dawn of ancient Ionia and continued in the early modern renewal and re-affirmation of enlightenment that remains, I think, the surest and brightest grounding of the current hour, and the path forward.

Let me expand upon the preceding somewhat vague, and formulaic or valedictory, remarks. Philosophically, I defend a position that I call (at least in one of the essays) *liberal naturalism*. This position is consciously adopted and intended as a respectful repudiation of the rational agency–based anti-naturalism brought fully explicitly into the philosophical world by Kant (a protoform of it appears in Plato), and prominently defended and regrounded, in different versions, in contemporary analytic philosophy by Wilfrid Sellars, Donald Davidson, Hilary Putnam, John McDowell, Robert Brandom, and others.

I specially note the respect in which this dissent or repudiation is couched. It is not so much the expression of academic courtesy, or of acknowledgment of the formidable array and the stature of philosophers on the other side of the issue, as an affirmation that rational agency is real, complex, and central for anything that can be an adequate account of the world and the place of human beings within it.

It also expresses the recognition that it is far from self-evident that rational agency can be accommodated, as I nonetheless believe that it can be, within a broadly naturalistic understanding of the world. This book includes essays that set out or explore different facets of this broadly (or liberal) naturalist understanding, with studies of naturalism itself; the conception of metaphysics within which liberal naturalism will have a plausible and identifiable place (as will some other metaphysical conceptions rival to it); explorations of the idea of human nature, which affirm the view that there is a human nature that encompasses both our animality and our reflective agency; and a schematic account of the origins and morphological structure of analytic philosophy that sees its two racinative wings as themselves of broadly naturalist coloration, at least in their "scientific modernist" and (as it happened) anti-Kantian foundations.

Other essays here, on the history of philosophy, explore aspects of the enduringly significant contributions of Hume, one of the early modern giants of the naturalist perspective, and also of Kant, who was a more thorough-going naturalist and scientific modernist—at any rate for the experienced knowable world—than his philosophical descendants of recent decades often emphasize or even, perhaps, discern. The philosophical aspects of the essays on Homer in this volume also rest on a universalism to be grasped in our understanding of what it is to be human beings in the world. That those two antique poems, from so long ago, should continue to resonate as widely, but also as deeply, reflectively, and existentially as they do, with awareness of differences but also of profound commonalities, speaks for the plausibility of situating ourselves in a natural world at least some of whose contours and content, within us as well as without, we can reasonably aspire to know.

I would like to acknowledge very helpful input on several of these papers from a number of readers, or from individuals present on occasions when they were given oral presentation. I particularly thank Andrew Bailey, John Bishop, Jack MacIntosh, Mark McCullagh, the late Graham Solomon, Catherine Wilson, and Julian Young.

I would also like to thank the University of Chicago Press for their generous permission to quote passages from the Richmond Lattimore translation of the *Illiad* published by them, originally, in 1951.

HUMAN NATURE

CHAPTER ONE

THE MIRROR'S REFLECTIONS AND THE CLOCKWORK BEHIND OUR SMILES
Human Nature, Agency, Spirit, and Mechanism

The original version of this paper was delivered as the keynote address at an annual philosophy conference at Brock University, in June 2002. The theme of the conference was human nature, science, and spirituality. One of the features of the conference was that not only was it open to non-philosophers in the university community, it was open as well to people in the community outside the university, with extensive publicity having encouraged their attendance. I have made a few modest changes to the text as written for that occasion, but this is essentially the paper as it was given.

We are told that during a very critical period in his early adult life, and possibly – the evidence is a bit oblique – during almost the whole of his later adult years, William James was preoccupied, sometimes obsessively and even morbidly preoccupied, by the problem of free will and determinism. It was for him a grim, deadly, haunting matter, depriving him of tranquility. The smooth, good-humoured, relaxed, knowing manner of so many of his essays — including ones where free will is a topic of focus — was, it seems, a façade. The inner man lived in dread that determinism was actually the truth of things, hence — as James supposed — that the free agency he cherished, and supposed humanity in general cherished with him, was an illusion and a hollow mockery. With all else that he was, James was a man for whom philosophy and its topics, some of them anyway, were living, inner stuff.

I do not share James's anxiety with respect to free will and determinism. I am persuaded of the view known among professional philosophers—though rarely so labelled beyond their discussions—as *compatibilism*. This is the view that actions can be both free—genuinely free—and determined—wholly, 100-percent predetermined. Some subtle issues—fine distinctions, and careful, delicate attention to ideas and applications of *modality* (that is, of necessity and possibility)—are involved in this matter. It takes patience, and a bit of focused navigation, to steer one's way through this ancient problem, and to arrive, as I (and a number of others) maintain, at a resolution of it that will allow us to unite a rich and confident vindication of our free agency with a wholly scientific view of the world.

James himself was aware, or at least partially aware, of the compatibilism option. It provided no solace or satisfaction for him. It was James who famously drew a distinction, which many have utilized since, between what he called hard and soft determinism. The latter was supposed to be something like what we now call compatibilism, and James had no patience with it. He thought it a paltry evasion. The real determinism, he held, the one that terrified him, was hard determinism. That was the theory he hoped was mistaken, but feared might not be.

I will not explore this issue further. Rightly or wrongly, I am myself at peace on the topic. A free predetermined act is not a square circle, even if it takes at least a bit of care to show this. I do, however, have a care or concern that is at least a cousin of James's, and one of my themes on this occasion is to raise and explore it.

I will enlarge upon that theme, and set it on the table before you along with other, related topics that I would like to discuss. But first I need to acquaint you with a background of perspective and assumptions that may, I hope, make my several topics resonate or appear to matter.

The broad philosophical point of view I adhere to is, in the way of philosophical points of view, just one of several in current contention in philosophy. Although I see it as fundamentally commonsensical as well as correct, this view is not, I think, readily *identified* as a perspective or general view, even among academic philosophers. *A fortiori*, it is not well known beyond the debates of professional philosophers, and certainly not as a perspective that a philosopher might explicitly or usefully bring to broad public discussion of human nature, science, and spirituality, this occasion's large theme.

Unfortunately, even within academic philosophy, what I am wanting to call a perspective, even a party, does not have a common, usual, or familiar name. Some party, one may well feel, if it lacks a name. Nonetheless, there's little doubt, I believe, that a considerable body of contemporary philosophers share the outlook I refer to. I will call this outlook *liberal naturalism*.[1]

Perhaps this broad view may most usefully and clearly be explained by contrast with another widely held philosophical view. So before coming to my own position, I will tell you of that one. The late Wilfrid Sellars drew a distinction between what he, and many others, regarded as separate, in fact mutually alien, thought-worlds, both of which, even though they are incompatible, make strong — in fact, compelling — claim upon the serious contemporary philosophical mind. One is the thought-world of physical science — supremely, theoretical physics. Natural science has been, from its inception, in the business of aiming at comprehensive theoretical understanding of the universe. In a punctuated equilibrium of stages since the early 17th century, it has met with extraordinary success, in both practical and purely intellectual terms, in its endeavours. For Sellars, and for a wide current of philosophical thinkers in and since the 17th century — and among whom I certainly number myself — that success cannot fail to be reckoned with, and indeed factored into, any plausible or serious attempt to make sense of things in general.

From the middle 17th century onwards, undertakings have been made to extend the stunning theoretical and applied success of physics — the natural philosophy of particles of matter in motion, and of waves and fields — to the living, animate, thinking, conscious, human, and social parts of the world. Hobbes is perhaps the earliest clear exemplar of this enterprise. Other 17th-century figures are muddier, though several make some further contribution to this work. In the 18th century, the large project that the 20th century came to call *scientific philosophy* was fully launched. (The phrase seems to be due to Reichenbach, who was certainly also a major practitioner.) Scientific philosophy is totalizing: for it, no sector of the real is beyond the sphere of naturalist, law-like, unitary understanding, an understanding within which theoretical physics will have a central place. Scientific philosophy, in its several forms and varieties — prominent names are Hume, La Mettrie, Mill, Russell, Reichenbach, Carnap, Ayer, Quine — is the systematic or developed expression of one of Sellars' two deep perspectives, which he calls the scientific image.

The other perspective, or thought-world, he calls the manifest image. This is the sphere and the conceptual space, and vocabulary, of agency, consciousness, and subjecthood or being a person. Carrying out deliberations, performing actions, for reasons, placing value upon alternatives, and upon other states of the world, understanding and interpreting one's own purposes and their consequences as well as those of other agents, participating interactively in the creation and maintenance of personal, social, cultural, symbolic, and theoretical institutions. This framework of concept and what we suppose is fact constitutes the manifest image.[2]

For Sellars, and for many other philosophers, setting out and trying to bring into a larger unitary framework of understanding the world of persons and their meaningful actions and interactions, and the world that theoretical physics brings to our attention, is a major — possibly the major — problem of modern philosophy. It is a *problem*, as Sellars sees it, because there is a *tension*, a deep and very real tension, if not inherently in these two *worlds*, then certainly in the complex and independently highly structured theoretical ideas we have of these two worlds. Sellars sees this problem as clearly and explicitly grasped first by Kant. Only with him, for Sellars, is the *bite* of the problem really taken in. Moreover, it is a signal part of Kant's towering philosophical stature that at least a version of his own proposed solution to this fundamental problem is still a viable contender for its final and definitive solution.

For Sellars, any adequate solution to the problem of the mutual relations of the scientific image and the manifest image will and must see that both images are serious, compelling, and non-dismissible, and that there is a conceptual abyss — an abyss beyond our powers to bridge — between them.

In different ways and with distinct formulations, two other prominent philosophical contemporaries of Sellars, namely Donald Davidson and Hilary Putnam, arrived at much the same outcome. (Like him too, Davidson and Putnam at least sometimes situate their own analyses under the commanding foundational aegis of Kant.) Their *solutions* differ, but, like Sellars, they too see, not a clash, but a chasm of content between persons and physics.

I hope that I have not oversold the Sellarsian stance, investing it as I have not only with argument, but also the weight of solemn authority. For a central part of the "perspective" whose identity I signalled and whose content I postponed — the position that I myself defend — is the view that the Kant-Sellars-Davidson-Putnam stance is wrong. Duly mindful of what I agree are big differences, I — and those of like mind — don't see why the broad project of *inquiry* can't encompass those differences, with at least partial looping together of commonalities that are to be found widely in the universe in its disparate sectors, in spite of those differences. We are animals as well as persons; also material objects. Some of our group structures and arrangements bear arresting similarity to those among baboon troops, ants, and bees. We may not *be* computers, and parallels between our cognitive states and some of theirs may sometimes have been overstated, but it is a mistake that there aren't still *some* significant commonalities. Other primates have proto-versions of morality and art, and certainly rich emotional lives, including a sense of humour. Still other animals have something approximating a sense of honour, and dignity.

I should perhaps remark that by "the broad project of inquiry" I mean the disparate, not necessarily organized, aggregate of questions and investigations brought to the world. Why is the sky blue (when it is)? What formed the stars? Why is gas cheaper in Saudi Arabia than in Guatemala? Why did Oswald assassinate Kennedy? Are there reliable and predictable economic cycles? At what rate or rates do objects fall if dropped from tall buildings? What caused the Franco-Prussian War? Are bats more like dolphins than like birds? Will there be another ice age? And what produces ice ages anyway? Etc., etc. Broad inquiry *as such* doesn't *assume* that it is conceptually or in any other way more appropriate, or "basic," to undertake inquiry about the world beginning first with inanimate material objects, still less with the simplest known items of theoretical physics, rather than, say, with features of human experience, or with daffodils — or anywhere else. It might of course *turn out* that there were good reasons to organize results of broad inquiry into theoretical structures where things involving inanimate material objects (or things they analyzed or reduced to material objects) were more fundamental. But just exploring the world, as such, wouldn't take this for granted. The rejection of the Sellarsian distinction between the scientific and manifest images would aim to restore inquiry to a pre-Kantian location (more precisely, to the century and a little more preceding the publication of the first *Critique*) — to a place correctly identified, I think, by another advocate of Sellars' polarity, John McDowell (in *Mind and World*), but wrongly repudiated by him.

In sum, the case is pretty good for a broad naturalism that will include human beings among other animal species — and, acknowledging that we are unique, affirm that so too are they. Further, differences between some of the special things we do and are and other parts of nature are not unique. Boundaries and theoretical subsumption under something more basic are also challenging, and complex, for living and nonliving systems, for example, and their mutual relations. We tend to assume that they are more easily soluble because they are remote, not so obviously connected to the observable, nor so much a matter of *us*.

My liberal naturalism, however, I want to stress, does not adopt a position of dismissive elimination of the mental, social, symbolic, or personal. In this, it differentiates itself from much of the scientific philosophy with which it otherwise has kinship. Although Sellars himself denied that this was possible — he in fact referred to such a hope as comparable to a child's petulant or wistful desire to have *both* of two uncombinable options[3] — my party, or school, thinks that an adequate theoretical understanding of the world can, will, and indeed must comprehend both — both physics, and persons and their products. Liberal naturalism proceeds with the methodological commitment, and conviction, that it is not clear, or obvious, or true, that there are distinct images, or realms, or thought-worlds, in the first place (or in the middle place, or the last place); that inquiry and understanding are fundamentally things of the same sort, whatever subjects engage in them, and whatever their objects; and that since consciousness is as real as amino acids, or quarks or comets, a theory must include real versions, and not mere simulacra, of all of them in order to offer a complete or comprehensive theory of all that there is in the world.

My purpose here, though, is not to try to win converts to liberal naturalism. Sophisticated neo-Kantians and other anti-unitarians will know at least much of the biological literature, and still not be persuaded. There is, it is important to say, what may be called a *meta-naturalism* that more or less everyone shares. Everyone knows that we operate on a substructure of bodily physical systems, without which no books are written, songs sung, laws promulgated, or trade unions or missions launched. Decapitation is at least as effective a preventive of a maestro's next symphony, or political tract, as is writer's block, or art-abandoning religious conversion.

Moreover, with the tide of anti-Cartesian affirmation of our embodiment that is to be met with from feminists, Derrideans, and others, following upon earlier like claims from Aristotle, Ryle, Merleau-Ponty, and analytic materialism in the philosophy of mind, hardly anyone among academic philosophers now officially asserts psycho-physical (substance) dualist views. *Methodological* dualism runs rampant—as it should do, since impressive theoretical assimilations of mind to body remain a still-distant fond hope (or, of course, for others, a fear).

But—mindful that human beings, like other animals, and their bodies, are material things—almost everyone's general theoretical stance, in current philosophy, is avowedly materialist. And hardly anyone, even few theists (and there remain of course *many* strong and committed theists), believes that ongoing life involves, in any regular or expectable way, interventions from outside the natural and human orders.

My aim is to paint a picture of these two large oppositional stances: liberal naturalism and what I have elsewhere called two-worlds inscrutabilism. (Kant and Sellars both speak for the two worlds, but only Kant speaks for the eternal inaccessibility of what may lie behind either.) Then I want to share with you my James-like occasional nightmare. And after that, ponder about what might be a non-Kantian way to dispel that nightmare, but with a chastened sense of our horizons and the deep uncertainty of much of what goes on in us. I will argue that it would be a mistake to restore Aristotle to the throne he once occupied[4] or in general to be over-sanguine about what we think we see in the mirror's reflections (that is, to a straightforward acceptance of manifest or common-sense views of ourselves). Finally I want to explore briefly and speculatively some possibilities, or possible possibilities, in the domain of spirit.

The issue whether all the world's states, events, and processes are predetermined—instances of exceptionless laws of nature, oak trees (so to speak) altogether the diachronic unravelling of prior sets of acorns—is abstract, complex, and conceptually high-planc. Equally so is whether the abstract structure of a deterministic world may be married with the reality and activities of free, rational, deliberating choosers. As I have indicated, I believe that that union is viable, and hence that James's anxiety in this regard was unfounded.

There is, however, a closer-to-the-ground basis for a different anxiety. It is that even if free rational agents are possible, perhaps compatibly with determinism, we humans are not such creatures.

Conceptions of marked limitation in our supposed free rational agency, which nonetheless do not see that freedom as shrinking to nothing, seem first to appear among some of the ancient Stoics. That school taught that we should accept that our genuine freedom is restricted to what is wholly within our power, or up to us, and that in turn is confined to *attitudes* we are free to adopt with respect to what befalls us — as opposed to *actions* we may undertake to perform. I am not even free, it seems, for the Stoics, with respect to whether to pass by a tree in my path by its left or by its right, since nature must cooperate with what I may have resolved upon, and that nature, including quite a lot of the operations of my own body that will be involved, is beyond my command.

The appearance/reality contrast is of course the oldest in philosophy. It is what started the subject, with Thales propounding the idea that all sorts of things that do not *appear* to be water nonetheless are. The contrast persists through all successive centuries to the present one. It is important to recognize that it takes two fundamental and distinct forms: the idea that the appearances are illusions, or counterfeits, the reality they conceal having to be discerned through those illusions; and the really quite different idea that the reality is made up of, constituted by, and analyzable into those appearances, which are its elements. (Sometimes the second idea works the other way round, with the elements being the realities that constitute the appearance. An example of such constitution is hydrogen and oxygen, in the right proportions, constituting water. An example of the other sort of composition is the phenomenalist claim that physical objects are sets of actual and possible sensory experiences.)

At any rate, this antique foundational philosophical contrast readily attaches itself to our agency. Is it reality? Or mere appearance?

Granting, as we have done, that our agency *could* be both — some things both are and appear to be water, of course — there will remain the question whether it really is anything other than mere appearance, i.e., pure illusion. Reasons to suspect the latter have presented themselves from three sources: social, psychological, and biophysiological.

The first of these no longer detains many; certainly not many philosophers. We are, no doubt about it, of individually distinctive sex, gender, historical location, socio-economic status and/or class and cultural origins and formation. We are first-, second-, or third-worlders, heterosexual, bisexual, speakers of some languages (quite regularly, just of one) and not of any of the rest, and doubtless have other basic-level background, identity-forming components in our makeup. These without doubt shape, mould, predispose, and sometimes blinker us. It is significantly less plausible that any of them unalterably compel us, or preclude any chance that we can stand back from these factors and formations, and view many or most (in some of our cases, all of them) with cool, detached analytical rationality, or with irony, and some significant degree of understanding.

This may seem to some too quick a summation and dismissal of the idea that our sociality, our contextuality, pre-empts meaningful individual autonomy for us. Indeed, for some the very idea of such individual autonomy starts too far forward in a tale needing more fundamental reconceptualization.

One of the prominent — indeed, some would say dominant — ideas of our time is the notion of the social construction of reality. For some, this is the total construction of all of reality; for others, it is more particularized, as, for example, the social construction of psychosis, or gender, or truth, or Canadian identity, or crime, or adolescence. Ian Hacking has an interesting list of the extraordinary range of candidate cases that have been proposed in the literature of the subject, in his valuable, if, I think, not as successfully-ecumenical-as-hoped recent book *The Social Construction of What?*[5]

At any rate, individual human identity is a natural and regularly encountered instance of this prominent notion. As Hacking, and others, show, I think, it is not altogether clear what social construction theses mean to assert. Does something socially constructed actually *exist*, for example? Is it that it does, and how it came to be was through this special mechanism of social construction? Or rather that it doesn't really exist, it just seems to, with some social constructing that was taking place creating the appearance — the illusion — that a truly existing thing was there? And is it literally supposed to be the *thing* that was socially constructed, or rather the *ideas* we have of the thing that was?

These things will matter, and not just metaphysically, because if there is actually not really any such thing as you, or me, or anyone else, then there would seem to be nothing of James's — or my — kind to worry about; nor indeed any basis, or foothold, for theories of any sort about what our natures are. On the other hand, if social construction was simply the *route*, or causal mechanism, by which we got here — rather like the fact that physical construction was how, say, the Eiffel Tower, got here, and is, once here, as real and solid and particular and individual as anything is — then, once here, it may not matter very much what our causal formation was: we can be as sanguine, or pessimist, as we may see ground to be, independently.

This is obviously a large and complex territory. I shall assume that we exist, each of us, individually, separately, and privately. I do not assume — and do not believe — that we would have been able to do this without networks, sometimes in the background, sometimes foregrounded, of familial, socio-cultural, biophysiological, ecological sorts, that operate in some manner and degree to shape and constitute us as we become or find ourselves. Still, we were born alone and we die alone, and there is in a basic and ontological sense a "we" to whom these, and events between, happen. At least, if there is *not*, it is not because of realities of social or cultural formation that there is not, but rather because of a quite different kind of reason.

Daniel Dennett's 1984 book *Elbow Room: The Varieties of Free Will Worth Wanting*[6] seeks to confront and overcome concerns one might have about what determinism might imply that we might not like. Dennett is characteristically fun to read, lively, imaginative, and well-informed about lots of relevant psychology and about neuroscience, and *Elbow Room* is vintage Dennett in all of these respects. Still, it does provide at least the outline of what I see, at least some of the time, as a real and unattractive possibility for our case. (Dennett's own view seems to be that this possibility is the actual truth, but that we can find grounds for not seeing it as unattractive, or worrisome, at all. We shall see.)

Dennett describes—or quotes an entomologist who describes—the behaviour of a digger wasp, *Sphex ichneumoneus*. This creature carries out an elaborate egg-laying routine, which involves paralyzing but not killing a cricket, and laying the wasp's eggs alongside the cricket, burying the lot (but not too deeply), with the result that the hatched offspring will be able to feed on the cricket's body. The wasp drags the cricket to its burrow, and before bringing it inside, lays it down and goes inside to check the burrow before returning to get it. What entomologists discovered was that if the cricket is moved from where the sphex has left it, when the latter emerges from the burrow it will once again drag the cricket to where it had previously placed it, and once again will go inside the burrow to—"*check*" doesn't really seem to be the right term. And it will keep doing this no matter how often the cricket is moved. On one occasion the observer—surely a wicked scientist if ever there was one—moved the cricket 40 times, and each time the sphex repeated her ritual.

The worry Dennett brings to the table from this example is this: might we be, in fact, altogether "sphexish" in our behaviour? That is, might we not be wholly routinized creatures, the routines, including what we think are volitional ones, simply being too complex, or operative in too non-obviously patterned a set of ways—a cunning of reason, that is, of natural selection—too subtle for us to notice, except very occasionally?

A related, if formally independent, concern, comes from cognitive science conceptions of human intelligence as a case of a so-called parallel distributive network. (One version of this conception is standardly called connectionism.) According to this idea, our intelligence is not actually unitary, but rather consists of a set of more or less autonomous subsystems that carry out discrete cognitive and affective functions. For connectionism, as for rival "modular" theories advanced in cognitive science modellings of the mind, there is no commitment to the idea that among this set of subsystems there is a conscious module (or instantiator of a "node") that coordinates any substantial subset of the others. The more "sphexish" variants of the modular idea explicitly deny that there is an "overseer" module, the illusion that there is one being achieved by content flow, often convergent, from activity in some modules to activity in others that they causally produce.

What I will, following Dennett, call the "sphexish" worry is the worry that, in effect, lights are on, but no one is home. It is the fear that our consciousness is not truly unitary, even on a single occasion or fairly closely connected set of occasions, that episodes, reactions, impulses are triggered, and rather fast-acting electrical currents in our brains compose affective, cognitive, or other mental states and sequences for us that constitute a façade and not a reality of a person. This is not particularly an anxiety that our mental states, singly or in their aggregations, may have been produced by networked electrochemical states in our brains. It is the anxiety that—however produced—our participations in the psychic events of our lives are not connected to each other by a logic of our resolutions, inferences, loves, or fears.

This is not the mere fear that we may not be rational agents, controlling and directing long- and short-term trajectories of what has significance for us. I myself have long been drawn, at least some of the time, to dark and pessimist philosophy of human nature, in the forms it takes in the Stoics, Spinoza, Schopenhauer, and Freud. These are views for which we are dark forests through which we wander, flee, or are driven in large-scale ignorance of our real motivations, enacting and re-enacting scripts of passion that we did not originate and can modify little if at all. But at least for these views — Freud's, and the others — there is a me to whom all this happens; it is unitary, and, interestingly, it brings to its world, and responds to, clusters of meanings. I may be a prisoner of my fate on such perspectives, but I at least have a fate, and it has meaning — indeed, part of what is ultimately implausible about these views is how heavy a load of meaning they involve. There is for Freud's human being, like Spinoza's and Schopenhauer's, what their life has been about (whether or not each individual can hope to put it together).

The sphexish alternative implies that all of *that*, and not just our rational agency, is illusion. It is an old fear, this one. It is the fear that we, and the very operations of consciousness within us, are mechanisms. This fear was generated historically by Cartesian philosophy. And that what it fears really is the case was asserted triumphally by that neglected second-rung eighteenth-century philosopher of genius, La Mettrie, in his "L'Homme Machine."

It may or may not be precisely the same idea, but another articulation of this feared view would understand it as the conception that our belief-desire clusters — the aggregations that common sense says produce what we do — are (at best) entirely *epiphenomenal*, the real causes of our behaviour (including our inner mental episodes) being nonmental states of our bodies, or — hardly any less worrying — that this is true of *almost* all (even if not literally quite all) of our behaviour.

There appear in fact to be *two* components of the fearsome possibility identified, logically independent of each other. One is that our lives, either as wholes or in significant parts (runs of years, say), might *make no sense* as bodies of things we have planned, wanted, and cared about (even though they will, of course, make naturalistic causal sense, and even if isolated chunks — episodes of several hours, say — might make rational belief-desire sense). The other is that there *is* a rational sense-making scenario that most, or big chunks, of our lives have been "informed by," but that this scenario (or these scenarios) have been almost or entirely epiphenomenal — *they* weren't involved, causally, in producing what we, by the ends of our lives, will have done.

Having exposed my nightmare to you, I won't linger further on it. Most of the time — 13 days of every fortnight — I seriously do not believe that it is correct; and the very difficulty of formulating with precision just what the "it" is — for a mechanist non-self view of humans is difficult to give detailed content to[7] — encourages me to believe that I am right. Yet, maybe, just maybe, we are sphex-like, mechanisms. And if so, the dread that we might be will itself be just a bunch of blips of mind/brain dotwork that something occasionally wheels into short-term alignment while the dot-obscuring light of consciousness is switched on.

As I have indicated, my view is that the significant contenders for offering substantive, explanatorily satisfying accounts of human behaviour and human nature, are almost entirely individualist, i.e., focused on the formation of each of the individuals that we are, even if — of course — fitting and suiting the members of a biological species and their commonalities. All such theories will and must be bio-based. We are animals, after all. And primates. We share 99 percent of our genetic makeup with chimpanzees. This has got to mean something in understanding not only what but who we are. Anyone without utterly blinding glasses on must recognize echoes, shadows, and parallels in the rich and growing ethological accounts of chimpanzee and other primate — especially higher primate — behaviour, with their clear, I think compelling, accounts of cousins of what we know in ourselves as humour, fear, sorrow, morality, boredom-affliction, and boredom-avoidance patterns.

Still, I believe that Darwin goes only so far, and does only so much for us. Darwin himself believed this also, I would say, as careful reading of *The Descent of Man* will confirm. Sociobiology, and its cousin evolutionary psychology, are I think, mostly non-starters. (Some leading contemporary evolutionary biologists — Steve Jones is one — share this view, by the way.) They — sociobiology and evolutionary psychology — plausibly explain so little, they are so easily, sometimes laughably, prone to unfalsifiable hypotheses. Too many of us are indifferent to having progeny, or siblings, or first, second, or third cousins, who carry out alleged genetic imperatives for us. Too many with progeny are indifferent to what befalls them. Too much of what we seem genuinely to want to do appears patently not to contribute anything at all to the survival of our genes. These considerations will not, of course, make it unlikely—surely indeed it is overwhelmingly probable—that *much* human behaviour is explicable in evolutionary terms. But sociobiology/ evolutionary psychology claim that the *core* of understanding us is to be identified in terms of natural selection.

Two recent developments on the human nature front seem especially to point to the fact that the brief sun of sociobiological accounts of us is soon altogether to set, or — really the same thing — retreat into mere philosophy, like Marxism or psychoanalysis. One is the particularly trumpeted recent disclosures of the Human Genome Project. Held so prominently to underscore and confirm our biologicality, our ineluctable housing within multiple genetic constraint and imperative, they in fact have the opposite consequence. It seems impressive that we share 99 percent of our genes with chimpanzees. It is a lot less impressive, I would say, that we have only a little more than twice as many genes as a fruit fly, that we share 10 percent of our genes with those same fruit flies, and that human and rodent—mouse—protein sequences are 95.3-percent identical.

These findings confirm our biologicality, to be sure—if that had ever, since Aristotle, been in serious doubt. They also show the conceptual and explanatory vacuity of much, maybe most, of that biologicality. One is reminded by these findings of Robert Boyle's corpuscularian theory. All of material being, the nonliving as well as the living things, are composed of *matter*, which Boyle supposed to be a real stuff or element, moreover rich with explanatory and unifying promise. But how helpful will it be, for understanding, say, why the Portuguese have become genuine democrats, or Churchill painted in his leisure hours, or blank verse lyric poetry developed in northwest Europe, or Bantu languages became dominant in most of southern Africa, or—to take a more universal case—that more or less all human societies have had religions, and incest taboos, that all the relevant humans were composed of matter? Boyle's material stuff theory says that everything (with the exception, for Boyle, of our rational souls) is composed of, and is to be explained by, principles of matter. True, one may well want to agree, as also with not merely our biologicality, but our specifically *genetic* biologicality. But how helpful will either theory be if we want to know about squirrels or boulders or people? Stuff 95.3 percent of which we share with mice cannot be expected to be very useful for understanding or explaining what or who we are, or what we do and why we do it.

The second development with dark consequence for sociobiology is what I see as a revival of a leading contender for human explanation before Darwin-derived theory appeared prominently on the scene: game-theoretic explanation. Again sociobiological eclipse gets concealed in this development, because proponents of new-game theory proffer their accounts as dictates of natural selection. But they, patently, are not. Individuals can—and do—seek benefit, and advantage, without being the thralls of selfish genes. In point just of *theory*, a model that analyses individual and interactive behaviour by reference to strategies for advantage, in terms of levels of comfort and well-being (caloric intake, ease from numbing physical labour, aesthetic tranquility, and other things), simply does not have to feature gene-proliferation prominently among the goals or goods of the components of the relevant systems; game theory as such will simply not point to any such aim as an irremovable part of benefit-seeking strategizing in its cunning and sophisticated members. Of course we are biological creatures. But either we see that fact as implying that we each and all of us are going about, alpha and omega, first and last, in our deeds and doings, as gene-proliferators, or we do not. And *game theory* certainly does not need to see us as doing anything of the kind.

I do not have time to do other than essentially list them, with my more-or-less dogmatic commentary, but the leading serious current contenders for human nature theory are, I believe, some sophisticated version of game theory, a cultural materialist theory of the sort developed by Marvin Harris — and these contenders might be united in a single comprehensive view — a physiological mechanist ("sphexish") theory, and, perhaps, some others.

One option has particular interest for me. This one, which I think may possibly be true, is a theory that sees us as mostly a complex of functional bio-based strategies and drives, but with occasional emergence into a genuine personhood that sufficient and the right sort of drive-satisfaction has purchased for and permitted us. This last would not quite be the common sense or manifest image — the mirror's reflection.

And here let me pause to say that I think that no philosophy of human nature that sees us, qua human-natured, simply and altogether on the surface of things, as *just* agents (even if in varying degree of command or knowledge of our agency), can be right. Nor likewise a theory — like Aristotle's — which adds to agency some extra baggage of distinctive species or individual non-rational nature that is just left permanently and in principle inexplicable.

The human nature option I want to suggest here instead would certainly envisage some degree of genuine agency, and episodes, sometimes of quite extended duration, of consciousness in which we have become participants in theory, art, social action, knowledge of others, knowledge of that created and only sometimes non-sleeping self, awakened from dormancy in this bought or borrowed time; and hold otherwise that our behaviour is more automated and mechanized, or unconsciously prodded, than we would perhaps be ready or happy to acknowledge.

This is so brief a sketch of what I have in mind that it may not have been worth even its intimation. But it will allow me to go on to some concluding remarks about spirit.

Philosophy turned its attention to human beings, their natures, and the principles of their behaviour very early; with

Pythagoras, in fact. Soon afterward, we find the idea that there is a significant contrast between what we think we are and what we actually are: the (mere) appearance and reality polarity applied to ourselves. Initially, this is just a modest elaboration on the idea that people are frequently self-deceived—an idea that shows up prominently, and significantly, in Homer's *Iliad* (where characters are often called fools for having mistakenly thought that they could best much stronger warriors, or gain wealth or other prizes that are altogether beyond them).

Heraclitus, Socrates, Plato, and the Stoics, all, in different ways, contribute to or expand the notion that what we take to be the mainsprings of our natures, possibilities, and actions—the mirror's reflections, again—just aren't so. We are, in general, most of us—for some of the philosophers all of us—neither as free or as rational, nor as capable of happiness, as we commonly suppose. We are the puppets of our passions or appetitive drives. The best we can, typically, manage is to acknowledge, in the phrasing both of Ovid and the New Testament, that we see what is better and approve it, but follow what is worse. The point, though, is not just, or perhaps even primarily, ethical. It is not that we fall short of higher ideals or values, that we err or sin; it is that we aren't really constituted to seek or equipped to realize those virtuous, and rational ideals in the first place.

From the days of Heraclitus to—perhaps one might say—the day before yesterday, there were widely held to be two possible avenues to escape from our blighted darkness: philosophy or transformation through religious faith. Reason or grace. Ironically, perhaps, the second would seem to be, at least relatively speaking, the more plausible of the two, at any rate as an avenue to satisfactory selfhood. For after all, if we really had been capable of doing it on our own—organizing our lives and interactions sensibly, so that we could achieve happiness internally and externally—surely we would have done it, individually in each of our life's odysseys, and collectively, communally, long ago. The Christian idea that we need another, a supernatural shoulder at the wheel, to co-produce, with us, satisfactory human life-scripts, may seem at least truer to the record of our patterns and failures they so commonly produce. Of course there is the matter of whether there is any good reason to believe that there are any other shoulders than our own; but that is a different issue.

I do not myself believe that it is probable that there are any such shoulders, or any magnificent significantly higher being. On the other hand, unlike some with whom I otherwise have much agreement philosophically, I do not believe that there are devastating or compelling arguments that refute the very possibility of such a being. We are rather in the dark, as I see it, as to what sorts of minds *may* share the universe with us, or have been involved in our being here ourselves. This stance is too weak to call it any variety of theism. It is not; and I am an atheist.

But many hypotheses that one doesn't expect to turn out true actually do. And many are true though we will never know that they are. The existence of occasional personhood in the careers of the biological/functional mechanisms that we seem otherwise to be cannot, if real, be magical. Its aetiology will not require a God, or higher spirit. Yet, if there is one, things would make a sort of post-facto sense: our personhood, fashioned indeed out of what Kant called the crooked timber of humanity, and the world such a being could have willed a wholly and altogether natural place — a place love for the possibility of which would moreover have created a superabundance of beetles, to paraphrase Haldane. The personhood we sometimes know, or occupy, is one of inward subjecthood — endedness, being an end — and also one of communion, of recognition or acknowledgment of others as ends. I conclude then with what may surprise you as salutation of the extraordinary power and depth of the philosophical insight of Kant. And maybe, just maybe, he was right.

I should perhaps explain a little more explicitly what I mean, in this context, by Kant's being right. Kant was an unqualified scientific modernist, at any rate for the experienced world. He produced what are widely regarded as the most comprehensive and devastating critiques of traditional theism, except for those of Hume, that philosophy has ever developed. At the same time, Kant came up with his own independent argument for theism, usually called the moral argument for the existence of God.

I cannot engage here the complex issues of scholarship this latter argument raises, but it does seem probable that it is not intended to be an argument on the same plane of rational or empirical inquiry as the arguments it is supposed to displace. Kant's largest philosophical commitments are to the reality and the inscrutability of the world beyond and behind our experiences. Rational agency — personhood — provides us with an oblique indication of what that world may partly include. As in his moral philosophy, indeed as an enlargement of it, Kant sees neither the postulate of personhood nor a world in which it is a reality as altogether intelligible if personhood does not find fulfilment in enduring community; that is, in an enduring community of persons under the coordination of a creative foundational person.

Philosophies of the anti-theistic varieties brought into the world in the European Enlightenment, more specifically in the wake of Bayle's *Dictionary*, affirm not only the unity of the one natural world, but also its ultimate normative emptiness. Nihilist, existentialist, and other naturalizing philosophies have affirmed, implausibly, that if God is unreal, then everything is permitted; more plausibly, a declared absurdity of the world, with which we must all of us, if we are intellectually honest, contend. This is, in fact, what I myself believe.

Kant's claim, in the moral argument, is, I think, that there is a more than merely ethical absurdity implied by the world producing actual *persons* — even if they are only occasionally, and superveniently, persons, in a full cognitively and axiologically integrated and integrating way — where that personhood would be wholly futile and appear in the world only to disappear in the endless night that all our evidence points to as the world's fate. Kant's claim, I think, is that the world cannot fundamentally make sense, that there is an ineluctable explanatory or intelligibility incoherence, if that is its case, ultimately and inherently.

As I say, I think that the world probably is absurd in just this way. But—I think—the sphexish option is a real, if unlikely, script for what we suppose is personhood. And the Kantian option is also a real, if unlikely, script for the same thing.

And with that triptych, I close.[8]

NOTES

1 The position I mean to identify by this term is close to the one that John McDowell calls "bald naturalism." (See John McDowell, *Mind and World* (with a new introduction by the author) (Cambridge, MA: Harvard University Press, 1996), p. xviiif. I hesitate to identify them partly on grounds of aesthetic disdain for the adjective in McDowell's term, but more seriously and substantively because McDowell is particularly concerned with explorations of our concepts and how we obtain them. Liberal naturalism, as I mean it, need not advocate a classically empiricist view of the origins of concepts; indeed, it would in principle be compatible with more theories than one about concept formation, or even an agnostic or fence-sitting stance.

2 The *locus classicus* of Sellars' distinction is his paper "Philosophy and the Scientific Image of Man," originally delivered in 1960, subsequently published in 1962, and reprinted in Wilfrid Sellars, *Science, Perception and Reality* (Ridgeview, 1963 and 1991).

3 "Philosophy and the Scientific Image of Man" (1991), p. 32.

4 This is undoubtedly a somewhat tendentious way to express what is a preferred option for some philosophers not only of Thomist or Neo-Thomist orientation. John McDowell's "second nature" conception is a central example of the *Aristotelian restoration* predilection.

5 Cambridge, MA: Harvard University Press, 1999.

6 Cambridge, MA: MIT Press, 1984.

7 Mechanism is not the same thing as determinism. Mechanism need not, in fact, *imply* determinism. (Mechanism is, informally, "machinism," and states of machines could presumably be produced indeterministically, just as states of non-machines might be.) It is not even clear that mechanism need imply materialism. It appears possible to conceive of a kind of dualistic automaton, some of whose states were non-physically mental, but all of whose

states were robotic and machine-like. What seems crucial for personhood — hence excluded from a (supposed) person's being (in fact) a mechanism — is being something whose beliefs and desires comprise clusters or patterns of *reasons* that successfully *explain*, and could be understood by the individual concerned as explaining, extensive aggregations of behaviour.

8   Thanks to Andrew Bailey for helpful comments on the penultimate draft of this paper.

CHAPTER TWO

WHAT IS HUMAN NATURE?

The original version of this paper was presented as part of a panel of invited papers on human nature at Otterbein College, in Columbus, Ohio, in May 2002.

Let me begin by noting that the question I am asked to address appears to presuppose that there is such a thing as human nature. The account of Otterbein's Integrative Studies Program in the college catalogue I was kindly sent also clearly makes this assumption, with its frequent references to human nature as the central and underlying conception of the program, with many individual courses explicitly constructed to make contributions to enriching the understanding of human nature. And, I hasten to add, I myself certainly believe that this Otterbein assumption is correct, and that there is such a thing as human nature. But I am a philosopher, and one of the things my kind does is ask questions—and, more specifically, in a regular way, questions about questions themselves.

The question "What Is Human Nature?" is actually ambiguous, between intension, or sense, and extension, or reference, to be just a little technical about the matter. That is, one can be asking what is the concept of human nature—the idea of it, its meaning—or one can be asking for at least some of the details: what does our actual human nature include?

The difference is not merely formal. In the "sense" sense, the question asks for parameters for what can count as a plausible or adequate notion of human nature—what do we, might we, should we, can we, have in mind for such a thing? Should a human nature, if there were one, be conceived as logically or metaphysically *necessary*, or essential, for everything it applied to? Or rather, might something be a nature, but in principle its bearer be able to do without it, or change without identity-loss? A little closer to ground, we may be concerned to know what, historically, has generally or typically been understood as the concept of this item.

In the "reference" or "extension" sense, we are asking for actual content. Is it part of human nature to be polygamous, say; or suspicious of strangers; or lazy; or competitive? Are there subtypologies, so that all humans fit into one or the other of some specifiable set of clear distinguishable types? (Males and females, for example?)

Still more concretely identifiable under the broad "sense" aegis is a cluster of issues posed by the study of human anatomy and human physiology. It seems clear that even the most thorough, comprehensive, and detailed study of human anatomy and physiology is not a study of human nature. This is a curious and arresting fact, if it is a fact. What else, one might ask, is being studied in a comprehensive account of the human physical system if it is not *humans*, and what else can be being learned of than their natures?

I have no wish to make merely semantic points. It does seem right that a study of human physiology is not *irrelevant* to the study of what we actually would target as human nature. Such study might show, for example, that something in our bodily composition makes it quite impossible that we should live to be, say, 400 years old, or run a one-minute mile, or be able to live a month without sleep. And these all seem pertinent to what it is to be human, and to have the nature of a human. On the other hand, lots of purely physical facts about us don't seem to contribute to what would in any natural or plausible way be thought of as our natures—for example, the fact that we are non-toxic to sharks who may eat us does disclose something about our physical composition, but not, it would seem, anything about our nature.

Human nature, if there is such a thing, appears to be, in the very idea of it, something having to do with our *behaviour*, and, perhaps, our behaviour only while we are alive, or (possibly) sentient. This appears to say that nothing could count as an account of human nature that did not invoke or involve ideas of consciousness, mental states, and self-directed or voluntary bodily motion. This should not be pressed *very* far, since some theories of human nature deny our freedom, or our having genuine or stable selves or psychological identities. There are also higher-order philosophical theories that have denied the reality of consciousness, though I believe that such views as those may be safely denied and ignored.

It would, though, seem mistaken to regard physiological study as altogether out of place in human nature study, as already indicated. An account of us that was *only* mentalistic would seem to miss the mark, or at any rate to be incomplete, just as one that was only physiological. We might, indeed, in a fanciful sort of way, conceive of a complete encyclopedic *true* account of human nature, if one ever could be realized, as comprising, say, 10 volumes of detail, one or two of which were entirely and purely physiological.

In fact, as many of you will be aware, one of the questions or challenges that has been raised now for at least several decades is this: is there such a thing as human nature at all? I do not want to accord this higher-order question too much of my attention on this occasion. I think the question has an affirmative answer. And I want to make a few modest and tentative comments about what I think our human nature is. Still, I do think the "meta-question" does deserve some consideration. Many postmodernists, femiists, and Sartrean existentialists, some Marxists, and some others who have simply thought that the *idea* of a human nature was not a clear or straightforward or even perhaps coherent notion, have brought their concerns or convictions in this regard to the table of our long-standing interest in ourselves; indeed, the imperative is mandated from Greek antiquity, to seek, for our own best good, to know and understand ourselves. And those concerns and convictions ought to be noted and responded to, even if it is not possible for me to definitively do so here.

Skeptics about human nature may be divided into two groups: those who haven't been in particular doubt about what a human nature *might* be, in principle, but who have simply denied that we have one; and those who have seen the very idea as problematic. I will address these constituencies of skeptics in turn.

Those who have thought us humans to be natureless have, curiously, tended to come to this result from two opposite—indeed, not easily reconcilable—poles of view. One of these attaches to what we have typically regarded as our being free, or having free will, or a power of free deliberation, choice, and action. If we *had* a nature—so this cluster of positions has usually held—we could not have such freedom; and contrapuntally, our very freedom precludes our being natured. A nature should confine and control, and we are precisely the terrestrial being not confined and controlled, at least in this respect. Man makes himself, as one former idiom put it. Otherwise, and also famously, said: in us, existence precedes essence, which, of course, one is to understand as implying that we don't really have an essence at all.

The opposite-poled stance of human nature skepticism sees us as socially, culturally, or historically formed, otherwise and priorly as blank slates, that *can* be rendered in any of an indefinite variety of directions, depending on what the social, cultural, or historical context has provided and inputted. For this position, there is no human nature, because we can be pretty much any sort of thing, and it depends on circumstances wholly external to ourselves what we shall turn out to *be*. As will be evident, the first of these bases of skepticism denies us a nature because we are free, and the second denies us one because, though unfree (or at least mostly so), we are chiefly empty pots that radically variable and differing *liquors*—social, cultural, or historical ones—fill.

I cannot offer thorough and definitive refutation of these views here, but—to go boldly to the issue—there is no good reason to adopt either. No one supposes that our freedom, such as it is, enables us to fly, sing underwater, or multiply pairs of 90-digit prime numbers in our heads. We live lives boundaried and constrained in a multiplicity of ways, kinds of ways that operate simultaneously with freedoms of choice and action there is no compelling reason not to view as genuine. Why then may our boundaries and constraints not include ones imposed by a human nature, within whose borders we are able to make plenty of genuine and meaningful free choices?

And at the other pole, the view that we are wholly ideationally fashioned—by things such as culture and history—too wholly ignores our animality as well as our freedom. It also seems to be contradicted by facts of experience that appear to show that we *can't* be moulded in indefinitely variable directions. Rather, we do seem to find from experience, history, psychology, and anthropology a number of patterns that humans manifest literally or nearly universally, and that they regularly revert to if artificially directed from them.

This may seem too abrupt a treatment of social constructivist and similar views of selves. But I want to move on to what I would see as the at least relatively more sophisticated position that holds that the very idea of a human nature is confused or problematic—conceptually problematic.

The way to address this stance is, I think, to ask directly what can and should reasonably be meant by a *nature*, such that humans might have one. It is not in serious doubt that humans are animals, members of a biological species, primates related genetically to other primates. If it is problematic what it can mean to speak of a human nature, is it comparably so in the case of lemurs, chimpanzees, or giraffes? If we ought reasonably to agree that there are lemur and giraffe natures, why might we not have in mind the idea of the *sort* of thing that those creatures have, only something true, comparably, of *us*?

This may seem simplistic, but I note that a nature of this sort—a creaturely nature, we might call it—does *not* imply, for example, *metaphysical unchangeableness*. Even if it is part of chimpanzee nature—as evidently it is—to fear snakes, this does not imply that there are no possible worlds with snake-loving chimps. Nor does it even imply that in a world with our natural laws—in the actual world, for that matter—a species might not remain the same species but undergo changes, over time, or in severely non-standard circumstances, that revised much or most of the species' creaturely nature.

It seems to me that *anti-essentialists* and other conceptual opponents of the idea of a human nature typically have unreasonable, and unnecessary, models and conceptions of what it is they are opposed to. A human nature ought to be the sort of thing that an extra-terrestrial scientist, investigating earth, might hope to identify, as *true* of human beings, and useful for understanding why they behave as they do generally, over time, in the range and variety of the circumstances in which they find themselves, i.e., in the real world.

I do not mean by this that such knowledge need be merely behavioural, or observational, in an overt sense. Inner mechanisms, or structures that weren't mechanisms—the sorts of things we call *reasons*, for example—might need to be invoked in a good and accurate account of us and of how we tick. Libidinal drives, concerns for the well-being of others, class interest, highly complex clusters of automatisms that constituted only a deceptive simulacrum of conscious rationality, the power of a focused rational will able to command and transcend appetite—any of these might turn out to be the sort of explanatory theoretical postulate by which the really discerning extra-terrestrial investigator might manage to get us right, to understand what we are, and how and why we operate.

My book *Theories of Human Nature*[1] explores 11 accounts of what we are and how we tick. Each seems to me a serious contender for at least part of what the imagined alien scientist might or should conclude. I will not provide even a sketchy survey of these theories here. I do want to reinforce the anti-anti-essentialist and anti-skeptical case I have been arguing for by drawing attention to three quotations I offer at the beginning of the book. They are there in part because they're pithy or catchy. But they also have, particularly in their conjunction—indeed, in the *triangulation* they afford—a serious and illuminating point.

The first is from Abraham Lincoln, who affirmed, "Human nature will not change. In any future great national trial, compared with the men of this, we shall have as weak and as strong, as silly and as wise, as bad and as good."

Next, from Oscar Wilde: "The only thing that one really knows about human nature is that it changes. Change is the one quality we can predicate on it."

And finally, a line from the Humphrey Bogart / Katherine Hepburn classic film, *The African Queen*. Bogart, the scapegrace low-life boat captain, who is guiding the high-minded missionary's sister Hepburn up an African river, has gotten uproariously drunk, and Hepburn has emptied all his remaining bottles into the river after he has passed out. Bogart—"Allnutt" is his character's name—awakens to this discovery, and protests that it is only human nature for a man to get drunk on occasion. Hepburn replies that this "nature, Mr. Allnutt, is what we are put in this world to rise above."

Human nature, then, is something basic, enduring, yet with a wide range, a regular pattern of contrasts, and permitting what can at least seem to be radical change. It is also something that it is not incoherent to conceive as transcended or overcome.

I would like to go on at least to affirm—it will not be possible to justify—what I see as some central human-nature truths. First, we already do know quite a lot about human nature, and this *is* knowledge. People do have, for example, both security and freedom needs and drives. They will do some things out of needs/desires for actual and felt security. And they will do some things out of needs/desires for actual and felt freedom. More or less no one is without elements of these operational and motivational parameters.

At the same time, there is not yet a *science* of human nature. The fact that putatively scientific theories can still come along, such as sociobiology or its sibling evolutionary psychology, and be so radical and popular and so clearly *wrong*, proves this. A third truth is that there very well *may* come to be something that *is* a genuine science of human nature, and in a not terribly distant future: a comprehensive, convincing account of why — why, *really* — we make war, and love, and tell jokes, and play with dolls, and wear ties, and develop religions and mathematical physics, and rob banks, and rape, and listen to music, and run for political office, and get intoxicated, and put together wealthy societies and poor ones, and play games, write poetry, help suffering strangers, stay with partners, leave them, do philosophy, and make and go to movies. Not that such a science need be simple, or involve a single *kind* of fundamental postulates. Current ultimate theory in particle physics, for example, involves 18 irreducible postulates.

A fourth truth is that a genuine science of human nature probably will keep our freedom intact. As much as we can and do reasonably want in a meaningful freedom of choice and action can be had, and explained, within a naturalist, scientific framework. A fifth truth: the fundamental truth about us *might* be a sort of enlarged and consolidated version of what we think of as common sense theory about humans and their natures, but it also may be seriously, significantly otherwise. The falsehood of sociobiology by no means implies the falsehood of all naturalist, mechanist, or rationality-diminishing theory. Rationality at the level of the devising of legal or air-traffic-control systems does not imply, or ensure, larger and long-term rationality in the operating of the common human world or in the smaller sphere of daily and interpersonal behaviour.

In the second and third editions of *Theories of Human Nature*, I endorse nine postulates as a partial list of universals of human nature. Most, though not all, of them were derived from the work of the late cultural materialist anthropologist Marvin Harris, whose ideas I would continue to recommend as making important and substantive contributions to the study — I will not mind saying the scientific study — of human nature. Unlike Harris, I am not a pure or strict cultural or historical materialist. I believe that some of our behaviour can be understood only by reference to ideational structures within us, which, while they rest on necessary biophysical bases, operate autonomously of those bases. As I am a *metaphysical* materialist—I think that all of our causally effacious mental states are actually also physical states—this will not yield an irreducibly dualist view of humans and the mainsprings of their actions.

But these convictions of *ontology* do not obviously, and in even the most optimistic picture of the actual future of science may not in fact ever, yield a scientific materialist theoretical understanding of all of what we are and do. So my own position is methodologically dualist, and my materialism, of any sort, of an "in principle" and metaphysical kind, without particular confidence or even hope of being able to be "cashed in" in real science.

The sort of thing I believe really happens, with sometimes significant result in the human story, and which cultural and historical materialist views cannot accept or accommodate, are cases where such things as *curiosity*, or *righteous indignation*, or *religious convictions*, or *aesthetic reactions*—all, in at least some cases, without genetic or sexual or calorie-enhancement or labour-reducing or other material accompanying co-determination—produce actual behavioural outcomes. So, as Aristotelian common sense also sees it, the Protestant Ethic may really have helped produce the Spirit, and the Fact, of Capitalism; Mohammed's religious visions may really have been necessary causal conditions of the Arab conquest of the Middle East; and simple inquisitive curiosity will have killed, and rewarded, both cats and scientific investigators.

Here are the nine human nature postulates I have referred to:

1. People need to eat and will generally opt for diets that offer more rather than fewer calories and proteins and other nutrients.
2. People cannot be totally inactive, but when confronted with a given task, they prefer to carry it out by expending less rather than more energy.

3. People are highly sexed and generally find reinforcing pleasure from sexual intercourse — more often from heterosexual intercourse.

4. People need love and affection in order to feel secure and happy, and, other things being equal, they will act to increase the love and affection that others give them.

5. People identify and act on possibilities of exchanging things they have surpluses of for things they want, in their interactions with other people. The oldest, most basic, and widespread case of this is exchanges of food for sex.

6. If people have received sustained high levels of love and affection in their early lives, they generally come to need to *bestow* love (as well as to receive it) in order to be happy.

7. People have cognitive needs, or are characterized by curiosity, whose object is only sometimes, and contingently, functional or of utility. (Or, as Aristotle put it, "All men by nature desire to know.")

8. People imaginatively project themselves into other people (sometimes other animals), having or sharing by proxy, as they suppose, others' experiences.

9. People need acknowledgment or recognition from others in whom they sympathetically project themselves, of their having status, worth, or value, and this tends to generate indignation or aggression in them if it is withheld.

Some notes on the foregoing. First, the list is by no means intended to be complete. There may be presumed to be many more universals of human nature than these. Second, it is not assumed that some of the nine may not be reducible to others, or that some may not be reducible to other still more fundamental postulates. It will be noted as well that these principles are generally of probabilistic, not exceptionless, character; that some of them, at least, seem to presuppose genuine powers of free choice in human beings; and that several of them, at least, have an obvious, straightforward, even trite and banal character. This last feature seems to me in no way a deficiency of the postulates. It reflects the fact that we have, after all, had — indeed, for rather a long time — at least some reasonable degree of self-understanding.

I note finally that while the nine postulates provided all purport to characterize (natures of) the entire human species, this will not of course preclude further postulates that would apply just to subcategories of humans — e.g., males, females, infants, pre-adolescents, teenagers, adults, the elderly, hetero-sexuals, homosexuals, and other apparently fundamentally dis-tinguishable kinds of human persons. I do not by any means assume, or suppose, that there will be even statistically significant "laws" of human nature for each, or any, of the human "sub-kinds" listed, or of others; just that there perfectly well may be.

I want to address briefly, and in conclusion, another human nature theme. I have been affirming essentially a forward-looking scientific project of a more-or-less completable account of human nature, which I have intimated would be the fruition — indeed, surely, the finest flower — of social science. It might indeed be conceived as a kind of union of insights and groundbreaking initiatives of psychology and materialist anthropology, both resting on and extending, even if in part transcending, Darwinian biology.

And yet my own book explores theories the majority of which are from a more classical and non-naturalist past. There I seem at least to claim that still-living, still-plausible images, accounts of our nature are to be found in Aristotle, Christianity (a version of it, at least), Rousseau, Marx, and liberal, conservative, and feminist theories. I also raise, as have others, the idea that central — arguably, among the best — reckonings, understandings of human nature are to be found in great literary works, by writers such as Tolstoy, Shakespeare, Joyce, and Mann. I *do* argue against philosophers such as Thomas Nagel, who hold that these latter depictions (he adds to them that of Freud) are not just the best but the only accounts, or knowledge, we ever should expect or aspire to have of human nature that will be even half adequate. I also certainly don't myself defend or endorse all seven of the theories (disjunctive clusters of theories in some cases) I have just listed. In any case, though, the question I want to address here is this: what is or should be the place in human nature theory of even the most enduring and arresting of the great classic images or visions of human nature, in intellectual history, or literary art, *in contrast to* the realized or still promissory possibilities of the best synthesized offerings of social science?

This is a deep question, to which I don't have a full answer. My partial answer certainly includes the claim and conviction that there will not be found to be clash or incompatibility between, as it may be put, the best philosophy and art — on the one hand — and the best social science — on the other — in the depiction and understanding of who and what we are. This certainly isn't obviously true, if it is true — and I believe it is. It also, though, even if true, doesn't really show us where we are.

I conclude with an expression of faith, or intuition: that the pursuit of understanding human nature via the route of naturalistic social science, and via the route of probing at least a select set of the blueprints of humanity in proto-science, philosophy, and art, are the same pursuit, and arrive, albeit disclosing different aspects or facets of it, at the very same place. Read, explore, teach those great novels and those great philosophers and thinkers of earlier time — at any rate, the ones that aren't just still influential, but that also still have serious adherents, for serious, good reasons — and follow where they lead the most recent and most comprehensive developments in cutting edge psychology and anthropology. They are ultimately, inner and outer faces of the very same thing: our very own faces — our face, the human face.

NOTE

1   Peter Loptson, *Theories of Human Nature*, 3rd ed. (Broadview, 2006).

METAPHYSICS AND
NATURALISM

CHAPTER THREE

METAPHYSICS AND ITS CRITICS

An earlier version of this paper was presented at McMaster University (to an audience of philosophers from McMaster and the University of Guelph) in September 1999. Portions of the text also appear, in adapted form, in my book Reality: Fundamental Topics in Metaphysics *(University of Toronto Press, 2001), chapters 1 and 2.*

"Metaphysics," F. H. Bradley remarked in a famous passage, "is the finding of bad reasons for what we believe upon instinct."[1] Bradley was, of course, being aphoristic. His quip is meant to express an insight of substance, even if not literally to be taken as true. In any case, it may very reasonably be doubted whether, in any literal or at least biological sense, there is much of anything we believe on instinct; and the fact that metaphysicians disagree so deeply would be at least a little surprising if their views were truly instinctive, innate, or anything similar.

Still, I think that Bradley's aphorism does capture something that is fundamentally right. I believe that we — metaphysicians and others — arrive at general pictures or conceptions of the world (and sometimes also pictures of our pictures) in a highly complex interplay of teachings we receive on authority, or because of temperamental leaning, location in history, culture, class, gender, or very particular features of our individual circumstances, together with argument and evidence of differing kind and quality, to which we attach differing significance. The whole picture, which will be in varying degrees of systematicity and of which we will be conscious to varying degrees, then undergoes processes of articulation and development, under stresses and constraints only some of which are particularly rational or evidentiary. Often, I think, views are adopted and accepted simply because they are currently prevailing ones. There is, in fact, I would say, an exaggerated, artificial, and largely historically and biographically untrue conception among philosophers of the role and importance of *argument* in reaching, retaining, and discarding metaphysical positions.

This affirmed, it might seem natural to go on to advance a historicist, relativist, or at least skeptic's and agnostic's stance on metaphysical topics and the competing plausibility of metaphysical systems—as many of course do. In fact, I am far more sanguine and optimistic about human intelligence and cognitive skill than that. I think the knowing hominid is—or at least is able to be—really rather good at negotiating his or her way through the thicket of subrational, pre-rational, and sometimes irrational epistemic predisposition, and charting through to at least relative autonomy from those forces and factors, and to at least relative receptivity to argument, evidence, and their ilk.

Of course, this is a matter of degree and it will vary by human case, and there is never achieved, not in metaphysics anyway (at least *yet*), a very impressive consensus. But the topics are difficult, and it takes a while, in individual lives as in cultures, for *free* creative intelligence to become engaged, and people do become wedded to their views, not always in rational—or very laudable—ways, or for rational or laudable reasons. (Hence I think much metaphysical posturing, as well as dissent, is inauthentic, often the expression of vanity—one does want to hold on to what one thinks others think one discovered or published first; or to disagree with what someone else has. But this too will speak more for a Sartrean than a Whorfian conception of our philosophical estate.[2])

There are so many philosophical topics on which philosophers differ radically, even vehemently, that it would probably be rash to claim that none involves deeper division than metaphysics. It is clear nonetheless that there is an extraordinary absence of concord about this particular branch of philosophy. So deep are these divisions, in fact, that many philosophers are even unaware that there are seriously held views different from the ones that they themselves hold, or that the truth with regard to metaphysics is other than settled and (at least relatively) banal. Some philosophers think that metaphysics is an old-fashioned and superannuated species of philosophical confusion and error (and arrogance). Others will say that if you think that there are at least four giraffes in Africa you are (thereby) engaged in metaphysics, or at least you are thinking something with metaphysical content, and implications. There is, in short, an astonishing and remarkable lack of light in this area.

Nor does it seem quite satisfactory to say that this (surely) is yet another of the myriad areas where it all just *depends what you mean*, and if the philosophers who have anything, ever, to say about metaphysics, would just set out what they mean by the term, they would see that some of their fellow-philosophers attach quite significantly different meaning to it than they do, and that perhaps they aren't as much at odds as they had supposed. One reason this doesn't seem as ecumenically helpful as in other areas, at least all by itself, is that philosophers connect their usage in this area to historical stances of which they believe themselves heirs. So, for some, "metaphysics" has a connotative force that makes it akin to "superstition" (or, for others, to "Western cultural imperialism") — hence, part of the point of talking about metaphysics at all is to distance what we are now thought to know, and do, from former dead-end illusions (some of them regarded, indeed, as dangerous ones). For others, by contrast, the term suggests a more benign, quotidian, and in any case unevadable activity, whose contemporary practioners are at work on matters of problem, and theory, in lines going back at least to Aristotle, if not indeed also to Thales. Exploring these contrasting historical dimensions might provide a better basis for making headway with regard to metaphysics and philosophers' attitudes and beliefs about it than just "defining one's terms" could achieve. For contemporary metaphysicians and anti-metaphysicians *do* know much of the same history, but conceive it quite differently and draw different conclusions from it.

At any rate, there does seem accord that the subject is supposed to investigate, and offer conclusions as to "what things are really like" or "what the world is really like," perhaps with a qualification for a sufficient degree of generality, or the "really like" being required to be at—whatever this may mean—a "fundamental (or ultimate) level."[3] So, it seems, metaphysics is agreed on all sides to be concerned with—possibly alongside other matters and possibly in a particular *way*—what exists and what its nature is. One of the metaphysical positions on what exists, namely monism (in one sense of this term), holds that there is, in a strict and literal sense, precisely one thing that is real. (The earliest thinker who explicitly took this view was the Pre-Socratic philosopher Parmenides.) Accordingly, we will be insufficiently inclusive if we characterize the metaphysical inquiry, as Kant did (and others, often polemically, continue to), as the investigation of "*things-in-themselves.*" But if we understand the latter phrase as not implying a plurality of objects, or entities of any sort, the Kantian conception—of how things are apart from appearance, and apart from how they may be conceived by us (always remembering that appearance, or our conceptions, and reality, at least *may* coincide) — seems apt, and often useful.

Beyond this, we seem to find conceptions of metaphysics that are incompatible, or at any rate that diverge from each other. Thus, there is a conception of metaphysics as (by definition, if one likes) a wholly *a priori*, or non-contingent, subject that would, if it were actual, produce results that were only and entirely necessarily true, in the strongest possible sense. Or—this conception is in fact logically distinct, though it usually accompanies the latter characterization—metaphysics is conceived as a subject that would yield results that would "transcend experience," identify what is real and what its nature is, in a manner "beyond" or "above" (whatever precisely these may mean in this context) knowing the reality and nature of things we are supposed to be aware of in regular or even scientific experience of the world.

An alternative conception — and this is the one I favour and advocate — sees metaphysics as what might be (and sometimes is) called most general science. This notion of metaphysics is, I think, essentially that of Democritus (ca. 460–ca. 370 B.C.), Aristotle, Descartes, Locke, Leibniz, and many 19th- , 20th- , and 21st-century philosophers. The general idea may be explained as follows. The notions of a species and of a genus have both, we may say, a *logical* (or categoreal) and a *biological* use, for classifying or grouping classes of things and larger classes they fall within, nonliving or living. The biological use is, it will be clear, just a special instance of the logical use.

Let us use the species-genus pair in its logical sense, not forgetting, of course, that it is also able to be applied to classes of living things. There is noted an ascent in species-genus characterizations of things we think we are acquainted with, or, in some cases, whose reality we reasonably hypothesize. For example, it is found reasonable to identify both beagles and collies as dogs, then both dogs and cats as mammals, mammals and birds as vertebrates, etc. This involves, and illustrates, species-genus ascent. It will be reasonable — indeed, important — to ask whether there is anything mandatory, or specially appropriate, in starting off with items like beagles. Would numbers, finger snaps, or death, have served? Or served as well? These are difficult questions, as well as being important ones. I ask your indulgence in deferring them. I return to species-genus ascent launched from breeds of dog. At quite high locations in such ascent, we achieve pure natural science — physics and chemistry. The relevant genera are of physical objects (actually or potentially) in motion — bodies, in the older natural philosophical vocabulary — elements — the things identified in the periodic chart of the elements, and perhaps compounds of them—and states and processes involving such things. Metaphysics, from this point of view, involves the idea of getting still more general, and comprehensive, than even physics ever gets (that is, in its theoretical categories, for kinds of things). So we reach, in the ascent model, kinds like *existent thing*, and possibly *stuff, property, relation, space, time, mental thing, physical thing,* and other sorts of reality. (The examples given are meant to be illustrative of possible metaphysical genera; some of them, at least, might well be empty, or non-basic categories.)

This latter conception of metaphysics—which seems to be the one first self-consciously articulated by Aristotle (whereas the former—the *a prioristic* and transcendent one—looks to be the legacy of Plato)—doesn't, at least at first blush, say anything about "transcending" experience, or affirm that its results will characteristically be non-contingent. After all, when we go from investigating dogs and cats to investigating mammals, it is hard to see why we should be regarded as "transcending experience," whatever exactly it would be to do that; nor is it obvious why we should be thought to have gone from contingent results to ones that will be like truths of logic. Aristotle does, to be sure, aim at results that will be systematic, law-like, and "rational." This has been the goal of metaphysical endeavour in most times and places, as it has also been the goal of science, and the conception of a contrast between theoretical (scientific or philosophical) investigation and "mere" history (including natural history) easily enough leads to a conflation of the theoretical and principled with the "necessary." But this is only anachronistically, and inaccurately, to be seen as providing a model of metaphysics as consisting solely of "truths of reason" in a strict sense.

It may be noted that Martin Heidegger, in the opening discussions of *Being and Time*[4], explicitly, if briefly, raises the idea of *being* (or *Being*, if one prefers) as the most general or comprehensive taxonomical concept, with a conception not unlike the one of species-to-genus ascent I have identified and advocated. Heidegger rejects the idea that being, being real, or existing can accurately be seen simply as a most general classificatory term. I share with him the conviction that being is *sui generis*, and something in concept additional to any categoreal taxon, however general or comprehensive, for things that there are. That is, *that* something is is always going to be something different from *what* the something is, even for universally applicable categories. But this will provide no objection to the idea of a science that is at most general levels of classification and analysis. It will be a point about the nature of existence (or being), not whether there is a plausible or viable general theory, or science — metaphysics — of the things to which existence applies.

One further component of metaphysics, as historically practised and as meant here, may contribute to understanding how at least a *part* of the subject is a matter of non-contingency. As well as exploring what in most fundamental terms the world contains — this is the special proper part of metaphysics usually called *ontology* (the study of being) — and what in most fundamental terms is true about the world, metaphysics also studies (in particular cases and in general terms) *the limits of possibility*. That is, metaphysics studies not only what there is and what is the case, it studies also what *could* be and what *must* be, in the widest conceivable senses of these terms. Possibility, necessity, and contingency are the fundamental varieties of *modality*. So this part or dimension of metaphysics is sometimes called *modal metaphysics*.

One is engaged in metaphysics in our sense, then, whenever one thinks about *what there is*, or *what there may be*, and what the natures of things that are (or might be) themselves are (or might be). Metaphysicians tend to be preoccupied with being (existence, reality) and what things are like — better, how things are. In Aristotle's sense, this sort of concern was a part of what he would have called, and also what we would call, science; only — possibly — more general, comprehensive, and foundational than actual natural science. Whether metaphysics might include subject matter — themes, content, results — that was substantively additional to anything to be found in (natural) science is itself a substantive matter of metaphysics. On the whole, my own view is that metaphysics does not go very substantively beyond science, but this is not supposed to be true "by definition." The idea of metaphysics includes and permits the idea of scientific (or naturalistic) metaphysics, but does not do so necessarily or automatically. This will be a matter of investigation.

Until relatively recently in the life of the mind, there was little conscious, explicit, systematic thinking about theoretical projects themselves — meta-level self-conscious probing of what the inquiry involved. As in other, more supposedly practical spheres, the aim was more usually to get to the matter at hand and produce its desired outcomes, rather than to ponder (still less to ponder in a systematic way) what the nature and point of having that aim in the first place was. Aristotle may be an almost singular exception to this generalization; at any rate his inquiries did extend to inquiry itself. But between Aristotle and the 18th century there was little self-conscious reflection of a systematic kind, on the character of inquiry in general, or its several varieties. Ideas of science, and the pursuit of knowledge and truth, certainly appear, largely within a broadly Aristotelian conception. In general, no marked contrast between what we would now identify as science and metaphysics can be found before the 18th century, however.

The idea of such a contrast does certainly appear in the writings of Kant, and perhaps implicitly in earlier thinkers of the Enlightenment. The explicit Kantian notion is that metaphysics aims to produce results that are absolutely necessary, or non-contingent, and transcendental, or independent of and in some manner inaccessible to experience. Though the idea that metaphysical claims will have the two properties indicated is subsequently almost commonplace, it is nonetheless not easily located before the generations following Leibniz.[5] It was perhaps *encouraged* by features of 17th-century rationalist metaphysics. The Cartesian ideal of an absolutely certain foundation for general inquiry about the world (science for Descartes, for he certainly didn't distinguish metaphysics contrastively from science) will have helped lead to this notion. Even so, as beginning students in philosophy working their way through Descartes' classic work the *Meditations* are taught to see, *certainty* is not at all the same thing as *necessity*. The Archimedean Cartesian results — the existence of self and thought — are supposed to be incorrigibly certain, but nonetheless contingent: there can be conceived worlds lacking me, selves of any sort, and thought.

On the other side of the matter, fundamental principles of metaphysics will be, many of them at least, of non-contingent character. What is to be resisted here is the idea that necessity is essential to metaphysics, that a claim cannot be metaphysical unless it at least purports to be non-contingent. This notion is absent from Descartes and from pre-Cartesian philosophy. Some form of it appears in Spinoza, but with some uncertainty (whether just for his readers or in his own confusions is arguable) as to whether the necessity Spinoza conceives metaphysical results to have is strongly modal, or what would now be called natural (or causal) necessity. Spinoza does, to be sure, conceive the notion of setting out a metaphysical system systematically after the model of Euclidean geometry, and certainly conceives the latter as *a priori* and strongly necessary. But even with Spinoza no commentary on the procedures assures us that a system of his type — even that of the *Ethics*[5] itself — *couldn't* introduce axioms that would be, in fact, logically or metaphysically contingent (as indeed some of Spinoza's axioms *are*, whether he recognized this or not).

As for transcendence (the idea of being outside or beyond anything experienced), this is something that comes late to conceptions of metaphysics. A contrast between appearance and reality is there from the start. From Thales on, this is an absolutely central and fundamental notion for the project of metaphysics. But the appearance/reality contrast as such doesn't require that things *cannot*, ever, be as they seem, or that reality cannot be experienced (as Thales' metaphysical system will itself nicely illustrate[6]). Again, the tradition may be thought to help *encourage* the idea of reality's being beyond or behind a veil of appearance, the latter necessarily differing in character from the former, and acquaintance, in experience, only possible with appearance. Platonic varieties of metaphysics may seem especially to nudge conceptions of metaphysics in this direction. But even here the notion is that reality — or that which is *most real*, in Plato's conception — can be experienced, even if it may require some non-standard kinds of experience (perhaps only available to mathematicians, or mystics) for this to occur.

The idea of metaphysics as essentially transcendent comes about more, I think, from 18th-century convictions as to metaphysical *failure* — failure to yield science, results that can be publicly known as certain — than from any central or defining notion of what the enterprise had aboriginally or historically been constituted as. No agreed results? Perhaps that is because what had been sought, and which alone would have been acceptable as results, were beyond the possibility of experience. The latter is Kant's view and that of other 18th-century, and later, thinkers. I will be arguing, indirectly (i.e., by example), that it is a mistaken view. But what prompted it is understandable.

I note further that also widely held is the idea, in this case perhaps more widely without academic philosophy than within, that metaphysics necessarily involves beliefs in the reality of abstract entities or of souls (the latter regarded as non-physical substances that human beings, among other creatures, either have or are). But these views of what metaphysics *is* are quickly and easily disposed of. Many philosophers are *nominalists*, i.e., they don't believe that (any) abstract entities are real; and there are systems of nominalistic metaphysics. Further, many philosophers (nowadays, possibly most) are *materialists*, who believe that all states of human beings and other thinking organisms are physical or material states, and they certainly don't believe there are souls; and there are systems of materialistic metaphysics.

Many philosophers and non-philosophers, including many scientists, have explicitly ranged themselves against metaphysics, and a considerable number have been educated to regard metaphysics as out of date and intellectually irrelevant for a serious modern mind. In recent years in particular, new arguments and positions have been developed by foes of the metaphysical enterprise, and these have generated a considerable literature.

One simplified account of the development of anti-metaphysics goes like this: until the 17th century, philosophy, which might better be labelled *speculation* and *theory*, enjoyed a unitary and somewhat privileged position in Western culture. For plain and practical folk it was alien and artificial, but sanctioned by its intimate relation to theology, a lynchpin ideological structure for that culture. Philosophical topics were curiosities, brain puzzlers, and sometimes matters of deadly earnest, as they involved individuals' and states' concerns about possibilities of power and intelligence beyond human life. Candour acknowledged that there was, for humans, at least, only one genuine systematic body of theoretical knowledge, and that was geometry. (For some, but not others, [Aristotelian] logic was a second science.) Piety and institutional power insisted, and doubtless typically believed, that there was much more of a theoretical kind that was actually *known*; but behaviourally people widely betrayed—as Hume was shrewdly to point out[7]—that philosophical convictions did not go deep. Hardly anyone *really* believed that they knew much at all about the extra-quotidian world, or even underlying structures of the quotidian world. If they did, they would have *behaved* differently than they did.

Along with so much else, the 17th-century scientific revolution changed all this. Galileo and his confrères, and finally, supremely, the 1687 *Principia* of Newton, showed that humans were capable of more actual *science* than just geometry and logic. There were other branches of mathematics that could be established to constitute actual bona fide systematic knowledge—i.e., knowledge in the praxis sense, things that, once you understood them, you could see to be correct, teachable to others, and not non-frivolously doubtable. And, most remarkably, actual systematic knowledge, rather than mere speculation, about the world was achievable: namely, Newtonian physics.

In the intellectual environment these developments engendered, a distinction came to be drawn between the philosophy (speculation) that was turning into — or seemed to hold promise of being turned into — (systematic) knowledge, or science, and the philosophy that looked to be dead-end, really condemned forever to remain (mere) speculation. Thus was born the distinction, as many have acquired and transmitted it ever since, between science and metaphysics. For this distinction, so conceived, and its advocates, metaphysics has chiefly survived since 1687 as a historical curiosity, or at best as a source-pool for possible proto-sciences of the future (a genuinely scientific psychology, say). If such a proto-science were able to be drawn from that well, it would show that it hadn't properly belonged with metaphysics in the first place; if the effort proved abortive, then it was correctly lodged, i.e., sunk, in the swamp of speculation (metaphysics).

The next major phase in the development of anti-metaphysics is due to Kant. The so-called critical philosophy that he developed involves a detailed and specific case against the possibility of metaphysical knowledge, and in favour of Kant's distinctive and complex account of rational psychology. The Kantian argument is complicated, and also I think unpersuasive. Kant argues, by reductio, that *if* there were knowledge of the world (i.e., of reality, as it is in itself), it would follow that various contradictions would be true. For example, we would be able to prove both that the world had a beginning (in fact, must have had a beginning), and that it did not (indeed, could not have). Since neither these nor any other contradictions *can* be true, it will follow in turn, by *modus tollens*, that we do *not* have any knowledge of the world.

As indicated, these Kantian arguments are entirely unsuccessful. They involve question-begging or quite implausible premises. Not even devoted Kantians nowadays suppose otherwise. Rather, a Kantian case for the inscrutability of the world is typically held more seriously to rest on other grounds — less formal, but no less decisive — than these so-called antinomies. Two such basic grounds seem identifiable. One is that we cannot think outside of our own structures of thought, hence whatever we *did* suppose was an objective (part of) reality would actually be a projection from those structures. This is the Kantian "Copernican" general idea, that we ought to come to the view that we can have no satisfactory basis for believing that we can escape, or think beyond, the cognitive filters and screens with and through which we apprehend the world. Earlier versions of the Kantian anti-metaphysical position appear with Gassendi and Malebranche, and among British empiricists, who give most focused attention to the idea that if one wants to know about something, one should accord some critical study to the instruments, and their user, with which the desired object of knowledge is to be pursued. In this regard Hume plays something like Galileo to Kant's Newton.

There is a strong and *a prioristic* Kantian argument, and also a weaker position. The former enlarges upon the Berkeleyan case for idealism,[8] which argues that trying to conceive of an object that would not be screened and conditioned by our experience-filters, our categories, is like trying to conceive of an unexperienced experience. Many undergraduate students of philosophy have been persuaded by such lines of thinking, as have some mature philosophers of the past and many students of the social sciences past and present. But in fact, this case for Berkeleyan idealism seems quite confused. Just because I learn of the planet Neptune through books does not make Neptune a bookish object; and in general there seems no difficulty with conceiving an object really to have a property even if object and property are screened or filtered by my mind.

The weaker Kantian position may fare much better. As Russell put it, with special reference to sense perception, "from the fact that the perceived qualities of physical objects are causally dependent upon the state of the percipient, it does not follow that the object does not really have them. This, of course, is true. What does follow is that there is no reason to think that it has them. From the fact that when I wear blue spectacles, things look blue, it does not follow that they are not blue, but it does follow that I have no reason to suppose they are blue."[9] Can we honestly, and seriously, suppose that we can come to knowledge about the existence and nature of constituents of reality, that would be accurate independent of our existence and nature? Won't such supposition necessarily involve a variety of cognitive *speciesism*, an anthropomorphism, that we can have no adequate reason to assume?

The second basic argument for anti-metaphysics grounded in the Kantian critical philosophy is independent. It asserts that different conceptions we come to about what the world is objectively like are irreconcilably in conflict, and we can have no hope of a rational basis, a decision procedure, for preferring one, or some, of the contenders over others. This second argument is, it may be said, a much modified, and weaker, version of the argument from supposed antinomies. It purports to prove not that metaphysics is contradictory, but that it is undecidable — radically and comprehensively so. In irreverent capsule form, we may call this the Gershwin case against metaphysics. ("You say tomāto, and I say tomăto…. So, let's call the whole thing off.")

Four post-Kantian phases or variants of anti-metaphysics may briefly be noted. First is 19th-century positivism, as expressed above all in the work of Comte and Mach. This current largely renders more explicitly what appeared earlier in the wake of Newton, especially in the writings of Hume: a conviction that metaphysics is naive, unsophisticated, representative of the childhood of human thought, really only a terminologically more ornate form of animism. The very idea that one could hope to know what would transcend human experience! All genuine, non-chimerical knowledge is founded in interpersonal observation: it is paradigmatically scientific knowledge.

The second module of late 19th-century anti-metaphysics is pragmatism, the most distinctively original American contribution to philosophy, though it has European affinities ancient and modern. Pragmatism is a close cousin to 19th-century positivism, if perhaps it is more the opposing dual of common-sense realism than — as positivism is — of scientific realism. That is, for positivism the grounding, the standpoint from which the intellectual terrain is to be assessed, is in natural science, where for pragmatism it is in common sense. In both cases, that grounding is *not* regarded as involving, resting on, or being a case of a metaphysical conception. So to suppose, for both positivism and pragmatism, would be to put cart before horse, or worse. And though markedly different from each other, both positivism and pragmatism share some degree of esteem for the other's grounding, and both repudiate metaphysics as antediluvian, as involving a childlike fixation on a "magical" view of the world.[10] All of this is of course rather vague, more picturesque than precise. And that is the basis for the most forceful of the responses to positivist and pragmatist anti-metaphysics: that the latter falls apart when the attempt is made to say (more or less) literally, or with precision, just what the problem is supposed to be with metaphysics, why it is a problem, and how positivism or pragmatism manage to avoid metaphysics in their own enterprises.

The third movement of anti-metaphysics is the logical positivism of the 1920s and 1930s. It differed from earlier positivism—for our purposes—chiefly in bringing a semantical dimension to the repudiation of metaphysics, something largely missing in Hume, Comte, and Mach. Though verificationism,[11] the distinctively semantical dimension referred to, continues to reappear in muted or veiled form, especially in British analytic philosophy, a consensus—a justified consensus, in my view—is that it is a wholly mistaken and a thoroughly refuted semantical doctrine. (It just seems so *easy* to think of statements whose content we can plainly understand, but which there would be no possibility of verifying or falsifying by any known publicly available method. Verificationism had, historically, usually insisted that something "in principle" was intended for the possibility concerned, but—as so often—the devil is in the details, and the demon hasn't satisfactorily been forthcoming.)

The fourth and most recent phase of anti-metaphysics has appeared in the work of several, chiefly American, philosophers, perhaps most notably Nelson Goodman, Hilary Putnam, and Richard Rorty. The positions developed tend to be eclectic and considerably divergent. Some of them (Rorty's, for example) identify themselves explicitly as reaffirmations of (at least selective parts of) classic American pragmatism.

The most philosophically substantial has perhaps been the one defended by Hilary Putnam, and usually called, not altogether informatively, internal realism. Although Putnam repudiated internal realism in 1994 for what he calls natural realism, both positions involve opposition to metaphysical realism. Putnam's views are eloquently stated and somewhat elusive; it may, in fact, be reasonably doubted whether Putnam's position has ever *really* been anti-metaphysical (or anti-realist) at least in the sense of metaphysics articulated and defended in these pages. But it is explicitly declared to be anti-metaphysical by its author, and *possibly* with justice.[12]

Putnam thinks reality is "underdetermined" by any theory we can produce, i.e., that several theories could be equally adequate to any consideration that could rationally motivate the quest to know about the world. This being so, there could be no sound reason to prefer one metaphysical theory to indefinitely many others logically incompatible with it. Moreover the project of wanting to know the nature of things-in-themselves, what things are *really* like, is, Putnam argues, intrinsically flawed, and possibly genuinely incoherent. So whatever it is we can do in cognitive inquiry, it certainly isn't metaphysics. This is, as will be evident, essentially the same as the Gershwin argument against metaphysics, made, in Putnam's deployment, a good deal more formal.

Let me proceed to a brief response to some parts at least of the arguments against metaphysics, general and specific. Recall that we have conceived metaphysics as first or most general science. If there were anything the matter with metaphysics under this— Aristotelian—conception, it might perhaps be that there was something wrong with getting *that general*. Rather as though it were perfectly okay to talk about beagles and collies, and maybe even dogs and cats, but that things get tricky, and dangerous, if you start to talk about mammals and birds. Something along these lines is indeed what some anti-metaphysicians, at least, have had in mind. They think that things go wrong if you get too general — i.e., apparently, more general than physicists get. J. S. Mill said, pithily, that this was a special trait of English minds ("The English invariably mistrust the most evident truths if he who propounds them is suspected of having general ideas."[13]) Whether this is so or not, there definitely appear to be minds that find extremely general kinds troubling. One reason, apparently, is because the complements of very general categories do not have non-null exemplification, at any rate in their category. Thus, there is (apparently) nothing in the category that includes substances that is a non-substance; similarly, for properties. *Existent entity*, it would seem, has no exemplification for its complement at all.

It is not easy to see, though, why this is a serious objection to metaphysics as most general ("first") science. It seems to rest on a simple *dogma*, with nothing independent to recommend it.

It is also sometimes held that the content of alleged first science would be in fact merely "semantic," analytic, at any rate non-contingent, in contrast to real science. This, if correct, would make Aristotelian first science converge on the first, Platonic, conception of metaphysics discussed above, save for the latter's supposed "transcendent" character.

Again it is unclear why, even if the charge were sound, this would be a good reason to object to metaphysics. It would no doubt justify demarcating metaphysics from science. That part of the Aristotelian characterization would be indefensible. But metaphysics as the empirical science simply more general and comprehensive than physics, as non-contingent theoretical content, seems unproblematic, as logic and mathematics of course demonstrate.

In any case, the charge here seems plainly wrong. That or whether there are material objects, or states, or mental ones, and the natures of both, are contingent matters; likewise, for the reality and character of time, space, causality, and other fundamental entities that metaphysics has investigated. Doubtless some of the things to be said — even among things substantive and contestable, at any rate, contested—about such things as these will be non-contingent. But that is true of some of what there is to say about clocks, and the Franco-Prussian war, and arsenic.

A significant part of the modern case against metaphysics takes the special two-pronged form of what are often called *concept empiricism* and *contextualism*. Both of these in turn have variants that give special attention to *language* and *semantics*, and variants that don't. I will largely collapse these variations here, though I appreciate that for some this must grossly oversimplify what I will say.

Contextualism, we may say, is the view, or family of views, according to which every view (hence, putative metaphysical views among them) is importantly *context-relative*—only true (at best) in a context. The context may be historical, or cultural; it may be a setting of class, gender, or some other. For contextualism, no assertion or group of assertions stands or can stand *sub specie aeternitatis*—"under the aspect of eternity"—saying that things are so. This is, for contextualism, illusion. The old logical positivists used to insist that truth be replaced with truth-in-L—truth in some specified language. Contextualists insist rather that truth be replaced with truth in some context.

Concept empiricism is the thesis that anything that can possibly be a *content* in or for our minds has got to have come from our experiences. The core idea here is that we've got to work with what we've got, and what we've got is to be found in us—in the furniture of the mind—whether it was already in the house when it opened for operation (habitation) and forays outward, or whether it was stocked in the course of these forays (including rummaging that didn't go beyond the doors). From that core idea stems the notion that all of the contents of the mind—the furniture—are ineradically stamped with the place, manner, and generation of their acquisition. Their reality, and identity, consists in the matrix of their creation. Since this is true of *all* of the mind's content, it will be true also of concepts (or ideas) of object, property, existence, identity, reality, world, and all the other concepts that purport to be concepts of metaphysics. Were metaphysics a bona fide enterprise (so the argument will go), these concepts would have a status, and a security of anchorage, that would permit the mind to consider their applicability independently of the matrix of their creation. But no concepts, on this view, have the privileged status of anchorage.

Concept empiricism (particularly if it permits innate mental contents) can be made wide and bland enough that it will be incontestably true—and not *a priori* or trivially true. Who can suppose that the contents of our minds have been placed there miraculously, or otherwise than as a cross-product of the workings of the world—the experienced world—on us, and our own operations; with us and world making widely quantitatively differing contributions, depending on the case? But world input is standardly critical. This affirmed, why should the fact that our contents are significantly by-products of the world's operations on us prevent us from reaching a stance permitting the factoring out of what we have contributed, so that we might hope to know what the world, in advance of or independently of doing whatever it did to us, is like in itself? Now, this may be impossible. But if it is, it will be impossible for Kantian or proto-Kantian Copernican kinds of reasons; not because of something about what it is to mean, to speak, or to think. There are, I think, devastating objections to both concept empiricism and contextualism, or to the claim that what is true in either implies any significant anti-metaphysical result.

There is simply no reason to believe that ideas—mental contents—got from one sort of context—experienced or innate—cannot, in principle, serve to permit the mind whose ideas they are to extend them in thought to contexts beyond their origin. This will not, of course, imply that extending ideas to origin-independent contexts will be *justified*; only that the idea of extending them in this way is shown to be coherent by our experience. That is, our own introspective phenomenology makes it abundantly plain that we can do what an anti-metaphysics derived from concept empiricism says we cannot do, and we can know that we can. How we can do so is, of course, another matter; the *mechanisms* of our psychological abilities are widely mysterious, this one among them. But *that* we can apply ideas, imaginatively or anticipatorily to unexperienced and postnatal cases, where we conceive the application as remaining unexperienced, is past serious doubt.

Contextualism (as understood here) seems to me still more frontally refutable. Like every species of relativism, it faces a genuine *tu quoque* problem. That is, it is plain that the advocate of the theory thinks that it is *true*. He or she may refrain from using the *word*, but there can be no serious doubt that contextualists think that something is *gotten right*, captured accurately, or something of the kind, by their contextualism. No special brief for truth condition semantics is made in claiming this. Whatever theory of truth someone sincerely advocates, or none at all, I submit that contextualists — relativists generally, in fact — really do believe (when they are sincere in their view) that their view is true. And if their view is true, then it will be false, since their view implies that no theory or stance or set of propositions or statements is true.

The sort of self-referential problem here posed — and held to refute contextualism — is often forwarded with a kind of smug "village rationalist" finality, which I find at least aesthetically displeasing, and overconfident. There may be formal ways around this type of objection, and meta-level distinctions that could be drawn to encapsulate and preserve the spirit of the contextualism. But — and it seems to me important to make this matter deliberately *ad hominem*, to speak to the eyes, as it were, of the advocates on the other side — there is something in the content of the objection that the contextualist *hasn't seen*, viz., the applicability of the theory to itself, and still more, the phenomenological fact that there once (or repeatedly) occurred actual occasions of (alleged) *insight*, where something — contextualism — was judged to be correct, i.e., judged to be true — objectively, literally, mind-independently true in itself — and if it is then something is, hence it cannot be.

The interesting (or more interesting) anti-metaphysician is not a concept empiricist or contextualist, nor a skeptic, or a solipsist.

He, or she, is some kind of empiricist. He/she grants — insists, in fact — that it will be wrong, *foolish*, not to regard key fundamental concepts we employ — the very ones central for metaphysical categorial analysis — as pointing to, standing for something. Kant held that there is such a thing as mind-independent objective reality; only (as he supposed) we can't have the foggiest idea of what it is actually like. The empiricist anti-metaphysician — at any rate the one I am thinking of — enlarges the Kantian stance in particular directions. Our fundamental concepts of features and constituents of the world all doubtless correspond to realities. There is *something* like time, space, material objects, persons, thoughts, causality. Only we have no hope or chance of recovering, or attaining, what the something is like apart from us. Our concepts are not mirrors of those realities, or that reality; indeed, they aren't even coded representations that we could hope to decode. Something is out there all right, and it is some way or other (or we can not unreasonably conceive its being so); but we haven't any serious chance at all of finding out what and how it is. Not really. We can perfectly reasonably talk of cats, trees, stones, and people, for it is with the notions we have of such things that we organize and group our interactions with the world. And it will be correct to think that, like *physical object*, *cat*, *trees*, etc. do correspond, approximately, to *something* that is genuinely real. But so does *sunset*. The fact will be, as with *sunset*, that the fit between our notion and the outer realia is rough and ready, approximate; and, more importantly and interestingly, we can have no reasonable hope of recovering, achieving, sorting out, *how* accurate the fit is, either in any particular case or in the large, for the whole systematic edifice of concepts we have. We can know we are representing a real world, know we operate with some kind of code (or set of codes) by which we do so, but we're doomed forever to lack the keys to decode the system. (This general position, in all its several varieties — Humean, Kantian, Putnamian, and others — may be called *inscrutabilism*.[14])

At the same time — and now anti-anti-metaphysics moves somewhat to the offensive — it does not seem widely to register among anti-metaphysicians quite how much, and what, they are asking themselves and their opponents to give up.

It asks a lot of a serious mind to give up the idea that there would be time, space, material objects, and a world system, which common sense and physical science have some genuine access to and information on, even if there were no people, concepts, or theorists, and independent of all three of the latter. It asks a lot to give up the convictions that it is true that *some trees have leaves*, that *it is known to snow on earth*, and a very large number of comparable claims about the world. It is reasonable to ask for very good and compelling argument for giving up such convictions. I submit that none of the arguments offered in contemporary anti-metaphysics come remotely close to justifying doing so. If metaphysics is first science, its theories are — like scientific theories generally — explanatory proposals that offer themselves tentatively, with open invitation to revision, refinement, and rejection. In that spirit, the claims that there are physical objects, time, space, people, animals, and that we may achieve — have already achieved — knowledge of much (not all) of their natures, do not seem implausible.

Much of the anti-metaphysics proffered by Putnam, Rorty, and others in recent decades suffers, and ultimately fails, I believe, by mischaracterization of the opponent. Rorty's conception of that opponent — though they otherwise differ considerably, this is also Putnam's — is captured well in the title of his early prominent book, *Philosophy and the Mirror of Nature*.[15] According to the conception of metaphysics I have argued to be both soundest and most consonant with the history of the subject, metaphysics is very considerably *like* science. Like science, metaphysics aims to produce general systematic theories that will be true, that will correspond to reality. Do physics, chemistry, biology *mirror nature*? Do they purport to? Does a physical theory — ever — purport to constitute a literal *isomorphism* with what it studies? Surely not. If we are realists — scientific realists, in this case — we will believe that scientific theories, sometimes, at least, are true, that they correctly describe reality. A comprehensive theory would aim to have something to say about everything in its domain. But a mirroring conception gets this altogether wrong.

The chief villain in the Putnam-Rorty conception seems to be the logical atomist theories of the earlier 20th century; that is to say, the metaphysical systems of Russell, then of his student Wittgenstein, and of others whom the pair of them influenced. I will not endeavour to illustrate this in detail, but I think that it is a caricature and a distortion to see logical atomism as implying (as Putnam and Rorty seem to believe that it does imply) that for some — possibly non-finite — number n, there are n objects; or as implying that there is one true complete description of reality. Logical atomism holds that there are facts of the world and that they are determinate; moreover that it is plausible that there are *symbolic structures* that can adequately, perspicuously, represent those determinate factual structures, and a goal worth pursuing to come up with *syntactic structures*, bodies of language, that will express this symbolism; moreover that first-order predicate logic looks to be a successfully achieved *part* of such syntactic structures.

Some or all of the foregoing may be untrue. It was/is an ambitious metaphysical conception, and set of projects, which may or may not be realizable. But they do not imply that there are a specific number of objects, a unique true description of reality, or that reality is mirrorable. And, of course, logical atomism is only one particular variety of metaphysical theory. The Putnam-Rorty case against metaphysics, even if successful against logical atomism, would throw out a baby with its bathwater.

It may seem that contemporary anti-metaphysics has often identified its target with what historically has only been a proper part of the subject: the quest for knowledge of what things are like *in themselves*. The metaphysical quest embraces additional concerns, as Kant was aware. It is instructive to note what he took to be the core topics of metaphysics. He itemizes six: 1) whether the universe had a beginning, 2) whether space is infinite, 3) whether there are ultimate simple particles, metaphysical atoms, of which all composite things are composed, 4) whether there is free will, 5) whether there is a God, and 6) whether there is an (indefinitely continuing) afterlife for persons. (Kant collapses the first two of these into a single topic.) Kant was quite clear about his own view: that is, he was prepared to bite the bullet of what the critical philosophy committed him to. He thought that either an affirmative or a negative answer to any of these six questions, if held to apply objectively to the world, led to contradiction; that it was quite impossible to suppose one had located here a topic having application to reality (rather than features of our concepts). For him, reason is powerless to reach a result, *even a tentative or (merely) probable result*, on any of these metaphysical matters.

Will many — any? — contemporary anti-metaphysicians really side with Kant in this?

For example, I suspect that Putnam and at least most (other) anti-metaphysicians believe that human beings have something adequately recognizable as a power of free choice, or free action.

There does seem, then, to be something to the idea that contemporary anti-metaphysicians consciously or otherwise limit their opposition to what has historically and traditionally been only a part of metaphysics. On other parts of metaphysics they will have, and sometimes defend, very metaphysical positions (viz., against God and immortality, for freedom; with Kant's other questions being left as difficult, but in principle answerable, scientific questions).

With regard to historical charges of metaphysical *failure*, I would submit that part, at least, of such failure — failure to prove desired results in metaphysical theories — stems from the fact not that the enterprise was flawed, but that particular conclusions sought were, frankly, untrue, or at least dubious. Kant took metaphysics to task, for example, for failing to prove convincingly that God exists and that the soul is immortal. He inferred that the problem was with the metaphysical enterprise, which was undertaking tasks beyond its powers. If it has not proved possible to mount intelligent, theoretically grounded arguments that offer strong support for a particular conclusion, it is of course possible that the enterprise engaged in the task is flawed or unsound. But another possibility is that the results weren't reached — not merely not a rigorous proof with apodictic certainty, but not even a powerful positive case — because the results aren't there to be reached. Maybe there is no God. And maybe there is no such thing as a soul. And maybe we aren't immortal. If particular metaphysical theorists or theories have sought to prove otherwise, that does not necessarily reflect on their instrument so much as the use they have made of it.

There is, of course, a very great deal more to say, both to press the case against metaphysics and to try to respond to it. I will be content if the foregoing discussion may have given the idea of seeking to explore the nature of reality at least some measure of purchase or plausibility.

NOTES

1   F. H. Bradley, *Appearance and Reality* (Oxford: Oxford University Press, 1962) (1st ed., 1893), p. x.

2   Jean-Paul Sartre held that human beings are radically free — unable to avoid or escape the ongoing condition of free choice in matters large and small. The attempt to evade our freedom is for Sartre one of the varieties or instances of personal or existential *inauthenticity* (a pervasive condition of self-deception). The Whorf (sometimes called the Sapir-Whorf) hypothesis holds that structures in particular human languages shape our conceptions of reality and, indeed, largely or significantly imprison members of very diverse cultural-linguistic communities within the ontological frameworks these structures supply.

3   Cf. Wilfrid Sellars' characterization of what he calls "the philosophical quest": "The aim of philosophy, abstractly formulated, is to understand how things in the broadest possible sense of the term hang together in the broadest possible sense of the term. Under 'things in the broadest possible sense,' I include such radically different items as not only 'cabbages and kings,' but numbers and duties, possibilities and finger snaps, aesthetic experience and death. To achieve success in philosophy would be, to use a contemporary turn of phrase, to 'know one's way around' with respect to all these things…" ("Philosophy and the Scientific Image of Man," in Wilfrid

Sellars, *Science, Perception and Reality* [London: Routledge & Kegan Paul, 1963], p. 1.) Philosophy, in Sellars' sense, is, to be sure, at least somewhat wider, and not quite clearly as ontologically focused, as metaphysics in the sense meant above. On the other hand, it is very much the intent of the conception of metaphysics that I seek to pursue that the full range of items Sellars lists be included within its reach.

4   Martin Heidegger, *Being and Time* (J. Macquarrie and E. Robinson, trans.) (New York and Evanston: Harper & Row, 1962), pp. 21–23.

5   It is interesting to note that we find what is essentially the conception of metaphysics advocated in the present volume, articulated clearly and in explicit opposition to the Kantian transcedent and *a prioristic* model of metaphysics, in Schopenhauer. (See Arthur Schopenhauer, *The World as Will and Representation* (E.F.J. Payne, trans.) (Dover, 1969), vol. 1, p. 428.

6   Spinoza's primary metaphysical work, which sets out his view of the universe along the model of Euclid's *Elements*, with definitions, axioms, and what are intended to be mathematically rigorous proofs of propositions and theorems.

7   Thales held that all things consist of water. Only some things of course *appear* to be, or present themselves as, water, and some things that appear to be water really are water.

8   *A Treatise of Human Nature* (Selby-Bigge and Nidditch edition, 1978), p. 113f.

9   Idealism—at least as usually understood (there are importantly distinct deviant versions)—is the metaphysical thesis that everything real is a thinking substance, or mind, or a mental existent (a mental state or process, or a subjective image) dependent on a mind. Probably the most famous of all idealists is Berkeley.

10   *The Autobiography of Bertrand Russell*, Vol. III (London, 1969), p. 130 (Letter to A. J. Ayer.) Russell must, it will be clear, be understood to intend an implicit *ceteris paribus* clause in the alleged entailment. (For I might, e.g., have looked at a bunch of blue objects, then put on blue spectacles, etc.)

11   The early pragmatists, including Peirce, and Dewey, shared the wide later 19th-century acceptance of a broad or basic Kantianism. Kant's claims as to the inscrutability of the world beyond our apprehensions of it were taken as permanent philosophical results, and what was at issue was what else, philosophically, there was to say, pragmatism making novel contributions with respect to a *praxis* component in theory. Current-day pragmatists are not as

unblinkingly Kantian, but of their anti-metaphysics there can be no doubt. Rorty is an especially clear case, his writings rife with claims about the "things-in-themselves" enterprise, and its follies. One passage may suffice to give the flavour of the pragmatist anti-metaphysical stance, in Rorty's rendering of it: "Philosophers like me...have learned (from Nietzsche and James, among others) to be suspicious of the appearance-reality distinction. We think that there are many ways to talk about what is going on, and that none of them gets closer to the way things are in themselves than any other. We have no idea what 'in itself' is supposed to mean in the phrase 'reality as it is in itself.' So we suggest that the appearance-reality distinction be dropped in favour of a distinction between less useful and more useful ways of talking." (Richard Rorty, *Truth and Progress* [Cambridge: Cambridge University Press, 1998], p. 1.)

12 Verificationism is the position (or family of positions) which holds that a declarative sentence has meaning only where there are public means for verifying or falsifying it.

13 Putnam's work, over the course of a long and productive career, may be viewed — at least from a metaphysical point of view — as dividing into four broad periods. In the earliest, Putnam is an outstanding creative contributor to broadly naturalistic and "scientific" analytic philosophy, and to a range of metaphysical realist topics and goals. The middle period (the 1970s, approximately) is transitional, with Putnam critical of much of his own and others' earlier work. It is in the third period (whose avatar Devitt names, provocatively, "the renegade Putnam") — dating from his 1981 book *Realism, Truth and History* (Cambridge: Cambridge University Press) — that the Neo-Kantian philosophy Putnam calls "internal realism" develops. This is the position referred to in the present context. Putnam's fourth and most recent position — natural realism — is set out in his 1994 "Dewey Lectures" (*The Journal of Philosophy*, vol. xci, no. 9, Sept. 1994). Although he continues there to affirm opposition to metaphysical realism and to the project of theoretical metaphysics, it is difficult not to view this opposition as equivocal, half-hearted, or merely nominal. Putnam characterizes his own philosophical odyssey, in this work, as a voyage from realism back again to realism, and he makes very clear, and unequivocal, that he thinks some stances, including some of his own, have insufficiently included the world and its operations independent of will or thought on our part, in constituting the nature of things. This anti-idealism is notably *not* coupled with a Kantian inscrutabilism — that is, with any affirmation that reality is beyond the possibility of our gleaning. To the contrary,

Putnam speaks for common sense knowledge of the world. There remains an insistence that natural (or common sense) realism is not a theory, and that it is just what (according to Putnam) Wittgenstein had been telling us all along.

14 F. E. Mineka, ed. *The Earlier Letters of John Stuart Mill 1812–1848* (Vol. XII of *The Collected Works of John Stuart Mill*) (Toronto: University of Toronto Press, 1963), p. 48 (Letter to Gustave d'Eichthal).

15 Inscrutabilism may be defined as the position that a world independently of the mental exists (one might add: and is known to exist), and in some way or to some degree corresponds to our apprehensions of reality, but we are entirely unable to determine how it does so, or what its actual character is, this inability being something no future development of science or technology will lead to our overcoming. Cf. what Devitt calls "weak, or fig-leaf realism" (Michael Devitt, *Realism and Truth*, 2nd ed. [Princeton: Princeton University Press, 1997], p. 17).

16 Richard Rorty, *Philosophy and the Mirror of Nature* (Princeton: Princeton University Press, 1979).

CHAPTER FOUR

METAPHYSICS AS FIRST SCIENCE

The original version of this paper was presented at the University of Windsor in September 2001.

This paper is intended to advertise and promote a conception of metaphysics that I believe many besides myself share, but that I think is not made as self-consciously explicit as it deserves to be. An earlier book of mine sets out and seeks to exemplify this conception. So I suppose I am also meaning to advertise and promote that book. It is called *Reality: Fundamental Topics in Metaphysics,* and was published by the University of Toronto Press. So I do naturally urge that you locate and read that book, and encourage others to do so, particularly if you find substance or interest in what ensues on this present occasion.

As I have said, I think that the model or conception of metaphysics I advocate is not original with me. Indeed, many will, I suspect, think what I will have to say unsurprising and just what they had supposed all along, and supposed most others did also. Yet the conception I favour is at odds with a number of others that tend, perhaps unthinkingly, often to be met with. Moreover, if metaphysics is what I, and I hope you also, think that it is, then it has a justified place among the cognitive enterprises that many, including many philosophers, have denied it, and reasonably clearly may be shown to do so. Further, if we — the authorial, or our collective "we" — are right, a good deal of philosophical ink, both anti-metaphysical philosophical ink and ink that has had other targets, may, with only a few additional highly plausible premises, be shown to have been mostly quite wasted. Of course, that philosophical ink has often been wasted ink will also be something that will occasion little surprise.

The conception of metaphysics I advocate sees the subject as the most general or comprehensive of the cognitive or knowledge-seeking disciplines. The word "science" originally meant just "knowledge." Individuals, of course, know things privately and personally. Bob may know that he had a headache earlier today, but thankfully it is now gone. Mary may know that she has reservations about that new fellow-employee. It is not clear that such items as these count, even in principle, as (parts of) science. Science, apparently also in its older and classical sense, meant something that can be called *public,* and also something more or less systematic — at least able to be organized into a structure or body of similar or related items.

If we allow, as I think even now we generally do, natural or empirical science to be just a part of science, or the body of things some group of cognizers takes itself to know, publicly, (and some of which they really may know) we may find it reasonable to call any knowledge-seeking enterprise or discipline a science. We do, for example, regularly call mathematics a science, so it doesn't seem that sciences must, as such, be observational, or empirical, or logically contingent. We also, of course, talk of social science, and break it down into component disciplines, some of whose results have a character whose observational, experimental, or empirical status is sometimes in dispute.

At any rate, the chief anchorage I would say is in knowledge, of the public sort. Within that framework there are variations and differences with respect to content, generality, and cognitive justifiability. Thus, some sciences concern themselves with a specific delimited territory, some are more general than others by virtue of encompassing the latter's territory and also others', and some varieties of inquiry are accepted or advocated by some inquirers as possessing bona fide knowledge, but this stature is doubted or denied by other inquirers.

There are a great many possible, and useful, taxonomies for the knowledge disciplines, by territory, methodology, and modal status. For some, there is something obvious, or intuitive, about divisions between sciences of nature and sciences concerned with conscious agents; likewise as between experimental/observational sciences, and those in which methodologies are abstract or purely conceptual; and yet again cases whose results are logically contingent in character, and those where outcomes are necessarily true, in the strongest sense. All the same, the boundaries in all three cases have been contested, or held to blur, or overlap. I do not assume here any particular view as to these matters.

There are also disputes and unclarities as to the science repertories of particular cultures or societies (or subgroups of them), both currently and transhistorically. Here I will make some assumptions. One has to be very careful in these areas, for it is easy to be misunderstood, and easy to cause offence. I will partly seek to diminish the latter risk by claiming, as I in fact believe, that there are no hermetically boundaried cultures or societies. Most everything in human groupings is porous and permeable, both synchronically and diachronically. The latest paleoanthropology confirms us as a uniformly single species, very closely interrelated, from 150,000 years ago, long before the rise of meaningful human culture, which occurred about 50,000 years ago. There is even a good case that all extant human language descends in lineal development from a single language spoken perhaps only about 75,000 or 80,000 years ago. Anyway, we have been mixing and mingling, borrowing, stealing and generally running into and affecting and being affected by each other all along. All cultures, and all social classes, are mongrels.

As it happens, some things showed up somewhere first, or in some cases in a handful of places or areas at about the same time. Agriculture, art, cities, state societies, wheels, the stirrup, mathematics, lyric poetry. The list, of course, is potentially very large. Various factors, none of them a matter of any group's more impressive ethnos-correlating traits, united to cause it to be the case that some things, of greater moment from the cognitive as also from some other points of view, showed up here rather than there, then rather than earlier or later, and to have been masterfully borrowed and augmented elsewhere, or not, to have been sustained and flourished, or not.

I mean some of these remarks to be more or less Hegelian ones — very liberal Hegelian ones, I may say — and to lead to very liberal, but Hegelian conclusions. Some people have things more nearly right than others, in some cases where the things about which they are concerned are the same. That is too bad, I guess. But there it is. In any case, that some group, and individuals among them, may happen due to historical circumstances to have a larger share of particularly theoretical varieties of knowledge at some juncture will not imply that they have greater abundance of other sorts of skills, or creative powers, or, certainly, of virtue. And there will be no reason to expect that they will retain their greater cognitive largesse for any particularly protracted period. Remember that porousness.

A second, not unrelated, assumption I will make is that the Western European 17th century has an anchored world historical significance that is, from the knowledge point of view, without rival. For it is in that century that modern science was created and launched.

I should remark that the conception of metaphysics I am setting out and advocating does not, strictly, depend on this, but the position I myself take in the history and philosophy of science is a classical and, many would say, rather old-fashioned one. It is, in fact, eloquently defended in the present day by Nobel-laureate physicist Steven Weinberg, who would be a contender, in my view, for inclusion among the greatest living philosophers of science. This position is explicitly anti-Kuhnian. It holds that empirical, observational, experimental natural science is an effectively unitary enterprise of theory and praxis, launched by Kepler, and Galileo — but especially the latter — and still going strong, organically evolved and proliferated, four hundred years later. Certainly there was proto-science before Galileo, and without it the 17th-century scientific revolution couldn't have occurred; but the latter was a revolution, and even the profound conceptual and theoretical reconfigurations in modern physics, in and since the 1890s, was, for the view I support, a part of the same ongoing conversation, and mathematical engagement with nature, that Galileo began.

Putting this assumption nonhistorically: scientific modernism is the view that modern natural science — the natural science of which Galilean and post-Galilean physical science is the central case and paradigm — is a diachronically unitary body of theories, methodologies, and pure and applied outcomes, and (according to scientific modernism) this body is without serious or credible rival in the areas it addresses and applies to. I am myself a scientific modernist, as are many others. Without committing metaphysics as I conceive it to scientific modernism, I would claim that for metaphysics under this conception, modern natural science has a security and centrality of place, among the knowledge enterprises, that metaphysics will acknowledge and take account of. Modern natural science is not just a theory, or mega-theory, or cluster of theories, just like the others.

This lengthy excursus has been intended to fill out, to some degree, the picture of public knowledge — science — within which metaphysics has its own place, and to affirm a special groundedness of natural science, uniquely, within that picture. Beyond that, I mean to make no commitments or assumptions as to the relative location, boundary conditions, or security, of any other knowledge enterprises or disciplines. It is no part of my purpose here to affirm — or deny — unity of science theses, or claims of a significant autonomy of disciplines having to do with conscious subjects. An imaginative model I would employ, and recommend, is of an ideal encyclopaedia, intended as a collected repository of public knowledge, of "what we know" — a sort of super-*Encyclopædia Britannica*, vastly expanded and expanding as knowledge does (an online *Britannica*, then). The sciences, then, would be what would have alphabetized entries in this huge, and changing, compilation.

Metaphysics is the science of entities—the science of what there is, and the fundamental natures and relationships of what there is. I have spoken of the arbitrariness, or at least contestability, of various classificatory groupings of what there is. That warning note repeated, there are sciences concerned with the behaviour of inanimate moving things: particles, units of matter, waves, fields. There are sciences concerned with specialized instances of the latter. Also sciences concerned with living things. Others with conscious things, and what they have done, tend to do now or at all times they exist. There are sciences concerned with abstract items: numbers, points, linear functions, sets. Metaphysics is the science that takes on the whole lot.

In doing this, it does not, of course, do more than merely fragmentarily duplicate or aggregate other sciences. Living organisms are cases of material objects and systems in motion. Physics does not *repeat* what biology affirms, adding also cases of nonliving objects and systems that move. *Some* repetition, or instancing, with occasional bits of detail judged significant, will occur. But the central idea is the one captured by the three-letter Latin word *qua:* physics studies things qua, or inasmuch as they are, physical entities in motion. So, too, metaphysics is concerned with things that exist, in ways that contribute to or constitute formations of general theories, that we aspire or affirm to know to be true.

Restating this in slightly different idiom, sciences admit of more and of less generality, and comprehensiveness. Sciences of cordates—creatures with hearts—are, for example, less general or comprehensive than sciences of living things, and the latter are less comprehensive and general than sciences of moving things. Sciences that will include also abstract things—if there are any— and temporal things (like the 14th century, and—perhaps—time itself) will be still more general and comprehensive. Metaphysics is the science of everything that there is.

This idea, or something closely similar to it, was expressed very effectively by someone one might think a not obvious philosopher to formulate it, Alfred Tarski. In "The Semantic

Conception of Truth and the Foundations of Semantics" (1944), Tarski wrote: "For some people metaphysics is a general theory of objects (ontology)—a discipline which is to be developed in a purely empirical way, and which differs from other empirical sciences only by its generality…. [M]etaphysics in this conception is not objectionable to anybody, and has hardly any connections with semantics" (p. 72, in Feigl and Sellars, eds., *Readings in Philosophical Analysis* [1949]). Tarski's confident assertion of the unobjectionableness of metaphysics in this—our—sense is, I fear, oversanguine. Some are declared foes of any and all conceptions of metaphysics.

One reason some anti-metaphysicians have had is precisely in the great generality of the subject as we conceive it. One of the (moderately) verificationist ideas the now defunct ordinary language school of philosophy had, and which some others shared and may still share, is the (as it was sometimes called) principle of specious contrast. According to it, no term is meaningful, at any rate has *genuine* cognitive content, if both it and its complement or negation do not both have exemplification. So, for example, *red* will, according to this principle, have genuine cognitive content, because some things are red and some things are not. But *entity,* and *existent thing,* would, by this principle, both be without cognitive content—since there *are* no things that there *aren't.* There could not, then, be a science of entities or existent things.

This does not seem to be a good or persuasive objection to metaphysics, since the principle of specious contrast seems false—moreover, question-begging. We plainly do know what we mean—whether or not the idea is reducible to, or definable in terms of, other distinct ideas—when we say that something exists, or is a thing or entity.

Nor does it seem very plausible to object to the idea of a science that was maximally comprehensive just *because* it was that general—rather as though it was okay to have a science of dogs, another of cats, another of porpoises, but not all right to have a science of mammals. Rejecting a science of everything just because it was so general seems plainly and implausibly ad hoc. I shall take it that metaphysics as first or most general science has made at least a toehold, maybe a beachhead, of claim on our endorsement.

Some would add to the conception offered of what the subject of metaphysics is that metaphysics engages its targeted object or objects also, and by definition, as it were, in a particularly sharp or critical or maximally presuppositionless or presupposition-examining way. I think that there is some truth to this, but not the definitional component of the claim. Collingwood, for example, gives definitions of metaphysics along these lines. In three passages in his *Essay on Metaphysics*[1] he offers variants of formulas of this type: (1) "Metaphysics is the science which deals with the presuppositions underlying ordinary science" (p. 11); (2) "Metaphysics is the attempt to find out what absolute presuppositions have been made by this or that group of persons, on this or that occasion or group of occasions, in the course of this or that piece of thinking." (p. 47); (3) "… the business of metaphysics is to find out what absolute presuppositions have actually been made by various persons at various times in doing various pieces of scientific thinking" (p. 60).

I do, of course, approve of Collingwood's calling metaphysics a science, and linking it with other sciences. But otherwise his formulae seem to me misleading, and incomplete. I would say that philosophy as such, whatever its targets or contents, conceives itself by and aspires to the sharp, critical, maximally presuppositionless, presupposition-examining ideal indicated. It is not specific to metaphysics to do this, nor part of what defines metaphysics. (Collingwood does, to be sure, speak of *absolute* presuppositions.) There can indeed be—are—cases of rather lackadaisical, unfocused, insufficiently critical or self-reflective metaphysical theorizing. Such cases are not thereby any less metaphysical.

This note may serve as the first indication of the several characterizations of metaphysics that are to be met with in accounts of the subject, by friends of it or foes (more usually the latter than the former), or people undertaking just to describe and classify, which are I think mistaken or inadequate. Someone can, of course, identify or stipulate a subject of inquiry, just as they can dub any other variety of item or initiate a new usage, intending that it become adopted generally or widely. The operative test or criterion of adequacy will be, it is clear, the applicability of a proposed conception or characterization of metaphysics to what Greek, Roman, or subsequent Western philosophers who have produced what they or others have described as metaphysical results have had in those results.

A particularly common mistake—so at least I see it—has been the idea that what metaphysics does is study some of our basic *concepts*. P. F. Strawson famously drew a distinction, for example, between what he called *descriptive* and *revisionary* metaphysics. "Descriptive metaphysics," he said, describes "the actual structure of our thought about the world, revisionary metaphysics is concerned to produce a better structure."[2] It will be noted that, for Strawson, both varieties are concerned with our *thought*—our *concepts*—not with what our thoughts and concepts might be of, or *about*. This is consonant with other conceptions of idealist or Kantian root.

That metaphysics is a study of *concepts* seems quite false to the history of the subject, and will certainly be contrary to the conception advocated here of a most general science. Botany is the study of plants, not of our concepts of them, or concepts of them whosoever they were. The objects of historical study are people and their actions, not concepts of people and doings. Metaphysics is the study of reality: of what there is, and what it is like.

To be sure, in studying what there is we use—must use—concepts. It is likewise with botany. To study plants systematically there need to be employed, and deployed, a range of concepts. But this still will not make botany—or metaphysics—fields whose objects are concepts.

It may be claimed that part, at least, of this argument is casuistry; that claims that metaphysics is the study of our most fundamental concepts are simply to be understood as assertions in *oratione obliqua*—as a *façon de parler,* and one wholly compatible with claims that metaphysics is the study of what there is, and its nature. This might or might not be so. I think that claims that a discipline or inquiry studies concepts—as opposed to using concepts, which are in turn critically examined—is at best misleading; and contributes to the mystification, and to an idealism-coating, of metaphysics. It is counterproductive and it is unnecessary.

A second error in conceptions of metaphysics since the later 18th century, by opponents of the subject, is the supposition that metaphysics—again, by definition as it were—is a subject that goes, or purports to go, beyond or behind experience, to supposed realia that are not, and perhaps cannot be, experienced.

The idea that a defining feature of metaphysics is that it goes behind or beyond experience *may* be in part just a case of a bad inductive generalization. If metaphysics is concerned with whatever is real, and some things do, as a matter of fact, go behind or beyond experience, then metaphysics would be concerned with them, as well as with the things that don't go beyond or behind experience.

There are also cases of doubt or divided view with respect to accessibility to or participation in experience. Is the self—are persons?—accessible to experience? Hume famously denied that he ever experienced a self, so that, as far as he was concerned, if there are selves they are entities that are beyond or outside anything we experience. This is what Hume says or implies in Book I of the *Treatise.* A little disconcertingly, in Book II Hume at least seems to say or imply that selves are encountered and participant in every experience we have.

At any rate, many besides Hume have been doubtful that human persons have experience of any other selves or persons than themselves; so that even if I do experience me, I don't experience you, or anyone else. More complicatingly, some insist that human persons or selves are just human beings, a certain variety of animal, and that we experience them in a perfectly straightforward way every day. Still more complicatingly, some want to distinguish between what we *directly* experience and what we experience only *indirectly*. With this contrast it may seem attractive to say that we do experience others, only indirectly, not directly. Those with the *idée fixe* identified — that metaphysics is about what transcends experience — will likely then want to affirm that the metaphysical target is what is wholly beyond experience, directly or indirectly. Depending on how indirect indirection can be, though, it might be argued that anything real can at least in some sense or in some manner be experienced. Don't instruments of magnification afford indirect experience of lots of normally imperceptible items? And may we not perhaps be argued indirectly to have experienced the number 7 when we have lived reflectively through enough weeks, or encountered other collections or sets with seven items in them?

At any rate, I would cut wholly and directly through this issue, since, again, I affirm that metaphysics is concerned with whatever is real, and that seems certainly to include lots of things we do (directly) experience. Physical objects, for example, are, I would say, items of and in many metaphysical theories — all of the true ones, in fact.

Another idea — Whitehead, for example, expresses this one in his metaphysical treatise *Process and Reality*[3] — is that metaphysical results should be *necessary truths.* This too seems easily confuted. By usual intuitions, it is not a necessary truth that persons or physical objects exist, yet that they do figures prominently in many an ontology — all of the true ones, again, among them.

To sum things up so far, then, metaphysics is not particularly or necessarily or specially concerned with concepts, or the conceptual, or with what is necessarily so, or with presuppositions — of accepted theories, or any possible experience. Nor does it specially occupy itself with what transcends experience, actual or possible. It is concerned with all of those things, but as being among what there is and what is the case, at general and systematic levels and in general and systematic ways.

If metaphysics is "first science," most general and comprehensive of the sciences, empirical or abstract, one naturally asks of its methodology, or methodologies. Sciences have methodologies, much studied by philosophers of science. What are the ones of metaphysics?

Since so much is real, and of such diverse variety, it would seem unreasonable to expect that metaphysics would have one single or uniform methodology. In fact, we seem to have two kinds of avenues of access to the world, or to what we think is world. There are those who deny one or the other of them, or deny their adequacy or autonomy, but it still does seem so. On the one hand we look out upon the world, or a world, from within each single one of us — or if there are group or collective selves, from them. On the other hand we form ideas and theories of what there is and of what is so that purport to be views not just from here, or there, or me, or us, but accounts that are supposed to stand independently. We may or may not genuinely know all that we claim to know in these two ways, or have differential — or perhaps interdependent — bases in the two cases. That is the concern of epistemology. Here the concern is not, except secondarily, with how we know, or how adequately, or to what degree, but with what we know, or can know, when we do: with, that is, the human (and knowable), not *knowing* and what informs and accompanies it.

Looking out from ourselves, then, there are — it seems — selves and mental states and — perhaps — mentally dependent or parasitic items, like double images when eyes are (gently) pushed in or stars we say we see when our heads are (gently) hit with hammers. Maybe also ideas — in a mental sense — simple and clustered also are to be found or posited here. So perhaps too are the past, and the present, and the future.

But I don't want to advance an ontology here; rather, to speak of method. Method in metaphysics is, where the base of origin of the work is in and from subjects, *phenomenological*. It is concerned with and seeks to regiment and theorize about the items we seem to experience. Method here is empirical and is partly locatable in, but not neatly, transferably that of any one distinct other empirical science, social or natural.

Method for metaphysics where the base of the endeavour's origin is impersonal is as varied as, indeed is the aggregation of, all of the other sciences, empirical and abstract. Direct observation provides a basis for establishing the ontological credentials of many (kinds of) things, as does technologically augmented observation and postulations of wholly unobservable things whose existence is required for, and justified by, plausible well-corroborated empirical theories.

Yet, again, I do not mean to presuppose or give the nod to any particular metaphysical theory or group of theories. Some are minimalist, even — I don't mind the term, and am happy to claim it "metaphysicalized" — deflationary. Some take a Van Fraassen kind of stance, according to which unobservables of physical theories are fictional. For some, only manifest (common sense) items are real; for the others, the latter decidedly are not — ultimate entities of physical theories, rather, being the sole realia. Some have notions of degrees of being, with ground level or primary sorts, then ersatz or "Pickwickian" kinds that nonetheless fail to constitute being fictional. I myself, let me say parenthetically, find all varieties of theories of degrees of being deeply puzzling and problematical, and of dubious intelligibility. But some famous others, to be sure — Plato, Russell, Dennett — hold (or seem to hold) otherwise.

There are also particularist ontologies, for which only substances are real, or substances and their intrinsic properties, and event ontologies, some of these indeed denying the reality of particulars participant in or constituent of events (or states, or processes).

Some ontological schemata may just be alternative structures of division and classification of a single selfsame world; others really are logically incompatible with each other. But it is, of course, like that with other, more specific sciences.

There is one facet of metaphysics remaining to enter discussion; that is the special place in it of *modal* inquiry. Conceptual, typically counterfactual models show up in other sciences, both logico-mathematical and empirical. But they have a special, and specially central, place and role in metaphysics. This is not just methodological. If the status of something—a substance, or a fact—really were strongly, alethically necessary, it is part of the business and concern of metaphysics to explore and determine that. Likewise the Humean conception of a radically contingent world—one of Hume's boldest and most original contributions—is an altogether metaphysical idea. That things are necessarily as they are, and explaining that this is so, need not be a metaphysical target; but whether this is so—i.e., the modal status of things (whatever that status is, determined, if perhaps it only ultimately can be, by thought experiment) is definitely a key and central part of the project.

I conclude by commending metaphysics as first or most general science to all philosophical inquirers. Philosophy has been engaged in this practice since Thales, with gradually advancing sophistication and impressiveness of result ever since. No good or adequate reason for it not to do so has ever been forwarded. Long may it continue to be part of what philosophers do.

NOTES

1   R. G. Collingwood, *Essay on Metaphysics* (Oxford: Oxford University Press, 1940).
2   P. F. Strawson, *Individuals* (Methuen, 1959), p. xiii.
3   Alfred North Whitehead, *Process and Reality* (Macmillan, 1929).

CHAPTER FIVE

THE CONCEPT OF NATURALISM
Some Complications

A major part of the original version of this paper was presented in the cognitive science speakers' series at the University of Guelph in October 2004. Relatives of the paper (both of them considerably shorter than the text here) had earlier been given at Trent University, in January 2004, and at the University of Memphis, in February 2004.

We find in Thomas Hardy Leahey's widely used textbook *A History of Modern Psychology*[1] (p. 3) a definition of naturalism as "the thesis that no supernatural or non-natural causes are at work in nature." This definition could serve almost as a paradigm case, a perfect exemplar, of the circular and uninformative definition. What, one wants to know, is super*naturalism* such that naturalism excludes it; and what is the *nature* that the definition enjoins limitation to? And what are *non-natural* causes (or *natural* ones)? If one knew what the naturalism was that supernaturalism implied being *above*, and what the nature referred to was, and knew what either natural or non-natural causes were, one wouldn't perhaps have any need of, or find any further informative content in, the definition offered.

Leahey supplements his definition with two further claims about naturalism, in the context in which the definition is given. One is that science is committed to naturalism. The other is that naturalism is incompatible with dualism—which Leahey identifies as the view that "explains experience and behavior as the result of interaction between the body and its ruling soul." Both these further claims are among the "complications" that I will be addressing.

Still further on in his book (p. 13), Leahey refers to what he calls "the challenge of naturalism," which he explains by saying that "[t]he goal of science is to explain natural things in a natural way, without resorting to supernatural entities or processes, and within a universalizing framework that transcends time, location, history, and culture." We see again the circularity referred to, but also other conceptions that add, I think plausibly, but also vaguely, and in their own ways complicatingly, to the goal of articulating a clear and informative explanation of what naturalism is. Leahey's lapses, and positive if vague articulations, will serve well to launch the project this chapter is concerned with.

I should say that there will be some, I think, philosophers and psychologists, and some who are neither, who may feel a certain impatience with the curt relegation of the formula to an outer darkness of confusion or emptiness. *Don't* we in fact know, and get, what this definition is telling us? Maybe. But in fact, not only is the Leahey definition circular and uninformative, it actually contains, or implies, positive error (quite apart from any complications that relations between naturalism, science, and dualism may involve). The definition as it stands allows the possibility that while supernatural or non-natural causes — whatever precisely *they* are — might never be at work in nature, whatever exactly that is, they might be busily and widely at work elsewhere.

But this seems clearly contrary to what we will have in mind by naturalism (if there is anything clear to have in mind about naturalism — and I think there is). Naturalism wouldn't find acceptable any notion such as there being a *nature* part of the world, and some other part or parts, and naturalism means to tell us only about the first. No, naturalism, whatever exactly it is, is a thesis about the whole of the world, or (perhaps better) the whole of what is amenable and available to rational study and investigation, possibly apart from purely formal or conceptual areas such as mathematics and logic.

Let me reveal the general character of my view, and this chapter, very directly. I do think *naturalism* is an idea with clear, identifiable, non-trivial content. I also think it is not obvious or easy to set out with accuracy and precision what that content is. Further, I believe it is important to know that many philosophers, at least, actually do not agree that naturalism *does* have clear, coherent, or useful content. Some argue that the idea is vacuous or unintelligible.

It is also important to know that many philosophers, including many whose complete comfort with and acceptance of the broad tide and success of modern science is every bit as good — and as well-informed — as any of ours, reject naturalism. They reject it because they think it is vacuous, unintelligible or more than one distinct view, or because they think it is clear, intelligible, and contentful, but demonstrably false. It may be added that many of these philosophers who are scientifically informed, and highly respectful of science, are also atheists and disbelievers in cosmic purpose, astrology, or the paranormal. Many, indeed, are also thinkers who reject psychoanalysis, postmodernism, science studies projects or other theses that advocate (or appear to advocate) social-construction-of-reality views. These philosophers think, rather, that there are compelling arguments, from reasonably familiar and ascertainable facts, that show that naturalism is untrue. The facts in question consist in human agents who act for *reasons*, within a framework of shared norms and institutions. Naturalists will need to, and do attempt to, find ways to "naturalize" this so-called "space of reasons." The philosophers I am referring to argue that these attempts are mistaken and unsuccessful, and are so in principle.

There are other bases that some philosophers have had for rejecting, or just worrying about, naturalism, stemming from real or apparent irreconcilable tensions between naturalism and religion, or morality, or the idea of free choice (or "free will"). In my view, the first two of these tensions are real and irresolvable, and naturalism is the more plausible bet of the contenders; in the third case, that of free choice, the conflict is only apparent, any acceptable or plausible version of free choice being able to be accommodated in a naturalistic world. So, for me, only one of the grounds or bases of anti-naturalism in recent philosophy is a live or serious option.

In this chapter I engage with only some parts of some of the arguments just referred to. My focus is more on how hard it is to articulate a clear and non-circular statement of what naturalism is, even as there are agreed upon and uncontroversial notions of key components of that idea.

Here are some examples of magisterial dicta on the difficulties or unintelligibility of naturalism from some prominent contemporary philosophers. Stephen Stich says, "…it is my contention that there is *no* defensible naturalistic criterion [i.e., a criterion to identify a claim as naturalistic], just as there is no defensible criterion of empirical meaningfulness…. [If naturalists] can be provoked into proposing and criticizing criteria with the same energy that the positivists displayed, it's my bet that… naturalism will ultimately suffer the same fate as positivism did: It will die the death of a thousand failures."[2] And Bas van Fraassen tells us: "To identify what naturalism is, apart from something praiseworthy, I have found nigh-impossible… Most likely it can not be identified with any factual thesis at all."[3] Barry Stroud, for his part, says: "'Naturalism' seems rather like 'World Peace.' Almost everyone swears allegiance to it, and is willing to march under its banner. But disputes can still break out about what is appropriate or acceptable to do in the name of that slogan. And like world peace, once you start specifying concretely exactly what it involves and how to achieve it, it becomes increasingly difficult to reach a consistent and exclusive 'naturalism.'"[4]

Some other leading philosophers seem to be reasonably untroubled about whether naturalism is coherently and non-trivially formulable, but hold that it is refuted by recalcitrant data, specifically involving the facts that human beings engage in rational, cognitive, and normative activity. Hilary Putnam, for example, wrote a famous paper, whose title will indicate the idea, called "Why Reason Can't Be Naturalized." And Jaegwon Kim has argued forcefully that the proposed project of *naturalized epistemology*, introduced by W. V. O. Quine, cannot succeed, because it must fail to capture, or be able to analyze, the fact that epistemology, essentially, aims to disclose grounds of *justification* when we know, or have warranted belief. We've got our work, then, cut out for us if we want to articulate a serious or interesting naturalism, and the greater part of what I present in this chapter will just add to the burden of that labour, even if it will, I think, point in the direction of definitional success.

Obviously enough, naturalism must exclude — indeed, preclude — *non-natural* explanations and properties. Equally obviously, as we have indicated, we want to know just what *natural* explanations and properties are. The *supernatural*, we may suppose, includes gods and at least non-human spirits of various sorts, and powers they are supposed to have and activities they are supposed to engage in. Does it include also so-called *paranormal* phenomena: telepathic communication, precognition, astral travel, astrology, and similar items? Are the latter supernatural, non-natural but not supernatural, or simply cases of *false* natural (and naturalistically formulable?) hypotheses? It seems clear that an intelligent and intelligible naturalism ought to provide antecedent guidelines as to what might count as horizons or boundaries of natural systems. There also need to be clear indications of what in principle would refute naturalism.

Two kinds of ideas don't seem to provide the required horizons, boundaries, or indicators. One is to declare that whatever sorts of posits, parameters, and principles show up in science, especially or specifically and explicitly natural science, or (perhaps) especially or specifically and explicitly physics, are to count as naturalist in the desired sense, and to serve as guiding beacons for naturalist proposals, and inspections, wherever they may occur.

There are several things wrong with this line. One is that it is content-empty. It doesn't tell you what it is about posits, parameters, and principles of science that give them a designated status. A corollary of that problem is that there may be more commonalities to the sciences, or more generic attributes specifically of physics, than just one; so declaration along the line indicated won't differentiate the specifically *naturalist* traits we are looking for.

Another problem is that it seems methodologically unwise as well as unsound to give anyone, or any enterprise, a blank cheque. Naturalism, certainly for naturalists, is supposed to be a good thing. How can confidence justifiably be sustained that a body of practitioners, or practices, will reliably deliver that good thing in indefinitely continuing future time — even if they now are doing so — if it isn't clearly known what that good thing is? Further, every science, including physics, has its eccentrics (I use the word in its literal etymological sense, though I am happy to say that some of those eccentrics are in fact ideologues, even in some cases crackpots; sometimes, let it be added, where they are *otherwise* good scientists). Arguments from authority may not literally always be bad or fallacious, but they are rightly held in suspicion, and certainly deserve to be in this case.

The second undesirable option in this broad direction is to identify naturalism with (so-called) scientific method, or with science, in general: grounding in the observable, testability, repeatability of the tests by a multiplicity of practitioners and in distinct contexts, falsifiability, subsumption under Occam's razor, fit with Mill's methods, etc.

I think there is no doubt that naturalism does involve both belief in and commitment to scientific method and methodology — indeed, of an especially classic, even severe, kind. The problem with the idea that naturalism simply *is* science, or commitment to and practice of scientific method, is that non-naturalists may also share that commitment and may also claim that *their* science, even where not what a pure naturalism would countenance, conforms to appropriate scientific canons and strictures.

Also, rather obviously, if naturalism just *were* science or scientific method, it would be puzzling, if not incomprehensible, why there would be any sort of issue or controversy over whether naturalism is meaningful or true. Naturalism is supposed to be (at least a little) bold, exciting, and contestable. (Even those who think it is true think that.)

A still deeper problem, not unrelated, is that this identification ignores the territoriality issue that naturalism poses. Naturalism claims that nothing — or nothing significantly, or in a theoretical way, knowable about the world — lies outside or beyond nature and the natural, as naturalism conceives them. An advocate of scientific method can hold that its *writ* is limited to what science can explore, leaving doors open to alternative areas of reality and possible knowledge of it, including alternate methodologies, in those domains.

Further difficulties are more concrete and specific. They are posed by cases of reputable, good scientists who forward theories that they evidently suppose are naturalist ones, but that are not, in fact, obviously so. One example that I believe exhibits this problem well is found in the work of the Oxford zoologist and popular science writer Richard Dawkins. There could hardly be a clearer case of a natural scientist and biologist who thinks of and describes himself as a naturalist, or who is more deeply convinced that the limits of naturalist inquiry are the limits of serious possible public knowledge or investigation.

In Dawkins' widely discussed book *The Selfish Gene*,[5] he introduces a postulate, or theoretical construct, that he proposes will have extensive descriptive and explanatory value in understanding much about human behaviour, especially in relatively recent (from a Darwinian point of view) time. This is the concept of a *meme*. A meme is supposed to be an analogue to a gene. Dawkins proposes that both memes and genes be viewed as instances of what he calls a *replicator*, or a replicating entity. Memes are, he says, "a new kind of replicator [that] has recently emerged on" earth. They are, he tells us further, *cultural* replicators. Like genes, they *evolve* (at least in *some* sense of "evolve"). "Examples of memes are tunes, ideas, catch-phrases, clothes fashions, ways of making pots or of building arches. Just as genes propagate themselves in the gene pool by leaping from body to body via sperms or eggs, so memes propagate themselves in the meme pool by leaping from brain to brain via a process which, in the broad sense, can be called imitation" (p. 192).

I am not making this up. This is literally what Dawkins says, as the many who have read his book will know. It is, to be sure, a semi-popular book, which should not perhaps be held to the strictest canons of science. At any rate, *ideas*, for example, are memes, and they can *leap* from one brain to another, though not quite literally, as Dawkins makes plain, only metaphorically.

I don't want particularly to linger on the content, or the plausibility, of Dawkins' meme theory. It seems to me that it might be able to be given greater precision than *The Selfish Gene* provides; and also that it is a suggestive sort of theory, and may even be, properly understood, true.

What I want to ask is whether the theory of the meme is a *naturalist* theory, and, more pointedly, how one would tell that it was, if it were, and how one would tell that it was not, if it weren't. I think a definition, or account, of naturalism, should, if adequate, provide guidance on the matter, at least, and ideally, a decision procedure. That the originator of the theory is a professor of zoology at the University of Oxford, and one who describes himself and his theoretical goals and aims as naturalist through and through, is not, I submit, a sufficient reason to view the meme as a naturalist posit.

It is not obvious that naturalists should view memes as naturalist items. Some of them, at least, cannot be observed. Nor do they seem literally to have locations, observable or otherwise. They are also of so disparate a variety that it will not be evident that they constitute a scientifically recognizable *kind*. It is difficult to believe that the future will include scientists going to their labs to do meme work.

It is important never to lose sight of the fact that we will want to allow and even to insist that there will be naturalist theories —

perfectly good, conceptually respectable and unproblematic ones — that are *false*. And also that naturalist theories, true or false, will involve assumptions, and theoretical postulates, including quite possibly the positing of unobservable entities held necessary or optimally explanatorily adequate for understanding some range of phenomena. Still, memes don't really seem to belong in the same conceptual category, even construed very broadly, as quarks or muons, or as drives or market trends.

I leave Dawkins and memes there, and go on to give an account of what should perhaps most plausibly be included in naturalism, even if each of these ingredients meets with "complication," and also some items that probably should *not* be included as requirements or necessary constituents of the thesis.

My aim, then, is to identify what is or should be meant by "naturalism," as the term figures in current debates in metaphysics, philosophy of science, philosophy of mind, and metaphilosophy, and as well, frequently, in self-identifications by natural and social scientists. This chapter is sympathetic to the idea that a conception of naturalism that is coherent and precise is achievable, but it considers a number of challenges to reaching this outcome. It also raises some issues as to which naturalism appears to be silent, and which may or may not be compatible with a most reasonable construal of the idea.

I present seven key or kernel ideas that appear to go into the core of the naturalist idea. Even if fully and successfully articulable, they will leave several questions unanswered or not clearly determined. That is to say, we would have at best a set of necessary ingredients, or conditions, of naturalism (even if arguably the most important components), not a fully sufficient set. In any case, all seven will be seen to pose difficulty of one sort or other.

I note that several distinct definitions or characterizations of naturalism are to be found in the philosophical literature. (In some cases, specific subvarieties of naturalism — e.g., "social naturalism" and "hard naturalism" — are offered and explicated.) Features of some of these definitions and characterizations will be similar to what appears in the account to follow. I will not in any systematic way indicate points of overlap and divergence. I will mention, though, that one important characterization occurs in Arthur C. Danto's article on naturalism that appears in the *Encyclopedia of Philosophy* (1967). Danto itemizes 14 "tenets," most or all of which, he says, naturalists will endorse. Some of Danto's 14 tenets appear among the seven conceptions I will indicate; others seem too specific to particular forms of naturalism, or in some cases unclear or uninformative (not that the list that will follow is entirely a model of clarity).

Here, then, are the seven. 1) Naturalism involves a conception of a unity of the world, as a single, integrated system with nothing outside or beyond it. 2) It also involves a rejection at least of large-scale teleology — purposiveness or directedness — in that system. 3) It includes, as well, a rejection of overarching minds ("gods") who are supposed to have created or ordered the system of the world in whole or in part. (One might suppose this third ingredient would follow from the second — that anti-teleology would imply anti-theology. But this need not be so. The world could have been the work of infant or senile gods who didn't know what they were doing — as Hume saw.) 4) Naturalism also seems essentially to involve an idea of a closed causal structure for the world. (This won't automatically follow from the unity intended with the first ingredient, since unities can be other than causal ones.) 5) Further, naturalism will seem essentially to involve a close symbiosis with physics — with natural science broadly, but in an especially fundamental way with physics. Current and developing physics will be regarded by naturalists as giving the concrete truth of the world, or at any rate providing its core and foundation, ontologically and conceptually. 6) The sixth idea is a thesis of a certain atomicity and compositionality: whatever is in the system of the world is to be understood as built up out of, and at least in some manner reducible to, at least relatively small parts or units of it. I note that *some* naturalists would not insist on even a version of this reductivism as part of their view. 7) The seventh component in the naturalist cluster is posed by naturalism's relation or relations to the normative: more specifically, the axiological, and most specifically, the ethical. For naturalists, there is a sharp boundary between non-normative facts and states comprising the system of the world, and the value, or ethical status, that some minds may assign to some of those facts or states or to the world as a whole. Naturalists would also deny that there are intrinsic, irreducible normative facts or states of affairs.

All seven of the preceding naturalism-cluster constituent ideas raise questions, some of them leading to at least apparent objections or problems. Some of these are legitimate requests for (greater) clarity and precision. Others have to do with the *character* of the rejections or exclusions some of the constituents involve. Are those rejections and exclusions (meant to be) *a priori* in nature? Or do they (merely) reflect what investigation of the world happens to disclose? There might have been gods, big purposes, objective ethical realities, wholly disjoint segments of the world, but it has turned out that there were not? Possibly, of course, some of the rejections/exclusions have one character, others another.

The latter seems quite right. There are no possible worlds where normative items have an ontological status other than their status — whatever that is — in the actual world. But there are worlds with gods, and others without them. Ours seems to be among the latter group. In any case, in some of the worlds with gods, there is just one of them, and a large plan, and set of guiding goals and principles, that the world in question is implementing or living through. On the other hand, the — Aristotelian — idea of purposes and functions that are in the nature of things, telea, including possibly one for the whole scheme, and (all of) which are independent of any mind whose plan, design, or purpose they were, seems dubious or problematic, i.e., for any world.

It does seem, then, that some of the rejections/exclusions of naturalism will be *a priori* in character, others *a posteriori*. Moving on to other queries regarding our seven identified central cluster features of naturalism, I have already remarked that teleology without minds—and large(-scale) teleology without large(-scale) minds—is problematic. Still, teleology lingers in the life sciences, and some argue that the prospects for its complete and entire removal in a putative future fully physicalist biology are not good. Even if this were so, it is unclear whether that would refute the fundamental naturalist idea, or whether the (allegedly) ineliminable teleological and functional properties of living systems are in any conceptually interesting sense contra-naturalist purposes.

Gods complicate naturalism in a partly similar way. It seems perfectly feasible that there be a planetary system somewhere in the cosmos where there was a local intelligence, of remarkably stable physical composition, that was in control of an impressive range of the doings in that system, and causally responsible for quite a lot of the orderings and arrangements that took place there—a local god, one might say. Such a mind might have quite an extensive degree of power in its local setting, and an impressive mental life. There is no evidence that any such planetary system, and being, exist; but the universe is vast, and there really *might* be—it seems—some such structure somewhere. If so, it would seem that it would be possible that there be whole *galaxies* comparably ruled and ordered.

This is not meant primarily to affirm the contingency of theism—i.e., that it is conceptually and metaphysically possible that there is a God—for if a galaxy had one, why not the whole universe? The point is rather, at least in this context, that the existence of gods, of some sort at least, might be entirely *natural* facts, and that some subsystem of the world had a god in charge would not, as such, be more striking, or significant, than that some countries are monarchies while others are republics.

Inverting the matter, what is it about supernaturalism, or what is meant by supernaturalism, such that it is incompatible—and it is supposed to be strongly incompatible—with naturalism? I pose the idea of a—presumably false—naturalist theism; that is, whether, under the umbrella of post-Galilean modern science, there could be articulated theistic hypotheses (of one sort or other), which could be subjected to standard conjecture and refutation Popper-style scrutiny; and then if there could be, this would complicate and problematize the naturalist idea, because that idea is supposed to be profoundly antithetical to "supernaturalism" in any form. The *problem*, if it is one, is meant to pose itself even if such putative theistic hypotheses I am bringing to consideration might all turn out false, or without strong, evidentiary warrant. The issue is whether advocacy of, say, an anthropic principle in cosmology is to abandon naturalism, or whether a theism of a (Leibniz-derived) Whiteheadian sort might be fit under a stretched naturalist umbrella, as well as "local" theisms of one sort or other, in proper parts of the universe.

Such a naturalist theism is not to be confused with another theoretical contender, one of several that claim (or are claimed) to be naturalist, but whose claims seem appropriate to reject; namely, Thomistic Aristotelian "naturalism." The quotation marks around the last word of the preceding sentence are appropriate and important. Catholic philosophy continues to be a significant player in the contemporary philosophical world. A long and rich tradition that achieved full formation well before the 17th-century scientific revolution (even if with subsequent, including present-day, innovative reconfigurations and rejuvenations), the Catholic philosophy — Thomism — asserts itself as a comprehensive account of nature and its workings, and a location and understanding of humanity as a distinctive animal species within that setting, all underwritten by a body of "natural law," systematically and systemically promulgated by a supreme architect and ruler. The Catholic philosophy may or may not have a plausible basis of claim for the rational allegiance of a modern mind, independent of allegiance to Catholic religion. In any case, that philosophy was historically a rival to, not a variant of, the Democritean philosophy of which modern naturalism is the heir and successor. Part of the realization achieved in the 17th-century scientific revolution was that — to considerable surprise, one might say — at least in the "natural sphere," apart, at least, from our rational and free selves, Democritus had been, not just partly right, but 100-percent right.

The thesis of the unity of the world is also "complicatable." For naturalist modal realists, such as David Lewis, there is an indefinite plurality of really existing possible worlds, in which non-actual events and individuals resembling actual ones obtain, but are disconnected from the causal order of the actual world. Other theories, some at least purporting to be hypotheses of current physical cosmology, affirm the not-merely-modal reality of alternative structures in the actual world, causally disjoint, or mostly so, from the regular accessible physical world. Are such theories naturalistic, or able to be accommodated to a broadly naturalist understanding and set of commitments?

As for the anti-normative: clearly, there are *norms* of scientific methodology and practice (some of them arguably ethical ones). So it appears that the normative, at least of some variety, has a role or location of one sort or other in the articulation, if not the content, of naturalism. There also are facts such as the fact that a person may be *rationally justified* in having some belief that he or she has. If naturalism is true, there will have to be a purely naturalistic rendering, analysis or account of such facts.

Further, on an apparently less theoretical plane — though its theoretical intelligibility is also challenging — (naturalist) physicists (and other naturalist scientists) and philosophers participate publicly in ethical debates and issues, and do so in some measure at least qua — as — physicists and philosophers. A number of philosophers, in particular, view themselves as naturalists and at the same time as moral objectivists or moral realists. Some, but only some, of the latter constituency are also ethical naturalists — people who think that the ethical (presumably also all of the normative) just *is* a certain sort of complex case of the natural, factual, and physical; that is, that the ethical is reducible to non-normative empirical states and properties.

My own view is that this last position is indefensible; but also that it alone would permit consistency in the union of naturalism and axiological objectivism that some philosophers clearly affirm or commit themselves to. Consistency is, of course, a virtue whose merits many want to say are exaggerated. But we are seeking to articulate an idea, with our focus on that idea rather than its contemporary or historical practitioners. In any case, it is arguable that naturalist physicists and philosophers who participate in public ethical debate are doing so as relevantly informed, or skilled, concerned citizens, and not as physicists or philosophers as such.

It is to be noted that ethical naturalism is distinct from, indeed incompatible with, another position that has appeared in the history of ethics, according to which ethical properties and states are *sui generis* — accordingly not reducible to anything else — and objectively, and non-relationally, in the world. G. E. Moore held a version of this view, according to which ethical properties are primitive and indefinable and (what he called) non-natural. Although Moore proceeded to try to define natural and non-natural properties, it is problematic whether the contrast, as he drew it, is altogether clear or satisfactory.

In any case, there is a variant position, similar to Moore's, according to which ethical properties (and states) constitute a unique variety of natural properties (and states) that are discernible by a moral intuition faculty or in some other way. Still another moral objectivist position treats ethical properties as genuine, and genuinely instantiated in the world, in relational states of affairs involving observing or experiencing minds and (particular sorts of) conditions they observe or experience.

None of these moral realist/moral objectivist positions appears to be compatible with a full and consistent naturalism; indeed, it appears to be definitionally true that naturalism excludes all of them — not arbitrarily, or dogmatically, but because naturalism *includes* insights, or alleged insights, about the ethical as well as about the "natural." Still — and given also the evident normativity in any possible comprehensive characterization of scientific theory and practice, which seems ineluctably to underwrite the naturalist idea — it is elusive what *precisely* is involved in the relationship between norms and the natural, as naturalism sees the matter.

The seventh component of naturalism I am trying to give at least preliminary content to might be characterized as an idea of norm-exclusion — to contrast it with norm-rejection. Naturalism rejects gods and large-scale purposes, but it in contrast declines to bring into its reckonings the normative and valuational (except where, if and as such cases could be made out, the normative and valuational might be demonstrably reducible to the non-normative and non-valuational). Naturalism implies that a reckoning of the world need not countenance, and does not include, the irreducibly normative or valuational.

A further complexity deserves mention with regard to naturalism and the normative, specifically the ethical, and which might or might not provide content to the idea just indicated. Just what *the ethical*, precisely, *is*, is notoriously challenging, and views have differed widely. One interesting, though elusive, idea is the one apparently intended in Wittgenstein's *Tractatus Logico-Philosophicus* (especially in sections 6.4 to 6.52). (It also appears, and is endorsed, in Wilfrid Sellars' essay "Philosophy and the Scientific Image of Man."[6]) According to this idea, at least on one construal of it, the ethical component of life, thought, and discourse is not a matter of asserting the obtaining or non-obtaining of facts of the world, but is, rather, something that stands (somehow) *outside* those facts and is a matter of attitude toward and action upon the world. The *Tractatus'* conception is fairly clearly similar to a range of *noncognitivist* proposals and theories about ethics that were developed primarily in the 1930s, the best known of which is *emotivism* (an importantly distinct noncognitivist view is presented, though not fully developed, in Russell's *Religion and Science* [1935].)

However, the noncognitivist stances of the 1930s are generally seen as, in an important sense, *reductions* of the ethical to subjective states and attitudes (for Russell's noncognitivism, unlike Stevenson's, those states and attitudes are *sui generis*, with no more than resemblance to any other subjective states; they are nonetheless subjective). Although something conceptually problematic may be involved in putting it this way, they "delegitimize" or "devalidate" the ethical. People (most? just some philosophers?) had supposed that in the ethical sphere they were in touch with and giving expression to, something beyond or outside themselves and their (mere) attitudes and feelings; and, according to standard noncognitivism, they are wrong about this. The Wittgenstein idea, however, in the *Tractatus*, is—apparently; Wittgenstein is characteristically cryptic in how he puts it—that the ethical sphere *is* "valid," "legitimate," and not merely subjectively attitudinal, but at the same time not something expressible as a matter of true and false claims as to the facts of the world, or, indeed, as to anything else. (It is a matter of "the mystical"; Wittgenstein may have got the idea from reading some of the religious writings of Tolstoy.)

With all due apology for the vagueness of the preceding, the *Tractatus* idea about ethics might be held, if it can be argued to have a coherent and feasible sense (and perhaps it can), to create an *option* for naturalist philosophy with regard to the ethical, which would allow, or putatively allow, naturalism to be, in the specially *Tractatus* way, moral realist or moral objectivist. (So Sellars, for example, seems to have believed.) The *Tractatus* itself appears to be a naturalist text, or to give expression to essentially naturalist or naturalism-compatible views. (So it was taken—though, in some cases, at their peril—by members of the Vienna Circle.)

The complication, though, will be whether this really is feasible, or plausible, or in a—or the—genuine spirit of the naturalist idea. For, certainly as we understand that idea, naturalism limits "the facts" to potential scientific facts, and denies that there is knowledge beyond knowledge of such facts, except, possibly, for conceptually necessary knowledge (analytic truths, mathematics, and facts of methodology) and perhaps philosophical—specifically metaphysical—knowledge where the latter is conceived as just more general scientific knowledge (than the sciences usually explicitly affirm). It is true that for the *Tractatus* idea, there won't be (claimed to be) moral facts, and the whole of what is the case will be exhausted by science (together possibly, and if understood in the right way, by conceptually necessary knowledge and metaphysics-as-general-science). However, in that *Tractatus* idea, the ethical is still *there*, and, evidently, not illusion or error or mere subjectivity.

I will leave the matter here, and go on to other facets of complication posed by others of the alleged defining traits or theses of naturalism. Some will (and many more likely will not) be attracted to a construal of "the ethical" along these Wittgensteinian lines, and then perhaps to an embracing or a conceptual marshalling of a naturalism that might be alleged to permit union of this idea with a "scientific view of the world." In any event, it poses an interesting challenge, puzzle, and complication.

We turn next to causality. The idea appears to manifest a historical and conceptual elasticity, which poses query for naturalism. Is there an inherent causal *necessity*, a coercive causal glue that binds causes and their effects? Or is so supposing something the mind imposes? Naturalists have historically embraced both alternatives. They have also sometimes been determinist, and sometimes not; current physics is, of course, indeterminist.

In fact, the naturalist idea does seem to accommodate itself satisfactorily to the elasticity we find with the modal character of causality. A naturalist can, as well, see the causal structure of the world as a matter of iron modal rigidities, a "law's empire" in a peculiarly blind and impersonal and coercive sense, or adopt a Humean radical contingency view, the world an only partly self-disclosing mystery that just does happen — so far, anyway — to present itself in uniformities of varying degrees, right up to lots of 100-percent cases, anything modal about the matter being our additions.

With regard to naturalism and physics, even if any naturalist's credentials will doubtless imply full and energetic allegiance to current and future physics, as an identifying insignium of naturalism, this idea seems to have a cart before the horse. That any property that figures in a satisfactory theory, description, or explanation of physics as a natural property will no doubt be true, but will not tell us why this is so or what it is for it to be so. This criterion seems, then, uninformative unless the conditions of physical and naturalistic satisfactoriness are explained.

There is, further, the evident and significant fact that not all of natural science is physics. Earlier programmatic goals of reduction of all natural science to physics have not been spectacularly successful. It will be clear that a plausible naturalism will not insist on any such successful reduction, even in principle. But just what the relations are among the several natural sciences, and among their objects, must clearly be relevant to what sort of thesis the naturalist thesis is, and what credibility it should be seen as deserving. If, for example, it were the case that components of biological systems turned out to be ontologically and conceptually *sui generis*, and the domain of natural science to be an archipelago of critically discrete subterritories (even if sharing causal and methodological constraints), that must presumably invite prospects that there are other, much more distantly related island structures in the world that we are part of and can hope (at least partly) to know, and that would presumably constitute a refutation of naturalism. Yet it would seem wrong to take there to be something in the "logic" of naturalism that must force it dialectically, even if it weren't intended that it would do this, to a strong unity of science thesis. How then to sort out the fundamental character and relations of the several natural sciences (still more problematically, adding to the terrain of view at least some of the social sciences) vis-à-vis each other?

What of atomicity/compositionality? Even though all don't, many naturalists include doctrines of this kind in their view. The early Greek atomists, of both Democritean and Epicurean persuasions, developed reductive theories aimed to show that everything was formed out of atoms and void, and they went to heroic if not always persuasive imaginative lengths to show this. The aim of science as such is to seek maximal simplification and unity in its postulates and explanations. The fewer basic (kind of) entities, the better, all reduction of principles as of ontic types to a more economical stock is advance. Still, the drive to conceptual economy might well not meet with success in reducing all to minimal observable or smallest particles (together with principles for their Boolean products and causal interactions) — the two usual historical candidates of the empiricist and materialist varieties of naturalism. Is it evident that commitments to irreducibly larger sorts of observables or objects must necessarily compromise an individual's naturalism?

Naturalism is, we may say, a philosophical stance that seeks to explore whatever it investigates using canons and categories, ontological and methodological, which it purports to derive from, or sees as implicit in, natural science activity and results, and which affirms as dubious or problematic the investigation of any philosophical territory or issue in any other way or on any other basis.

Naturalism, it is to be observed, is not the same as *positivism*. Positivism, at least as it figured in its 19th-century version and in its 20th-century so-called "logical" variant, explicitly repudiated the pretensions, usually even the possibility or coherence, of metaphysics; that is, of a project of producing a theory of the fundamental nature of reality. Naturalism as such, on the other hand, does not exclude that project. Neither does it imply it. Positivists are naturalists, but not all naturalists are positivists.

I referred above to the two primary historic streams, or orientations, within naturalism. More should be said about them, because the differences between them also constitute a complication for naturalism as such, a deep-level query, if not objection, as to just what the naturalist idea is and whether it can reasonably be seen as a single coherent thing.

On the one hand, then, the naturalist project has historically, for some, been an undertaking grounded in, and aspiring to reduce or understand all targets of inquiry or analysis in terms of, an observational perspective. Paramount for this approach has been groundings in classic primary and secondary sensory qualities, and observations/experiences of them (or of their being exemplified), from — or, as though from — the perspective, vantage point, or observational location of an individual mind. Some of the qualifications in the foregoing stem from the fact that for many naturalist views, there are not really or literally any such things as minds.

Exploring, still less adjudicating, this facet of empiricist and naturalist history, is not of present concern. I will speak of a first-person perspective, but mean by it a disjunction of a self's (or observing animal's) perspective, or a passive-voice construal of a view from a here (which may or may not require a someone or something doing the viewing), or a Vaihinger-style "as though" (or "as if") construal, of the sort favoured in recent discussions by Dennett and others. Still another complexity in the "first-person perspective" variety or stream of naturalism is whether it implies commitment to what is called phenomenalism; then, whether or not it does, whether phenomenalism in turn implies commitment to, or is a form of, philosophical idealism.

The prototype of first-person perspective naturalism is Hume's *Treatise of Human Nature*. Russell's *Our Knowledge of the External World* and Carnap's *Aufbau* are classic texts where this variety of empiricist/naturalist project is undertaken in ambitious and comprehensive ways; the one, interestingly also a metaphysical realist instance of naturalism, and the other an anti-metaphysical realist instance.

Naturalist endeavour has also, on the other hand, set itself to analyze and construct (a theory of) the world, or to construct a comprehensive body of cognitively adequate discourse, in its own terms, and not from an observational position. Classical materialist projects have been of this sort, from those of the ancient atomists, to the materialism of the early modern period, to the materialism that has been usual over the course of the past half-century. Here the idea has been to articulate and forward a theory of material minima—material particles, or states—or minima in the vicinity of cognizing systems, where the attention has been restricted to those (and not also aiming to produce a comprehensive theory of the whole world, or of cognitively adequate discourse).

I do not mean to suggest that reconciling or formulating a correspondence between these two naturalist/empiricist approaches is not feasible. But it will be clear that it is a task needing to be achieved, and that it is naturalism-complicating.

A next stage of exploring naturalism would address issues as to which naturalism as such appears to be *silent*. That naturalism is silent in respect of some very fundamental issues has already been affirmed. You can be a naturalist and a metaphysical realist, and you can also be a naturalist and an anti-realist. Naturalism as such doesn't license or endorse the project of seeking to come to conclusions about what actually exists, and the natures and mutual relations of what exists and what is true; nor does it preclude or foreclose on such projects.

Still another issue on which naturalism at least *should* be silent, I think, is *materialism* or *physicalism*. There has actually been extensive discussion in the literature, in this case going back to the 1940s and continuing since, as to whether naturalism implies materialism. Since no one now is seriously a philosophical idealist (at least in any classic sense), the two options in this territory — the territory that explores things that have experiences, i.e., psychology and philosophy of mind — are materialism, in one version or other, and dualism, in one version or other. So if you held that naturalism *excludes* dualism, as we saw, at the beginning, that Leahey holds, you would be committed to the idea that naturalism *does* imply materialism.

This does seem premature or undesirable. There really are more dualisms than one — e.g., property dualisms that deny immaterial minds or souls; one such property dualism is epiphenomenalism, perhaps most "naturalistic" of all dualist stances — and there is no question that *much* theoretical work in the social and life sciences is at least *methodologically* dualist. It proceeds as though there are beliefs, desires, etc., without worrying (or indeed, asking) whether, or assuming that, those things are actually brain states, or even supervenient on brain states. Further, materialism has proved difficult to establish in a clear, unitary, and empirically confirmable way. In spite of that fact, most philosophers now remain committed materialists in the philosophy of mind, even if with only disjunctive or unfilled-in commitment. At any rate, it seems soundest not to require that naturalism as such be materialist (hence, anti-dualist).

Other questions are posed by *property-realism*, and by *indexicality*. For some philosophers of naturalist sympathy, it is evident that naturalism implies a nominalist stance on abstract entities like properties, or a positivist or similar position that the issue itself is incoherent. Others, however, also of naturalist leaning, or with a self-identification in "scientific philosophy" (e.g., Russell, Armstrong, and (early) Putnam), affirm the reality of (at least some kinds of) properties. The issue is multiply complex, and yet also, in the end, one about which the advocates of naturalism can be somewhat sanguine, I believe.

The facts appear to be that *physics*, for naturalists, as we have said, the lodestar and central model for their conception, needs both mathematics and properties. Some philosophers of mathematics, and of science, most notably Hartry Field, have sought to show that a view of mathematics adequate for science can be wholly nominalistic. Other philosophers, metaphysicians and philosophers of science, typically, have tried to develop accounts of properties, or qualities, that will enable viewing them not as abstract entities. (One such view is the notion of so-called property *tropes*, or *concrete "universals,"* according to which the red, or loudness, or acidity, or divisibility by four, of this particular item is something individual and particular to the item. Other views take what more classically were thought of as so-called conceptualist views of the abstract, construing the things under this head as entirely mental items, without genuine reality beyond the mind. Still other positions seek to take the supposed sting out of the abstract, by taking their central and clearest cases to be sensory qualities, which appear to be able to be experienced directly, even if they may also appear in the experiences of others.)

The options are several; and even within classical abstract entity theory, there are the Platonistic sorts of stances (according to which abstract things—such as, e.g., being a 20th-century female lunar explorer—don't require actual instances in order to be real), and the Aristotelian sorts of stances (according to which the only real abstracta are ones with instances). In any case, it does seem clear: physics needs both mathematics and properties (construed or conceived in one way or other). Although it is the path of least work, imagination, or courage, the naturalist can, quite reasonably, I think, simply adopt, or aggregate to his/her naturalism, whatever account of so-called abstract entities is the most plausible one to hold for physics. There will not, at any rate, be a *special* problem for naturalism posed by abstract things, or an issue that need require taking a particular designated stance. There may, of course, remain problems posed by *particular* sorts of properties (as opposed to properties as such) for naturalists— especially, of course, properties that go with being a free rational agent embedded within culture and normativity, or, according to some, the property of being *conscious*.

Somewhat more prosaic, but still naturalism-challenging, is whether naturalism can, or should, accommodate *indexical* states—e.g., that I am here now, or that dinosaurs are long extinct—as irreducible *sui generis* parts of the world. While such states may appear at first to pose merely technical, or artificial, challenges or questions for a naturalistic view of the world, they in fact are parts of a considerably larger and deeper apparent reality, about which naturalism might, arguably, need to take a committed position. That larger and deeper apparent reality comprises the perspective or point of view of a subject—the world, or a part of it, as it seems to or is experienced by *me*, and *you*, and each several one of us, where the idea is that it is an irreducible or ineliminable fact that such perspectival facts include the particular subject concerned, i.e., *as* me, you, etc.

In this instance, it seems, naturalism cannot lean upon physics. Physics does not need irreducible facts such as my being here now. It can express all that it purports to express by naming me by a proper name (perhaps even eliminating that in favour of a suitable definite description), and using spatio-temporal coordinates for my location. My inclination is to hold that the spirit of naturalism is at odds with (irreducible) so-called *phenomenological facts*, or *facts of subjectity*. If there really were such irreducible facts, they would compromise, if not formally refute, naturalism. At the same time, it might be argued that if this were the only objection to naturalism, it might not provide much of a reason to be other than a very modestly qualified almost-naturalist. Maybe. At any rate, this will be yet another area where there is more work to be done.

NOTES

1 Thomas Hardy Leahey, *A History of Modern Psychology*, 2nd ed. (Englewood Cliffs, N. J.: Prentice Hall, 1994).
2 *Deconstructing the Mind* (Oxford University Press, 1996), p. 197.
3 "Science, Materialism, and False Consciousness," in J. Kvanvig, ed., *Warrant in Contemporary Epistemology* (Rowman and Littlefield, 1996), p. 172.
4 "The Charm of Naturalism," Proceedings and Addresses of the American Philosophical Association 70, 2, Nov. 1996, 43–44.
5 Oxford University Press, 1976; 2nd ed. 1989.
6 Reprinted in Wilfrid Sellars, *Science, Perception and Reality* (Ridgeview, 1963 and 1991).

CHAPTER SIX

NATURALISM AND THE NORMATIVE

An earlier version of this paper was presented as part of a "research in progress" series at the University of Guelph, in November 2004.

One of the deepest and most intractable problems of philosophy is this: what is the place of humanity within nature? What, at the most fundamental level, is the relationship between human beings and the rest of the animal and vegetable "kingdoms" and the wider, larger domain of inanimate objects and processes and the facts and events that they involve?

Two apparently irreconcilable positions have been taken on the question. *Naturalism* holds that everything true about human beings, including their creative activities and institutions, can be understood within the same broad scientific framework used to explain and understand non-human nature (especially its living parts). Now, *exactly* what naturalism means, beyond the formula just given, is itself a matter of considerable complexity. I have a lot to say about this matter and its complications, but will not, for the most part, try to do so in this chapter. Perhaps it will suffice to say that naturalism, for present purposes, is the thesis that when trying to provide a true factual descriptive or explanatory account of any part of the world, no concepts, models, or procedures are necessary, at least in principle, apart from concepts, models, and procedures of the natural sciences, including the life sciences, and empirical psychology, including basic so-called "folk psychology" (in which simple or minimal sensations, beliefs, desires, and comparable states — of no greater complexity than appear in the same kinds of states in non-human animals — are accepted as scientifically legitimate[1]).

(The very idea of "basic" folk psychology as just explained is itself controversial. Part of the detail of why that is so will be seen below. At any rate, as explained so far, naturalism will allow that, in an unequivocal sense, both a dog and a friend of the dog's owner might believe, in suitable circumstances, that the owner was soon to arrive home.)

With naturalism thus explained, it might seem obvious that the thesis is false. Thus, for example, consider the claim that in some countries, but not in others, it is illegal to criticize the head of state in the public media. That claim appears to be *true* — there *are* countries in which such activities are, respectively, legally impermissible and permissible (e.g., Thailand and Sweden) — and yet the *language* of the claim involves terminology that would not be found in any natural science, or in the language of sensations, beliefs, or desires.

That is where the "in principle" of the assertion about naturalism comes in. The naturalist idea, and resulting thesis, is that to the extent to which the indicated factual claim is true (and some naturalists would deny that such a claim *is* literally or strictly true), there will, perhaps only in some somewhat remote future, be achieved analyses of what such things as being a country and its head, and of a legal system, criticism, and public media, involve, that will be entirely expressible as physical, biological, or psychological facts about physical and biological systems and objects.

I hope it will not introduce confusion to note that naturalism does *not* imply that all *concepts* are (even in principle) expressible as or reducible to physical, biological, or straightforward folk psychological concepts. *That* thesis is fairly certainly false. Naturalism is, rather, a claim that all of the facts — for some, all of the basic facts — of the world, or all of the facts about human beings, are physical, biological, or psychological facts.

The opposing position, which I call *agent anomalism*, holds that features of *agency*, of acting for reasons within a network of interpersonal cultural practice — of sorts illustrated by the example just provided — imply that we *transcend* nature or are otherwise not able fully to be understood as natural systems (hence, that we are "anomalies" within the larger natural framework of the universe).

The example given involves instances of legal and cultural *norms*, and many philosophers have seen *normativity* as the strongest arrow in the anti-naturalist quiver. Normativity consists in our ethical and valuational lives, practices, and institutions, and also in our capacities to reason and reach conclusions that are *justified*.

This chapter explores particular facets of normativity and the challenges it poses for naturalism, as well as the prospects of resolution of naturalist and anti-naturalist dispute that derive from this source. One currently very popular view among a number of philosophers is what is called *supervenience naturalism*, according to which all of the basic facts are physical or biological, and there *supervene* upon them all sorts of psychological, and also cultural and social, and for some versions institutional and normative, facts or states. These are entirely *fixed* or determined (strongly determined: for every possible world, in fact) by the basic facts. Supervenience is itself a little complicated. In any case, supervenience naturalism is a sort of way of trying to have your cake and eat it too; and perhaps, in this case, you can. But I shall ignore supervenience naturalism in this chapter, because it is both complex and controversial, and also because it does not directly confront the kinds of considerations that agent anomalists think make naturalism in any form completely implausible.

An older vocabulary, and conceptualization, saw humanity as *transcending* nature not merely because we are rational agents. The latter — our rational agency — was seen as the overt public face of a deeper fact: that we are made in the image of God, by which was evidently meant that we are beings set apart from nature, at least metaphorically sons and daughters of the deity, which no other element of nature is. (At least on our planet. Committed theists have standardly been allowed to be agnostic about possibilities of other intelligent life — other persons — that God might have created elsewhere than in the solar system.)

The current philosophical issue that I am addressing is a secular one, cast in secular terms. But certainly many people, even many philosophers among them, *care* about the issue and think it is important, because of the larger theological and cosmological matters just referred to.

Others, again sizeable numbers both of philosophers and non-philosophers, have cared whether naturalism or its supposed opposite (agent anomalism; it might also be called transcendental personalism) is true, for a different reason. They have cared because they have supposed that if naturalism *were* the truth about us — if we were wholly and entirely parts of nature, like other parts, and wholly able to be understood within a broadly scientific framework, at least in principle — this would imply that we don't really make genuinely *free choices*, or have (as it was usually put in the past) *free will*. If we *are* unfree, then a cherished conviction that at least part of what happens to us is *up to us*, something we have some hand in directing, is an illusion, a mere façade. Art as well as science exists — it may be said — in part to puncture our illusions, and often we are the better for it when we learn, when we do, that something we had thought splendid about ourselves is not really so splendid, or in some cases not even true. But a result, if we had good reason to come to such a result, that we have not merely less control or direction than we have supposed, but in fact no control whatsoever over what we do or what happens to us, would be more than merely humbling and properly deflating of our sometimes overweening pretensions. It would imply that we are not agents, nor persons as we have supposed, at all.

A further concern some have had goes beyond mere unfreedom. It is a concern that if naturalism were true, then we must be a certain sort of complex natural mechanism, with only a façade or illusion of having a *unity* as a person or subject, being rather a kind of robot all of the mainsprings of whose doings are physiological, biochemical, and automatic.

Still another concern naturalism has raised has been with ethics. If naturalism is true, what happens to morality? What happens to right and wrong? "To understand everything is to forgive everything," Voltaire warned (or triumphalistically affirmed).[2] If everything is on a natural plane of causes and effects, operating exceptionlessly in accordance with laws of nature that hold independently of any of us, or of our planet, what room will there be for duty or justice? Worse than that, won't ethical ideas themselves need to turn out to be reducible to psychological dispositions that are merely species-specific, or else vacuous, extensionless?

The preceding, then, points to four bases from which naturalism is seen, not just as an issue of some interest and concern for lots of people, but as a *scary* issue; as something we, or lots of us, don't want to be true, hope isn't, even as we sometimes may — some of us, anyway, in incautious or insecure moments — *fear* may be true after all.

In fact, the philosophers who have been engaged in the contestations to which I referred at the start do not, mostly, take it up to allay – or to promote — anyone's fears. These philosophers are mostly secularists, or, where they are not, religious convictions or commitments are kept off the stage of investigation and debate. Further, most — not all — of these philosophers do not see the issue of freedom and unfreedom as central for the topic they engage.

Many philosophers nowadays accept some version of a position that was apparently first articulated by the brilliant ancient Stoic philosopher Chrysippus, and which has been called *compatibilism*. (That term first appears with the intended meaning, in — curiously — an introductory philosophy textbook, in 1959.[3]) This is the thesis that freedom – genuine, real-alternatives rational agency freedom — is *compatible* with determinism: genuine, 100-percent causal determinism, of every single event, state, and act, and all their aspects and parts. After Chrysippus, compatibilism was developed in an explicit modern way by Leibniz, and subsequently defended by Hume, by Mill, and by a small army of philosophers since 1900.

It is important to note that many philosophers also are *not* compatibilists. They have looked into the matter, have heard the arguments, and remain unconvinced. Nowadays many philosophers are compatibilists, many are incompatibilists, and many aren't sure what to think. I myself am a compatibilist; at least 13 days out of 14, so to speak. (Every fortnight, or thereabouts, I find myself wavering, or perhaps just unclear about the matter.)

Anyway, the primary locus, and the primary focus, of contestation vis-à-vis naturalism and anti-naturalism, now, is not a concern, one way or the other, with freedom. Most naturalists think that our freedom is real, and that naturalism can accommodate it, and most anti-naturalists agree with them about that, or else think that the most important places of engagement and dispute are elsewhere. In short, then, both God and freedom are rather off the stage of what is seen importantly as at stake in this territory, at least as philosophy in recent decades has concerned itself with my theme.

As for physiological mechanism—the idea that we are essentially naturally selected living robots—this one seems to me a genuine, and genuinely scary—well, unwelcome—theoretical possibility. That is, I don't see anything in a scientific or a naturalistic point of view that would undermine or threaten the possibility of our freedom. But I do think that even if science, and nature, *allow* the possibility of real freedom, they do not ensure it. Moreover there *may* be, I believe, scientific evidence that would sabotage, not merely our freedom, but our rational personhood in any meaningful sense. (In fact, it would even be possible that we are more or less "free," some of the time, even where we might be non-persons.) However, the naturalist idea as such does not imply physiological mechanism any more than it implies unfreedom. And anyway, this too—physiological mechanism, and whether or not we should believe it, or even give it serious consideration — has not been a principal site of engagement between naturalists and their opponents.

As for the ethical: this facet of the world or our conceptualization of it, and actions induced by it, *does* have a larger and at least somewhat more direct place in the naturalist-agent anomalist cluster of contestation, but it is oblique, and it is extraordinarily complex and is variable from thinker to thinker and position to position. *The ethical* is, of course, one very important branch of *the normative*, and as I have already indicated, it is primarily in normativity that the anti-naturalists I am concerned with think that naturalism comes to grief. Normativity plus a special holism that being us, and doing what we do, involves.

The specifically ethical is nonetheless treated very differently by philosophers who regard themselves as naturalists or as anti-naturalist agent anomalists. There are moral realists and objectivists in both parties, and also moral noncognitivists and moral agnostics. In what follows, accordingly, I will have more or less nothing to say about right and wrong, and what happens to them according as the outcome of my inquiry is one thing rather than another. The larger, more complete resolution of the polarity and contestation I am exploring will necessarily have something explicit and definitive to say about the ethical, but that will be in settings other than this chapter.

However, the normative, more generically, will directly engage us. For, as indicated, centrally posed in this debate has been whether naturalism can cover, handle, encompass the *normative*; and also (as also mentioned) a certain sort of *holism* that rational agency seems to involve.

Before proceeding to some of the details of what this cluster of concerns is about, and to acquainting you better with what some of my own research in the area involves, I want to note a few features of the area and the stances it leads to that are, as it were, on the outside and at some distance from the nitty gritty of debate. One is that we find a considerable confidence, on both sides, that the position advocated is correct. Indeed, for that reason — at any rate, for *some* reason or other — it is not easy to find respectful consideration of the possibility that the other side might be right and one's own be wrong, to a point where careful attention to articulating what the other side's position precisely *is* is not easy to come by. In fact, most philosophical (and some scientific) work proceeds unselfconsciously within a framework that seems to take for granted that a broadly naturalist, or a broadly agent anomalist, position is not simply correct, but what sophisticated theoretical rationality obviously presumes. The opponent, if thought of at all, is regarded not just as wrong, but as *naive*.

More than what many (certainly, many non-philosophers) would regard as usual philosophers' arrogance is involved in this. And in fact, many non-philosophers, I think, do or would share adhesion to one of the two solitudes I refer to. What is involved seems to be a manifestation of something resembling C. P. Snow's famous division of the two cultures of the sciences and the arts, or views its pair of constituencies will deeply if sometimes inchoately feel. Those of an arts or humanities orientation find it quite easy and natural to suppose that much, and much of what is most substantial and interesting, about human behaviour and human life cannot—could not in principle—be captured by scientific formulas or theoretical models. And those of a scientific orientation seem readily to find just the opposite natural and intuitive: that however complicated, and however remote achieving it might be, whatever we are and do can exist and can be intelligible only as some sort of elaboration upon the basic building blocks of the natural world.

Part of my own purpose, in the work I am doing in this area, is to try to make explicit what these parties too often leave unexplicit or unargued for. My aim is to articulate naturalism, or naturalism as relevant to being human and doing what humans do, and agent anomalism, and grounds for each, in as clear and sympathetic a way as possible; and then to see what case there may be for some degree of mutual accommodation of the two. This is not quite a peacemaker role, since, if I am right, the two sides have only in incomplete and opaque ways, mostly, been willing to acknowledge that they were at war, or at least to acknowledge that there was an opponent (other than a straw man) worthy of being at war with.

I should remark, too, that much of the literature in this area comes from what is, for me, close to home, namely, the site of my own doctoral studies (many years ago) at the University of Pittsburgh. There have been several prominent agent anomalist anti-naturalists. I will sketch a bit of the relevant historical background presently. At any rate, a leading philosopher who articulated the quarrel I am addressing, in a contemporary idiom, was one of my own teachers at Pittsburgh, Wilfrid Sellars. After I had left for the ranks of the academically employed, two subsequent Pittsburgh philosophers, Robert Brandom and John McDowell, have continued the legacy of Sellars in prominent and influential ways. Like Sellars, Brandom and McDowell are the authors of deep, difficult, complex books and articles that have had a considerable impact in contemporary philosophy.

I should also say that, although Sellars was one of my teachers, and I had a good deal of contact with him as a graduate student, I really got to know his work only after I had left Pittsburgh, and I have only quite recently — and largely as part of the expanding character of my investigation of my theme — been getting to know Brandom's and McDowell's work. Some sort of odd variant of prophets not being without honour, except in their home country, is perhaps discernible here. Actually doubly so, since, as you will see, I find myself resisting, even as I have been trying to understand, and maximally sympathetically to understand, these three masters from my own philosophical cradle.

The origins of the formation of the idea that the kind of advancing and enlarging understanding that the natural sciences have brought to the world comes to irresolvable conflict with what understanding ourselves and our actions and practices involves, are usually traced to Kant. Indeed, seeing clearly that this conflict, and impasse, have occurred, and what their larger significance is, is often seen as a major — perhaps the major — part of the reason that Kant is so great a philosopher. Certainly, that is how Sellars sees things—and, I think, Brandom and McDowell, but also many other important agent anomalist thinkers; most important of all, at least for many, is Davidson.

Actually, we can find articulated in Thomas Aquinas, and possibly earlier, implicitly, in his master, Aristotle, the basic contrast that Kant brings to very developed, and theoretically dense, formulation. In the *Summa Theologiae*, Aquinas says, almost casually, that "all natural things can be reduced to one principle, which is nature; and all voluntary things can be reduced to one principle, which is human reason, or will." (Aquinas is expressing a view that is supposed to imply, but which he of course denies does, that there is no need of a God.)

There, in Aquinas' formulation, you basically have it. There are the natural things and the voluntary things, and neither is reducible to the other; so we need to understand the world in terms of the operations of, and principles relevant for, each.

This insight, if insight it is, may be said to have been lost, or veiled, with the arrival of the scientific revolution. Its first dramatic century—the 17th—saw the formation of modern natural science. Its second century, the 18th, witnessed the foundation of social science—self-consciously conceived as on Newtonian (i.e., natural scientific) lines and models. The latter development was, especially, an achievement of the Scottish Enlightenment.

Perhaps forgetting, or discounting, the proto-expression of the agent anomalist insight, or conviction, that I have noted in Aquinas, McDowell characterizes relevant historical and conceptual developments succinctly and well, from the agent anomalist point of view, referring to "the rise of modern science, in which natural-scientific understanding, as we are now equipped to conceive it, was being separated out from a hitherto undifferentiated conception of understanding in general. According to my picture [McDowell continues], an important element in this clarification of the proper target of natural science was an increasingly firm awareness that we must sharply distinguish natural-scientific understanding from the kind of understanding achieved by situating what is understood in *the logical space of reasons* [my emphasis]; that is, precisely, that the structure of the logical space of reasons is *sui generis*, as I have read Sellars, and in different terms Davidson, as claiming it is"(*Mind and World* [2nd ed., 1996], p. xxii).

Now, I will not seek to fill in the historical or the conceptual picture as either agent anomalists or naturalists, or I myself, understand it, in any detailed way. I will also not attempt on this occasion to give a determinate philosophical analysis of the relevant ideas and arguments concerned, though I will try to do a bit more of that, at least to some extent.

But to expand a little on the historical picture: as Sellars and McDowell see it, we might think of there having been a single conceptual territory of investigation, with many components and aspects. There were natural objects, and events, consisting primarily of reasonably stable middle-sized things that were observable, and sometimes at rest and sometimes in motion. Some—many—of these things were also living things, among them animals, including human animals—human beings. The latter also, it was standardly supposed, had capacities for free and moral choice, and created societies and institutions and other artifacts. Maybe the fact of natural things, and the fact of free beings, with volitions, indicated a certain fissure or contrast, even a tension; but a more or less unitary world, with more or less unitary canons of inquiry for investigating it, seemed in place. We may think of this conceptual territory as primarily Aristotelian, but that label shouldn't be taken to imply too close a fit with the actual philosophy of Aristotle.

Then, to continue the Sellars historiography, the 17th-century scientific revolution got underway, and gradually, by incremental degrees, the unitary conceptual territory of what it was for there to be a world to investigate and what it was to investigate it more or less came apart. Increasingly, again by stages and becoming really advanced by the beginning of the modern period in physics, from the 1890s on, the world as physics disclosed and described it was seen to be more and more alien and weird, and remote from the original picture of stable middle-sized natural objects moving around in more or less commonsensical ways. Natural objects turned out to be literally porous — non-solid — and increasingly to be displaced at the centre of the theoretical and explanatory action by unobservable things — forces and postulated atomic and subatomic entities — behaving in accordance with odd, nonstandard mathematical principles.

The conceptual disconnect also occurred on the other fork. For Sellars, the centre of gravity for this other fork is the idea of a *person*, who *acts* for *reasons*. Those reasons have *meaning* for the person, and explain what he and she is doing, internally for that individual and interpersonally in a shared life. It is in this context that the *normative* distinctively presents itself and appears to offer — is argued to offer — insuperable obstacle to the success of any possible naturalist project.

Here is the sort of fact, or alleged fact, the agent anomalist is thinking of. Someone — Mary — may believe, *justifiably*, that a movie she has an interest in seeing is currently playing at a cinema in town. *Mary*'s relationship to facts about buildings and cultural artifacts in her neighbourhood involved *evidence* that she has had, and psychological states, in her mind, that aren't merely in a kind of structural correspondence to the facts indicated. Mary has something *right*, and what it is to do that is, it seems, ineluctably *normative*. Moreover, those who observe Mary's state, including scientists and scientific philosophers who want to have a clear, true, and *complete* theoretical understanding of this part of the world, seem to need to include in their theory what being *justified* involves. It seems hard to see how something like that could be *naturalized*. That is, it seems hard to see how there could be a natural fact of having justified belief.

It also seems plausible to hold that states of thinking involve — and essentially, unavoidably, *internally* involve — *commitments*, such that being in one state of thinking will imply commitment to some others, but likely not to all others, that are conceptually or logically implied by the state. To take a simple case: if someone thinks they see a red surface, they seem to need to suppose, and to need to be regarded as supposing, that they are also (or else, thereby) seeing a coloured surface. Enlarging an idea like this, Brandom, for example, pairs or identifies psychological states with *inferential roles*. These involve, or seem to involve, *shoulds*; i.e., if someone thinks that p, then they should, or ought to, also think that q, for lots of cases of (distinct) p and q.

Enlarging ideas of this kind even further, it seems plausible to see our lives and practices as embedded within *institutions*, where what we are doing will not make sense, either to ourselves or – arguably, more importantly for the present purpose – to theorist observers, except by reference to those institutions and to their norms and goals. For example, it seems difficult to see how sense could be made of some facts about Fred without including his being a university professor (if we suppose that that is what Fred does for a living), which will require, in turn, sense being made about universities and roles they play within social orders.

I mentioned that normativity is at the heart of what agent anomalists see as what is involved in being a person acting for reasons and interacting with other persons who are doing likewise. I mentioned also a certain holism that the agent anomalists' picture and commitments include. Normativity and conceptual holism appear to be distinct facets of the states of persons (though it may be argued that the second, at least, implies the first). Sellars, and also Davidson, believe (and both believe, I think, that they derive this insight partly from Kant and partly from Wittgenstein) that to have the mental life of a person is to have something that is an indissolubly interconnected network. A network of *concepts*. Different philosophers, Wittgenstein among them, have quite different ideas about what a concept, or having one, is.

For the present purpose it is important not to see the idea, *as such*, as tied to any particular, say, Platonistic sort of theory. Maybe having a concept just *is* behaving in certain sorts of ways, with appropriate stimuli and outcomes. I don't actually think that is true. But the point – for Sellars and Davidson – is that we have them in large interconnected bunches. Maybe it is even true, they think, that to have one basic concept is to have all basic concepts, at least within a certain cluster, a certain so-called logical space. So, for example, you couldn't have ideas of just some colours or sounds or geometrical shapes—certainly not only of *one* instance of these classes. And you couldn't have the idea of a reason without the idea of a persuasive or convincing reason. This is the *sort* of thing meant by what we can call the (or a) thesis of conceptual holism. And it too appears to pose challenge, major challenge, for a fully naturalist view.

Holism as such appears not to pose challenge for naturalism, at least in some forms or versions. Quine, for example, was a certain kind of holist—he thought that theories (he meant specifically theories in the sciences) stand or fall more or less in their entireties, as networks of postulates, theoretical and observational—and his naturalist credentials, indeed, creative naturalist contributions, seem impeccable and important. The challenge in this instance stems from the idea that individual mental states of rational agents involve holistic conceptual linkage with a huge array of other conceptual content—that, for example, a person can't see that a book is on a table without the *content* of that state of seeing and knowing leading ineluctably, but *conceptually*, not (merely) *causally*, to institutions and ways of life and background learning experiences, without which the state (it is argued) does not *make sense*.

For agent anomalists, these issues are especially met with in respect of what it is to have a belief, or any comparable so-called "state of propositional attitude," and the significant commitments these states involve. The idea of these commitments is Kantian, or appears in a rich set of traditions stemming from Kant, and self-consciously presents itself in opposition to classical empiricist views. According to such views, even to have a belief—*any* belief that a human being has—is to be in a state or condition webbed or networked with many many other beliefs and other states of propositional attitude, and involving and figuring in a rich *conceptual life*—something which, for the Kantian and neo-Kantian, a non-human animal, for example, quite certainly cannot have. *Some* of the components of this web or network will be normative in character. Opposing empiricist views, it is equally important to note, do not accept any very replete or conceptually necessarily extensive version of these claims.

At any rate, sorting out — coming to a fully satisfactory and persuasive theory about — what it is to be in a state of propositional attitude is going to be a key part of settling issues with respect to naturalism and agent anomalist anti-naturalism. The Kantian, and neo-Kantian, holistic idea also poses itself in respect of states not explicitly of propositional attitude type, where the experiencing mind is regarded as engaged in *interpretation*. So, for this view, to experience something *as* something of a conceptually imposed sort is likewise to be in a psychological state of *content*, that content again linked to a large, totalistic network of other meanings, other cases of an experienced or interpreted *as*. The (anti-empiricist and anti-naturalist) claim will be that such holisms obtain, and that there is nothing remotely comparable in (other parts of) the natural world. In general, the idea, in the natural world, is that its basic individual component states occur autonomously of other basic individual component states, linked causally but not otherwise to them.

(Intuitively, if metaphysically, a basic *bit* — individual component state — of the natural world could have been the first, or the last, state of the world. It would seem not conceptually, or metaphysically, possible that experiencing and interpreting someone's smile as resembling an expression in a famous painting should be the first event or state of the world.)

I will not expand on these somewhat sketchy probings on this occasion. These issues are too big and, as I have presented them, too amorphous for resolution without work of great detail and range. I would like, though, to be at least somewhat more disclosing of my own leanings in these territories. I actually feel the draw of both the agent anomalist and naturalist views or *stances*. I think that we inhabit an altogether natural world, and that what we are and what we do must be intelligible within that setting. Yet we do clearly and certainly operate as rational agents, embedded in rich cultural, interpersonal, and institutional settings. If it came to it, we should, I think, stretch or modify the idea of the natural to encompass what, if anything, is inescapably distinctive or special about us. Modern science began — perhaps *happened* to have begun — with trying to understand inanimate material particles in motion. Maybe beginning there marked what gets to count seriously as scientific in ways that would not have been true had modern science begun with another part or zone of the world. By this I don't mean to imply that the edifice of resulting science might have turned out to have different content had there been a different starting place; I don't, in fact, believe that this is the case. In any case, I am not yet persuaded that norms and concept clusters *cannot* be naturalized, at least in some sense.

How *might* a naturalist try to handle norms, i.e., naturalistically? Here is one possible approach, at least in outline. (It derives in significant part from ideas of Hume's, in the 18th century, and J. L. Mackie's, in the 20th.[4]) We start with the case of moral or ethical norms, where it is acknowledged and affirmed that we — humans — do have concepts of good, bad, right, wrong, duty, etc., and that these concepts purport to be, we think of them as being, objective and factual. However — so the theory goes — we are wrong about this. *Clear* as these concepts are — more or less, anyway — in sense or intension, they actually lack extension, or reference. Some of us, the theory continues, have realized this, even if others — possibly a majority — have not.

We have also a concept that is conceptually derivative from, parasitic on, the ethical concepts just indicated. This is a concept that social scientists — anthropologists, say — use in investigating and describing people's value systems. The social scientists will say that a certain individual or group *regards X as good* (bad, obligatory, etc.) for suitable X. (It might be argued that a *regards as good* concept may be just a special case of a *regards as* concept (e.g., *regards as a fish*, *regards as toxic to eat*, etc. In this case, *regards as good* would *not*, as such, be conceptually derivative from or parasitic on the ethical. But I will ignore this question for my purposes.)

Returning to the social scientists: their descriptions will be factual and objective, and not themselves normative. It will be a matter of fact that community C regards something as good, or doesn't. All the *regards as* facts will be in the same broad category or group as other psychological and social facts that will be taken to be non-normative. And if any of them is naturalistically subsumable, or reducible, to physical or biological facts, then all will be. What will work in this kind of way for ethical norms will then be extended to every other kind of normative case, including *theorists'* normative judgments of human cases. The result would be, in this part of the (putative) naturalist response to, and accommodation of, the normative, that there *are* no normative facts, only, rather, relevant *regards as* facts. This, it will be argued, will suffice to *explain*, theoretically, everything that genuine normative facts were supposed to have explained.

As for *justification*: no one is simply *justified* in some belief, or inference; rather, something in the situation or context produces or yields justification. Whatever it is is something that operates, causally, on the person or agent, or group of them, that are concerned. Causality is, of course, paradigmatically naturalistic territory. So the idea would be that cases of justification would be construed or analyzed as cases where the right sorts of causes were at work.[5]

And the conceptual holism alleged to be constituitive of the thought world of the rational agent? The naturalist will attempt partly to deny it. Chunks of conceptual territory *can* be lacked by rational agents who have nonetheless other networks of concepts. The congenitally blind lack colour concepts, and, perhaps, the sociopathic lack ethical ones. If conceptual holism is significantly sabotaged or undermined, smaller concept-sets can be grasped, and explained, naturalistically, as induced by distinct, nomologically intelligible sets of causal contexts that operate on the human animal.

The latter phrase points to another facet of the picture that the agent anomalist tends to ignore or implausibly to deflate, and which, for the naturalist, puts the ball in the opponent's court, so to speak. Humans are animals, and other so-called higher animals exhibit versions or approximations of almost everything in the allegedly distinctive and impressive human template. Darwin, in *The Descent of Man*, develops this theme at considerable and persuasive length, showing to what extent traits humans have thought unique to themselves show up in other creatures.[6]

Elaborated upon, this constitutes what I call "the problem of the beasts," viz., that, by hypothesis, all nonhuman animal—"beastly"—behaviour is accountable naturalistically, so, since there are—it is argued—only differences of degree, along a continuum, between beastly and human behaviour, should it not be expected that the latter can be accounted for naturalistically as well? Even the dogs carry out logical inferences, the ancient Stoics argued. They made the case for the validity of disjunctive syllogism—"p or q, not p, therefore q"—partly from the canine case. The dog on the chase, following a scent, and coming to a fork in the track, sniffs one of the pathways and, finding the scent missing immediately sets off on the other without sniffing, confident that the quarry has gone that way.

This is, of course, only the outline of a possible naturalistic response to the idea of the singularity and normative unevadability of the human condition. Nothing along such lines may in the end work, as the Pittsburgh trio—also Davidson, Putnam, and many other deep and searching contemporary philosophers—are confident will prove to be the case. And I should add both that, Darwin notwithstanding, there appear to be undeniable major and massive differences between the mental lives of humans and even the smartest of the other animals, and that some agent anomalists—McDowell, for example—do not shy away from the problem of the beasts and argue that it does not undercut or diminish the power of the fact of normativity in our, but not the beasts', condition.

As the project, of which this is a modest and informal general introductory account, advances, I will be trying to see whether normativity and the natural really can be reconciled, and how, if so; and then, if they can't, what *that* seems to tell us about the world and our place in it.

To give you a final, concluding idea of where I myself stand, I would say that we need first to affirm clearly and unequivocally some of the *data*, which the correct theory, whatever it is, has got to be able to explain. Further, that among the data that I, at least, am in no doubt about, is that sentences *like* the following sentence are definitely sometimes *true*. Here is the sentence: "Hearing Professor McMillan's talk, and still more reading the full text of it afterwards, persuaded me that the end of history had not yet arrived." That is, of course, a sort of sentence that agent anomalism will, evidently, have no trouble with. It is naturalism—or some third theory, aspiring to unite the two contenders—that will face the challenge of how it might analyze and explain a sentence of this type. It is not, of course, obvious that naturalism can do so. I want to explore doors that may seek to realize the possibility that naturalism *can* pull it off. But whether it can or no, the eye of theory must keep such data unfailingly in view.[7]

NOTES

1   Human cases of such basic states *might* in particular cases be allowed or taken to be more complex than those of other animals. The idea here is one that may be found in Kantian moral psychology and philosophical anthropology—something important to note, since we are seeing the anti-naturalist agent anomalist stance as deeply rooted in Kantian philosophy. Kant has a conception of "empirical psychology, which would be the second part of physics if we consider it as philosophy of nature so far as it rests on empirical laws" (*Foundations of the Metaphysics of Morals*, 2nd section [Beck trans.] [Hackett, 1959], p. 45). This psychology, which comprises the second part of physics is for Kant, and, presumably, the present-day Kantians such as Sellars and Davidson, to be contrasted with the rational psychology of persons as free agents.

2   Although this famous tag, or aphorism, is standardly attributed to Voltaire—and is undoubtedly in the spirit of his outlook, and the sort of thing he *should* have said—it appears that it is difficult to find the saying in his works.

3   James W. Cornman and Keith Lehrer, *Philosophical Problems and Arguments: An Introduction*, 1st ed. (Macmillan, 1959). When first introduced, the spelling for the term was *compatiblism*; it was subsequently revised to, and has remained *compatibilism*.

4   I refer, in Mackie's case, to the so-called "error theory" of ethics. See J. L. Mackie, *Ethics: Inventing Right and Wrong* (Penguin Books, 1977), pp. 35, 48f., and passim.

5   This is the core or underlying idea in the *naturalist epistemology* programmatically enunciated by Quine, and developed more fully in the reliabilist theories of Alvin Goldman and others.

6   Charles Darwin, *The Descent of Man, and Selection in Relation to Sex*, photoreproduction of the 1871 ed., (Princeton University Press, 1981), pp. 34–106.

7   Thanks to Mark McCullagh for very helpful comments on an earlier version of this paper, clarifications they have prompted having substantially improved the paper.

HISTORY OF
PHILOSOPHY

CHAPTER SEVEN

SCIENCE AND THE HISTORY
OF ANALYTIC PHILOSOPHY

*Earlier versions of this paper were presented at Wayne State University,
in September 2001, and at York University in October 2001.*

I think that at its most general and comprehensive level, this
chapter means to be a contribution to the attempt to define
analytic philosophy; to provide, if you will, the essence of
this particular historically and culturally located variety of
philosophy. Providing such a definition or essence is, I believe,
extraordinarily difficult. By the canons of some of the varieties of
analytic philosophy, it is probably not possible to do it. It may or
may not be possible to do it. And even if possible, it may not be
something worth doing. At any rate, that is what I am interested
in contributing to on this occasion.

It is striking how recognizable analytic *philosophers* are. There
are very few — if, perhaps, any — philosophers who have lived and
written since the 1890s about whom there is much serious doubt
whether they belong in the category.[1] There must presumably be
some cases difficult to classify.[2] At any rate, it is an astonishingly
clear intellectual genre, extensionally. It is the intension that is
hard to produce, chiefly, it would seem, because the extension
is so diverse. What will unify, or be interestingly, theoretically,
and illuminatingly common to Frege, Moore, and Wittgenstein
in all phases; Davidson, Sellars, and Putnam in all phases,
Russell in all of his; Carnap, Dummett, Strawson, Austin, and

Ryle? Likewise Quine, Chisholm, Ramsey, Reichenbach, Lehrer, Richard Taylor, Broad, Hintikka, Gettier, Von Wright, Kripke, Searle, David Lewis, Kim, Armstrong, Hampshire, Fodor, Geach, Anscombe, Castañeda, Van Fraassen, Churchland, McDowell, Richard Cartwright, Robert Brandom...? The list, obviously, is easily prolonged. Cultural common denominators certainly present themselves. These philosophers overwhelmingly write in English, with a strong minority in German. They have been associated with universities in the United Kingdom and the United States, and to a lesser extent Australia, Germany, Canada, Israel, New Zealand, Finland, and Sweden.

But the aim of the large project to which these remarks are meant to contribute is not extensional, nor genetic (in the old sense — the one that gives rise to the so-called genetic fallacy — not the biological one), but conceptual and (in Foucault's sense) genealogical. And my topic is so huge. Here I will be sketchy, fragmentary, with many claims needing filling out and more extensive documentary citation needed than I shall provide.

This chapter examines and contests some prominent recent accounts of the origins, structure, and development of analytic philosophy. These accounts, chiefly from the eastern side of the Atlantic, have conceived analytic philosophy as (entirely) concerned with the study of concepts or meanings of a more-or-less permanent and self-contained common human life. Michael Dummett and P. M. S. Hacker are leading advocates of this historiography, which tends to place Frege and Wittgenstein at the creative centre of its analysis. By contrast, I set out a taxonomical and historical analysis of analytic philosophy that is I believe more accurate and persuasive and that locates this broad philosophical movement by reference to modern science. Analytic philosophy, I argue, is a development from *scientific modernism*. (Not, of course, only from scientific modernism. It has other roots and grounding as well, about which I will also comment.)

Scientific modernism is the thesis that modern science — methodologies, theoretical frameworks, and a continuous set of practices and traditions in and since the 17th-century "scientific revolution" — is without serious or credible rivals (is "untrumpable") in its own domain. The boundaries of that domain may be contested — whether, for example, it extends to consciousness and all of its products, or to mathematics and all of *its* — but if you are a scientific modernist you think that modern science is a more-or-less single or unitary thing (even with extensive, sometimes quite dramatic, changes in its constituent proper parts and theories), launched in the 1600s, that it has met with not-yet revised or reversed success, and that in whatever is its proper territory there are no genuine alternative contenders. It is to be noted that scientific modernism is compatible with both realist and anti-realist interpretations of science. Corollary to that fact, scientific modernism is compatible with "inscrutabilism": the thesis that reality is inherently inscrutable, or unknowable, for us. Kant, in fact, was both a scientific modernist and an inscrutabilist; or at least sought to be so. The jury is still out on his success in this endeavour.

Four features of the scientific modernist conception and practice of science may perhaps specially be noted, as distinctively present in the approach and commitments of Galileo (though the conjunction of the four is found nowhere in the world before him), and continuously evident and central in science ever since. These are an invariable preference for non-teleological theory of the natural world or its parts under investigation; inertial explanation, whereby the continuing of a state as it has been is held to require no further explanation than that nothing extraneous to the system has acted to alter it; a mathematicized understanding of nature, whereby its laws take invariably quantitative form; and a "grubby interface" between theory and its grounding and justification in observation of and controlled technologically guided interference with the concrete material world.

Briefly to highlight further what is meant here, there are philosophical currents or movements in modern thought that reject or oppose scientific modernism. Two prominent cases are

Neo-Aristotelianism—especially in its Thomist form—and (what may be called) narrativism. This last is the view that all theoretical postures and endeavours are "stories," with alternative plausible or serious stories always possible. For narrativism—some prominent postmodernist stances are narrativist, as are positions espoused in the philosophy of science by Feyerabend and others—modern science is "only a story," alternatives including astrology and some distinct cultural narratives of the natural world. Neo-Aristotelianism disputes the irreversible achievement of the 17th-century scientific revolution, on large or small scale, arguing for the reinstatement of teleology, for example, or the systemic possibilities of (and a necessary theoretical aetiological role for) divine interventions in nature, or other miracles.

In calling analytic philosophy a development from scientific modernism or (as it might also have been put) a form of scientific modernism, what is meant is something similar or comparable to calling the American Baptist Church movement (say) a development from or form of Protestantism. The parallel might be seen as particularly apt, since in both instances the development occurred, or began to occur, about 300 years after the appearance of the larger cultural phenomenon, which (in both cases) flowed or advanced continuously from that beginning; and at the same time the later movement cannot be adequately or significantly understood without reference to the earlier.

Returning to direct focus on analytic philosophy, I argue that it has had historically two broad wings, both definable by a relation to scientific modernism. One wing holds that scientific modernism is true, and that it is significantly relevant to (tasks, projects, and outcomes in) philosophy. The other wing also accepts scientific modernism, but denies that it is significantly relevant to philosophy (although, as I will argue, it minimally views modern science as imposing a constraint on its philosophical results, namely, that those results be consistent or cohere with at least reasonably well-corroborated outcomes of modern science). The first wing is unitarian and naturalist; the second is anti-unitarian and anti-naturalist, seeing a world (or a "world") of common life, of culture, value, and consciousness, which modern science, while compatible with it (and doubtless in some inscrutable or uninteresting manner a framework or backdrop for it), is largely irrelevant to.

Both of these wings derive historically from Cambridge University in the 1890s: from the creative initiatives of Bertrand Russell and G. E. Moore, the real founders of analytic philosophy as an ongoing tradition or movement in philosophy. More of this, and the historical and genealogical picture I mean here to sketch and advocate, subsequently.

This chapter has two central theses. One is that analytic philosophy, as a historical movement in the career of philosophy, has had, and continues to have, a distinctive conceptual structure and shape—which I set out—and which, I argue, a prominent British historiographical account seriously distorts and misrepresents. This first aim is, then, partly positive, historical, and taxonomical, and partly negative and polemical. The second thesis is that analytic philosophy needs specially to be conceived and characterized by virtue of what I argue is its relation, often only implicit, to science.

The two theses are independent, and one could accept the first but not the second. Indeed, the first will, I believe, be reasonably straightforward to set out and justify, even if it is at odds with what several distinguished philosophers and philosophical writers have said. The second is not as easy to formulate and defend. Given what will appear as my account of analytic philosophy and its nature, my second thesis will quite clearly, indeed obviously, be confirmable for half—so to speak—of analytic philosophy. Not so easy, though, will be justifying it, in fact explaining what can be non-trivially meant by it, for the other half.

The view of the history and character of analytic philosophy that I contest seems to be particularly popular in Great Britain. There, it has been advanced a number of times in the half-century between 1950 and 2000, in varying degrees of detail, in the writings of Austin, Warnock, Strawson, and Hacker, but above all, of Dummett.

According to this view, the founder and originating creative avatar of analytic philosophy was Frege. Not particularly because he was the originator of modern symbolic logic; rather, Frege is accorded this role because of his work in semantics. There is more specifically assigned him a conception of philosophical semantics, as the semantics of natural language at a deep structural level. Philosophy, as this British school conceives it, just *is*, properly anyway, the sustained study of structures of natural language, aiming to disclose their truest or deepest "logic." Sometimes this enterprise needs to get a bit formal and make use of logical resources, the prototypes of which Frege also supplied; but more usually it is a matter of careful, disciplined, nuanced attention to voices of semantical and social intuition, as to how we speak, and operate, in fundamental areas of shared life. Philosophy, like what it properly confines itself to, has strictly no history, or culture. Frege launched, for this view, a *philosophia perennis* in a newer, better sense of that old phrase. Aristotle and Kant, especially, are seen as grandfathers or forerunners of this enterprise in fundamental respects, but it is with Frege that it strictly and properly starts ("Analytical philosophy is post-Fregean philosophy," as Dummett puts it[3]), and then in Wittgenstein that it fully and most luxuriantly flowers.

Dummett gives a characterization of analytic philosophy the analysis of which will itself help disclose the position I am disputing. "What distinguishes analytical philosophy," he says (*Origins of Analytical Philosophy*, p. 4) "in its diverse manifestations, from other schools is the belief, first, that a philosophical account of thought can be attained through a philosophical account of language, and, secondly, that a comprehensive account can only be so attained. Widely as they differed from one another, the logical positivists, Wittgenstein in all phases of his career, Oxford 'ordinary language' philosophy and post-Carnapian philosophy in the United States as represented by Quine and Davidson all adhered to these twin axioms." Dummett immediately goes on to indicate that he is aware of other trends, some involving departures from the pure faith just specified, and which, for him, simply declare such departure non-analytic(al).

My concerns are with Dummett only as one instance of a historiographical current, which I believe goes back at least to the late 1940s. I do not, in any case, wish to add to the considerable castigation Dummett has received as historian; and I think several other passages, in other writers, can be used to illustrate the broader position under review. As I say, the view in question long precedes Dummett; I will call it the Oxford view, though not all Oxford philosophers have held it, and many non-Oxford (though almost invariably British) philosophers also have. At any rate, as I see it, this view does capture a significant (proper) part of what analytic philosophy has been, and been concerned with, though even here in a distorted way. What I want to focus on is the idea that, according to analytic philosophy, philosophy is a matter of giving an account of *thought* (a philosophical account, to be sure), implicitly intended to be thought of sorts that any and every functional human being engages in, and of doing this via an account of language.

I believe that this view is very deeply wrong—root and branch, so to speak. There are, of course, kernels of truth in the picture, and I certainly want to acknowledge these. But apart from the kernels, there are few analyses in the history of thought that can be more mistaken than this one.

First, Frege. This is not the place for detailed exploration of the Frege corpus, but a few things do seem clear from a review of that corpus. Frege nowhere gives evidence of a conception of philosophy along the lines indicated, nor of a conception of some other discipline or endeavour with these purposes or assumptions. He does provide conceptual analyses of a number of basic notions of natural life or natural speech, somewhat haphazardly. And he formulates a number of key conceptions of semantic theory; among them, of course, the sense/reference and concept/object distinctions. Frege is no special friend to ordinary language or common sense, however, and is sometimes cavalier or dismissive of claims of both. (Dummett, by the way, sometimes affirms clearly that this is so. "Frege," he says, "aimed at creating an artificial language free of what he regarded as the many defects of natural language, and hence a reliable instrument for carrying out deductive inferences… He was not interested in any precise account of the mechanisms of natural language, and was skeptical about the very possibility of one."[4]) Frege's goal (one of them, anyway) appears to be to provide categorical resources for ideal vehicles for theoretical truth — that is, truths that can be parts of theories — in mathematics and science, including, derivatively and secondarily, social and historical science. Pursuing this goal is indeed a central part of one of the main streams of analytic philosophy, as I will argue, and Frege is significant, and to some degree foundational, for that stream. Moreover, for that same reason, he is anything but the philosophical progenitor of the later Wittgenstein.

Frege was also, in any case, a philosophical Platonist of a very clear and pronounced kind. For him, a really existing "third realm" of abstracta is a key component, not only of ontology, but of the possibility of adequate theoretical understanding in both mathematics and semantics. Frege's Platonism is for most of his latter-day followers and enthusiasts, particularly those for whom he is John the Baptist to Wittgenstein's Christ, an embarrassment or a quaint minor note mostly to be ignored.

In any event, as the Oxford view is aware, Frege was largely unknown and ignored in the philosophical world, except for the attention given his work in logic and semantics by Russell, and to a lesser extent by Wittgenstein, until formalist revival of interest due to Church and Carnap, and then the British ordinary language school's largely myopic consideration in the 1950s and afterward. For the Oxford view, Frege is not to be seen as a historical influence or founder, but rather as an ideal prototype with whom, once rediscovered, conceptual conversation can unendingly inform and enrich the project of engagement with "what we mean."

I turn to what I think is more accurate historiography, and to more accurate conceptual alignments.

The most accurate historical and taxonomical depiction of analytic philosophy is, I think, the following. Analytic philosophy was founded at the University of Cambridge in the 1890s by Bertrand Russell and G. E. Moore. It had then, and has had ever since, two wings or branches, typified in the work of the two founders, and more or less self-consciously stemming from them: a scientific branch (Russell) and a common-sense one (Moore). These branches have often known mutual stress and contrast. What unites them, and characterizes analytic philosophy generically, is commitment to very clear and rigorous argumentation, methodologically, against a background, sometimes foregrounded, of canons and results in settled natural and mathematico-logical science. The foregrounded branch — the Russellian one — typically identifies what it aspires to as "scientific philosophy." An attention, sometimes methodological and sometimes conceptual or ontological, to language has also been usual, though it does not define the subject. Some analytic philosophers have little to say about language or meaning.

The "spirit" of what I am calling Russellian or scientific analytic philosophy may be found expressed in a brief citation from Russell. In *Our Knowledge of the External World* (1914) Russell characterizes his conception of philosophy (and incidentally pays foundational homage to Frege). Russell refers to

> ... the logical-analytic method in philosophy. This method, of which the first complete example is to be found in the writings of Frege, has gradually, in the course of actual research, increasingly forced itself upon me as something perfectly definite, capable of embodiment in maxims, and adequate, in all branches of philosophy, to yield whatever objective scientific knowledge it is possible to obtain.... [T]he great systems of the past...are abundantly worthy of study. But something different is required if philosophy is to become a science.... The central problem by which I have sought to illustrate method is the problem of the relation between the crude data of sense and the space, time, and matter of mathematical physics (p. v).

The correlative "spirit" of Moorean or common-sense philosophy is perhaps more diffuse or variegated, and I do not have a brief Moore passage to parallel the one from Russell. In both cases, I want to avoid tying the respective wings to the specific views, at any stage, of either Russell or Moore as individual historical philosophers. Moore was a very explicit common-sense metaphysical realist. What he launches generically for what I am calling a common-sense wing of analytic philosophy is a *centre of gravity*, so to speak, in everyday or common-sense life, beliefs, practices, and assumptions, departure from which is what must be justified, if it can be, Mooreans characteristically holding, and arguing, that it generally cannot be. From this centre of gravity, philosophical activity is seen most importantly as fending off attempts to dislodge or decentre it, or to set out more explicitly and illuminatingly its key and most significant components.

Let me enlarge on the Russell and Moore wings of analytic philosophy, respectively, to seek to bring out commonalities as well as features of difference. The Russell one first (and it needs to be appreciated that the idea is to have a characterization applicable, not just to Russell, but also to logical positivism, Quine, and later people). I used the (vague) phrase "centre of gravity" with reference to the Mooreans, and would use it also for the Russellians. For them, the "centre of gravity," philosophically, is in science (the latter understood as including mathematics as well as empirical natural science). Virtually everyone on this wing would endorse Sellars' claim (in "Empiricism and the Philosophy of Mind"; it is, of course, made deliberately — and slightly provocatively — to contrast with a famous old saying of Protagoras, in antiquity) "that in the dimension of describing and explaining the world, science is the measure of all things, of what is that it is, and of what is not that it is not." Still, the presence of *the world* in Sellars' formula might trouble some scientific philosophy positivists; also, it is not transparent (in at least some cases) what the scientific measure endorses, or permits, ontologically.

There are three common components to both Russellian and Moorean branches (in all instances): 1) philosophical logic/grammar (a.k.a. conceptual analysis) of basic concepts of experience, common sense, or the world; 2) epistemology (both include, centrally, issues of epistemic justification and other epistemological issues); and 3) philosophy of language (certainly differentially foregrounded and backgrounded in different instances).

Then: for each of the branches, there is a metaphysics/ontology category, only in the anti-metaphysical sub-branch of each the category is empty. In the other sub-branch, though (for each), metaphysics/ontology has content. For the Russellians, its content is driven or dictated by science, precisely along the lines of the Sellars dictum. The aim is to produce the most accurate/adequate metaphysical results that will fit current physics. For the Mooreans, the desired metaphysical results are those that best cohere with common sense (in the senses of Reid and Moore).

Further — in addition — there is for both branches a category for actual empirical results. Again, in each branch there is a sub-branch for which this category is empty, and one for which it is not. The former are the pure underlabourers (in Locke's sense), those who just dwell in logical space (whether the space be scientific or manifest). The latter philosophers either blur or deny the empirical/nonempirical contrast (à la Quine), or accept the contrast but think that philosophy includes empirical questions and results as well as conceptual ones — e.g., those whose philosophy includes cognitive science, sociobiology, other theory of human nature, naturalistic epistemology, or specific theoretical issues in physics (including cosmology). All of those identified are on the science/Russell side. I would say that much Wittgensteinian philosophy is also empirical in a similar way, but on the common-sense or manifest side of things. But this claim would certainly be disputed by some Wittgensteinians, who insist that all that they do is "(philosophical) grammar."

Finally: Russell/scientific philosophy has also one other component unique to itself: philosophy of science.

Analytic philosophy has, for both wings, been (unsurprisingly) significantly, though for neither exclusively, nor even primarily, a matter of *analysis*. Whether seeking to provide explicit necessary and sufficient conditions that will non-trivially illuminate, in a theoretically rich way, some fundamental item of thought or world, or in some more diffuse and approximating way to replace allegedly wrong models with better or more adequate ones, analytic philosophy has involved analyzing. Russell's work on "*the*" (the term, or what it signifies), many philosophers' endeavours with knowledge and perception, and others' with promising and other cases of agency illustrate this certain truth.

But what corresponds only to some analytic undertakings is a limitation of the horizons of all possible projects of the kind to concepts of a common and non-theoretical life—where the aim of such projects is supposed to be to get them right, and the projects' assumption is that there is a right to get. (Not necessarily a fixed or sharp-boundaried right, of course. Very likely, indeed, for many central concepts, quite otherwise.) Nor are all analytic undertakings confined to *us*.

For Russell, the analysis of our *thought*, in this way, is just part of what analysis may take on. Indeed, for Russell, the symbolizing mind and its structural relations to what is (or is conceived as) other than it, is itself one, but just one, of the interesting, important, difficult elements of the world *all* of whose discernible fundamental features and elements it is the aim of philosophy to explore. Moreover, for Russell (as for Hegel), part of what mind does in its engagements is think theoretically (also—and this is different—think self-consciously or reflectively). We don't just know and act and feel, we also theorize; and although we sometimes do the latter ineptly, in the grip of imprisoning models, etc., we also sometimes do it *well*. And we can *study* our doing it well—not just the processes it involves, but also the products, the results, when we have plausible theories about things.

Again, though, our thought, our language, our meanings, our culture, and other parts of the wonder that is us are just parts of what philosophy can and does study, and parts of what significant strands of analytic philosophy, scientific and manifest, has historically studied and continues to.

For Russell (and Frege), specifically, quotidian, manifest concepts may, sometimes, be not merely underdetermined, imprecisely boundaried, or involving of constituent concepts resembling each other only in a family way, but also, rather, confused or inadequate for expressing anything true about the world. Of course, expressing things that are true about the world is not the only thing — possibly not even the most important thing — that goes on in language, and maybe some of the (allegedly) confused or veridically inadequate terms and concepts common language contains serve quite successfully their own primary purposes, as Wittgenstein and those he influenced affirm. But that will be beside the point where the focus of interest is not language, or even meaning, as such, but truth, facts, and existence. In any case, my purpose here is not adjudication among quarrelling analysts, but rather illustration of how large and varied the house is in which such quarrels occur, and how inept it is — parochial, in fact — to claim just part of that house, normatively or factually, for the whole edifice.

The two wings or branches that stem from Russell and Moore have had, both of them, what may be seen as paired subdivisions, into a metaphysical and an anti-metaphysical orientation or set of commitments in each wing. Russell and Moore were themselves both metaphysical realists, of more classical type than their revolutionary rhetoric at least sometimes discloses. But out of the former's scientific/formal mode, and the latter's common-sense/manifest one, strongly anti-metaphysical currents as well as continued metaphysical ones ensued. The primary anti-metaphysical sub-branch of scientific philosophy is, of course, logical positivism, but more muted naturalist nominalist empiricist positions continue an opposition to supposed metaphysical extravagance. The anti-metaphysical sub-branch of manifest philosophy is the ordinary language school and its Wittgensteinian, and more recently Putnamian and Rortyan, variants.

Russell and Moore naturally did not found analytic philosophy *ex nihilo*. Important figures in the background for Russell are Democritus and Epicurus (with their ancient atomist tradition), Leibniz, Hume, Mill, and of course Frege. For Moore, Reid is particularly central. (By this I mean more to assert that Reid provides an earlier version or prototype of the kinds of philosophical projects in which Moore was engaged and many of the views that he defended, rather than that Moore was importantly influenced in coming to those projects and views by reading Reid.) For both Russell and Moore — scientific and manifest philosophy — Aristotle and Locke, may, I believe, be seen as significantly figuring in the formation. Although he is chiefly dismissed as an opponent by both Russell and Moore, Kant appears as a prominent influence in most post-Moorean manifest philosophy. Pragmatism is also an important contributor to developments in both wings in the work of several epigones.

As well as its historical prototypes and sources, the analytic philosophy founded with special flourish in the anti-idealist revolt of Russell and Moore, like other intellectual movements, did not emerge in a vacuum or without quieter more or less contemporaneous parallel streams or echoes. Elsewhere than Cambridge, much in a similar vein was particularly rooted in Aristotle and a revival of attention, scholarly and more purely philosophical, to his work and ideas. In Austria, a school of realist ontology developed in this way, with Brentano the spearheading figure. At Oxford, Cook Wilson played a comparable role. Both Brentano and Cook Wilson were metaphysical realists, of "manifest" or common-sense type and Aristotelian coloration. The numerous philosophical progeny of both thinkers mostly continued work in this same mould. Even so, the note in both of these substreams, typified by Husserl and Price respectively, mutes or (in Husserl's phrase) "brackets" the world in favour of the character of features of experience had by an experiencing subject — rather like, or at least parallel with, the phenomenalist projects of the more self-consciously scientizing Russell, Carnap, Reichenbach, Ayer, and Quine.

This last remark will point to a further structural feature of analytic philosophy conceived diachronically. In addition to the two polarities already identified, the scientific and common-sense one, and the metaphysical and anti-metaphysical contrast, analytic philosophy has also exhibited a contrast between practitioners and practitionings that have been subject-grounded and others that have been object-grounded. This is not a Kierkegaardian truth-as-subjectivity versus truth-as-objectivity split. Analytic philosophy has always been entirely in the truth-as-objectivity camp on this one. It is a split between conceptions of philosophical centres of gravity in observation states that are in the first instance in the category of what would normally or pre-theoretically be regarded as first-personal; and conceptions of states, observed or of the world, that are logically and methodologically separate and separated from observers and observings.

Much of the analytic work of the first half of the 20th century, in epistemology and philosophy of science, is of the first variety. Rooted in Locke and Hume, and a little more distantly in Descartes, the projects of Russell's *Our Knowledge of the External World* and Carnap's *Aufbau* exemplify particularly clearly the conception of the construction of the world or some of its significant parts, or of the theorizing that will ultimately or in principle culminate in physical science, that are the hallmark of the first model. Projects of naturalized epistemology, or of modal metaphysics, well exemplify analytic philosophy in the second, contrastive mode, where no particular account of observings, still less of an observing subject, are held to be necessary for the relevant philosophical endeavour to get underway, to progress, or to succeed.

It will be reasonable to place most of the anti-metaphysical analytic writings in the first, observer-centred grouping identified, including both Wittgensteinian and ordinary language work and that of the logical positivists. All of the latter depart from what we sense or allegedly know, or what is sensed/observed. So too do some metaphysical realist endeavours, like much of Russell's epistemological work. On the other hand, much scientific philosophy does not; likewise common-sense philosophy of the sorts exhibited by Moore and Chisholm.

The conception of analytic philosophy as the study of conceptual clusters in a supposed "common life" ignores, and is false to, a very great deal produced in the analytic tradition, and distorts much in that tradition to which it bears at least some resemblance. What is signally ignored is the extent to which analytic philosophers have sought to address older, classical problems and topics in metaphysics and epistemology, even if, typically, in putatively innovative ways. Also ignored is the extent to which they have sought to study or characterize science, and as well have had projects of bringing the latter's goals into creative conjunction with those to be assigned to philosophy. That is, a very large part of the work of analytic philosophy has been philosophy of science, and a considerable body of that work has also been explicitly companionate with science—early, in some of Russell's work, in the 1920s, in *The Analysis of Mind* and *The Analysis of Matter* (and later, in the 1940s, in *Human Knowledge*), and other work it influenced, and more recently, in projects of cognitive science and naturalized epistemology.

Even where analytic philosophy has taken on projects of the analysis of items of a common life, this has often, as for example in the work of Moore, Chisholm, Davidson, and Cartwright, had clearly and explicitly metaphysical purpose. Reid-style assumptions are made about the metaphysical validity and centrality of quotidian or manifest categories and postulates, and the aim is to deliver the metaphysical goods as to this part of the nature of things. (It may be particularly important to note this in the case of Davidson, as Dummett frequently and pointedly names him as a paradigmatic analytic philosopher in his "Oxford" sense. One has only to read Davidson's "The Method of Truth in Metaphysics,"[5] among other essays, to see how incomplete, importantly inadequate, a conception this is.)

The explicit—typically, indeed, classic—"metaphysicality" of much analytic philosophy duly noted, analytic philosophy does, as has been stressed, have its two anti-metaphysical sub-branches. Using, again, Sellars' helpful terminology and conception of a scientific image and a manifest image, while Russellians and Mooreans are, respectively, scientific metaphysical realists and manifest (or common-sense) metaphysical realists, their respective sets of cousins have been anti-realist naturalizers and positivists, and anti-foundationalists — indeed, typically, anti-systematic anti-theory theorists of the piecemeal and disjoint and occasional.

The overall architectonic of analytic philosophy and its origins, structure, and developmental patterns that is sketched here will be, I think, only a little contestable. It is not so obvious that the key motif for locating and capturing analytic philosophy has to do with modern science. I turn, then, to difficulties or complexities for this part of the thesis.

One sort of potential objection, though, I think may be dealt with quite briefly, if not summarily.

Although doing so can be contested, there are two categories of item or of discourse attitudes toward, or treatment of which, should mostly, I think, be muted or given only secondary consideration for our historical and taxonomical purposes. The two are abstract entities and morality. Carnap famously saw no problem with countenancing abstracta as theoretical entities for semantical or other formal theory,[6] and he was a positivist for whom ontology is either a trivial or an incoherent endeavour. Abstracta seem to many philosophical labourers difficult or impossible to dispense with in formal and natural science; for others, commitments to nominalism and projects of justifying it are essential ingredients of credible philosophy. My suggestion is that since an array of incompatible views and attitudes to abstracta are found among analytic philosophers, including some who simply ignore the subject, we do well to leave out of account stances in this area.

Perhaps more surprisingly, morality also should, I think, be "bracketed" in our enterprise. Many analytic philosophers are moral skeptics or subjectivists of one sort or other, finding moral realities or an objective moral truth inconsistent with empiricism or a scientific view of the world, or with a fully modernist outlook. Rather a considerable number of analytic philosophers, though, including some of hard-core physicalist persuasion and broad outlook, hold strongly to moral objectivist views. Advocacy of moral realist or moral objectivist view from within the Moorean or "common-sense" wing of analytic philosophy will not be surprising. A prominent strand of philosophical activity within that wing is, of course, analytic ethics and meta-ethics, famously inaugurated by Moore's *Principia Ethica*. But moral objectivist or realist views held or advocated by philosophers in the Russellian or "scientific" wing of analytic philosophy will be more unexpected. Only some of these philosophers appear to be drawn to naturalist treatments of morality of the sort that seem currently popular, or to quasi-realist or pragmatist accounts.

Whether the strong moral objectivist positions the many otherwise pronounced materialist and hard-headed scientizing analytic philosophers espouse can be accommodated to or rationally combined with these latter commitments and convictions seems unclear or doubtful. The philosophers in question seem mostly to keep the two, schizophrenically, in separate intellectual compartments. (Russell himself famously developed a version of an emotivist theory of ethics, in his book *Religion and Science*, and otherwise took subjectivist meta-ethical stances at other stages; yet throughout his life, as he acknowledged, he held strong moral positions that he was unable, and unwilling, to think of merely as personal, or subjective.) It seems appropriate, then, to assign analytic philosophy, in its wings and sub-branches, differing positions and attitudes towards the ethical (including in one wing a conceptually sophisticated and very prolifically advanced body of research activity), whether or not some of those positions and activities are fully compatible with fundamental models or blueprints of analytic philosophy conceived (as we are trying here to do) as unitary — as what Russell and Moore launched in the 1890s.

More deeply complicating the historical picture and architectonic I am claiming is the fact that a number of prominent analytic philosophers of the present and past have been devout theists, usually Christians or Jews. Peter Geach, Elizabeth Anscombe, Christopher Williams, Michael Dummett, for example, were or are committed Catholics; Norman Malcolm was a Lutheran; Hilary Putnam and Saul Kripke are believing and practising Jews. Many other individual analytic philosophers share similar commitments. Typically, these dimensions to their views are private and do not enter into the philosopher's published work. Only occasionally is an analytic (for that matter, any contemporary) philosopher's theism a public or central component of their professional endeavours. Alvin Plantinga is an obvious exception: a technical analytic philosopher, but more importantly a philosopher of religion, on the believing side. On the other hand, many analytic philosophers have been public, committed, even missionary advocates of atheism and anti-supernaturalism. Russell, Reichenbach, Ayer, Ernest Nagel, Mackie, and many others may be cited.

How about it then? Can an analytic philosopher be a Christian or a believing Jew? Yes, obviously: several are. Can a scientific modernist be a theist? And if not, can my characterization of analytic philosophy as a movement illuminatingly definable by reference to relations to science, more specifically by reference to scientific modernism, be tenable?

I have distinguished scientific modernism from naturalism. The former is, again, the idea, roughly, that natural-science-since-Galileo is a single diachronically (reasonably) unitary thing, that is without rival in its domain—whatever exactly that domain is, though it will be clear that it has large and significant dimensions both of theory and of practice. A naturalist holds that the domain of natural science is without boundary: it comprehends everything that humanity can have actual knowledge of, just possibly excepting mathematics and other purely conceptual or abstract areas. (Some, of course, hold to a strict definition that would require that naturalism be nominalist.)

In a rather obvious way, someone could be a scientific modernist non-naturalist or anti-naturalist just by holding that science has nothing to say about (some or all of) persons, agency, consciousness, normativity, or morality, or about a supra-empirical or the supra-natural world or dimensions to things; or perhaps by holding that science has only something, and not a fully determinate or complete word, to say about some or all of these things.

Two positions appearing in or prompted by the history of philosophy suggest themselves as candidate stances for putatively non-naturalist scientific modernism. One may be associated with Aristotle, the other with Kant. Stripped of his teleologism — which of course takes away something central — the Aristotelian picture of things seems to be that there is one, natural, world, but that the rational agent part of it involves in principle anomalist patterns and structures, that, not just for our cognizing endeavours, but inherently in the nature of things, do not share the exceptionless law-like character of the rest. Aristotelian anomalism is not quantum randomness, and we will legitimately decline to regard even a deteleological version of his system as truly naturalist. The Kantian picture is fully naturalist for the phenomenal order, but non-naturalist— indeed, anti-scientific modernist—for the whole larger scheme of things, including its unknowable nomenal part. Because all contentful *knowledge*, for Kant, is confined to the experienceable world of objects and events in space and time, and that world is altogether the one that post-Galilean science successfully nomologically investigates, it can seem correct to call Kant a scientific modernist, even if there may be intelligibly postulated, according to him, a world beyond or behind the experienceable one, and even if it is there that free rational agency, if anywhere, is to be found.

I begin to travel too far from my central theme. Analytic philosophy is diverse, multi-form. It is also famously characterized, some would say caricatured, as concerning itself only with small, narrow, technical, individual problems and issues, which of course would permit compatibility with a wide variety of large philosophical stances and commitments, or with none. The narrow focus of so much analytic work notwithstanding, I would argue that that work occurs always within a field of definite constraints and horizons, and that these are inevitably and invariably scientific modernist ones.

Part of the argument that all of analytic philosophy is to be grasped or defined by reference to science is subtle, rough-boundaried, open-textured. It is a matter of nuance, of the "culture" or cultural coloration of analytic philosophy, even in its ordinary language, British or Wittgensteinian forms and modes. Analytic philosophy in all versions celebrates—even if it does not always practise—clarity and argumentative rigour. Things may get dense or technical, but the complexities are always supposed to be explained by reference to the less complex, and there is always supposed to be a recoverable route back to an open terrain of more-or-less plain speech, and possibly bodies of results in logic, mathematics, or the physical sciences.

The latter two are supposed to be explainable, and may sometimes be explained, in varying degrees of detail. But an analytic philosopher of any persuasion can, as it were, pull rank or leave passages in his or her texts in a state of expectation that the reader is supposed to know, or figure out, or refresh himself or herself with the relevant resources, when the technicalities or details are those of logic, mathematics, or the natural sciences. Sometimes such expectations also include the history of philosophy; that is, the history of Western philosophy, up to and inclusive of Kant, or in some cases beyond to Hegel and Mill. But it is striking that for Wittgenstein and Putnam (in all phases) even also for Ryle, Austin, and Strawson, a sense of a stable body of logico-mathematical and natural science, lurking generally off the stage, is present in their texts and in the presuppositions of their approach to philosophy.

This is not the case, I suggest, with other varieties of philosophy than analytic.

There is, to be sure, a larger story within which, I would argue, the account offered here of the genealogy and development of analytic philosophy is just a proper part. I will only intimate this larger framework. It may seem plausible, arguably, to locate most or all currents in modern thought, those of modern non-analytic as well as analytic philosophy, by reference to scientific modernism. Virtually everyone—apart from Thomists, advocates of astrology or the occult, and radical narrativists—is (it may be said) a scientific modernist now. Everyone accepts that science has got things right with respect to airplanes managing to get into the air and deliver you between New York and Paris, causal connections between smoking and patterns of severe ill health, and broad understandings of the histories of and also the aetiological principles applicable to our and other living species, the earth, the solar system, and indeed the universe as a whole. What is not clear, though, is whether the sort of scientific modernism the latter involves—we might call this position, somewhat inelegantly, "meta-scientific modernism"—counts for a given philosopher or their school as a philosophical position at all, or one that their philosophical topics and concerns are concerned with.

The several kinds of prominent schools and types of philosophy and philosophizing on the current scene, I suggest in closing, are perhaps best grouped in their contrasts by reference to what they think is left for philosophy to occupy itself with. For the non-analysts, such scientific modernism as they accept is not in a philosophical foreground or background, but rather in an individual or personal one—it is what is accepted in after-hours or on weekends, so to speak. For the analysts, even the Wittgensteinian, Austinian, and Rortyan ones, scientific modernism, even when passive and with a conviction of science's having little or nothing significantly to contribute to philosophical purposes and goals, is a part of the philosophical landscape. No view, or objection to any of one's positions or theories, would be regarded as deserving being discussed or taken seriously, if it was demonstrably at odds with currently accepted (that is, *really* currently, non-controversially accepted) modern science; and establishing that no such conflict existed, where one was alleged, would be a challenge and philosophically significant work that any analyst, of any persuasion, would regard as important to take up. For the non-analysts, by contrast, scientific modernism is not part of philosophy at all. (It is, rather, like whether or not you have life insurance and how much, vacation plans, what kind of car to drive, or what academic programs or careers one's children should pursue. It is *on the outside* of one's professional writing and work, not even in the passive background.) And on that undoubtedly vague, and perhaps also somewhat dogmatic, note, I conclude. [7]

Postscript: I do not now (2007) regard this piece as successful, even in its own sketchy and schematic terms, as I did when I wrote it and presented it to audiences at Wayne State University and York University in the autumn of 2000. Many readers will not unreasonably complain of the piece's underdocumentation, both from the philosophers I characterize and the scholarship concerned with them whom I cite, praise, and blame. The piece doesn't mean to be a closely detailed exercise in historical scholarship, but even as a set of large-terrain ruminations with an accompanying historical narrative, more citation and quotation might have been useful (and, in fact, readily supplied).

Other deficiencies seem to me to include the following. Although this is noted in the essay, it still does not take seriously enough the claims of some explicitly religious (chiefly Christian) philosophers to be analytic philosophers (the leading example is perhaps Plantinga), or the background theistic commitments of still other philosophers (Charles Taylor would be an example), which would nonetheless not preclude *their* being viewed, not unreasonably, also as analytic philosophers.

Further, the essay, schematic as it is, does not take sufficient account of what has grown up as a now very scholarly literature on the history of analytic philosophy. That subdisciplinary development manifested itself very emphatically with the furore in the discipline, expressed in reviews, public electronic exchanges and conference presentations and debates which followed the publication of Scott Soames's *Philosophical Analysis in the Twentieth Century*,[8] argued by its many critics not to be a good history of its subject precisely because of its insufficiently historical character, including its neglecting the important research of the contemporary historians of analytic philosophy. (At the same time, Soames's work finds its defenders, and not only with Soames himself, who has responded vigorously and forcefully to his critics.) Soames's "Whiggish" account, having analytic philosophy come to its supreme expression, if not its apotheosis, in the work of Kripke, seems no less historically parochial and unsound than Dummett's earlier claims that analytic philosophy is essentially, and effectively, a body of footnotes to the work of Frege.

In addition to the need to provide more grounding in the scholarship of the history of analytic philosophy than the foregoing essay provides, I now think that one of its central theses needs considerably stronger support than I provide here. While I remain confidently and emphatically of the view that the general structure and shape of the historical picture that the paper presents of analytic philosophy's foundational matrix and two primary wings (each with its two sub-branches) is correct, the alignments of the second of the wings, the Moorean one, with *science*, even tacitly, that this essay claims, seem now to me not only less well supported, but also less clearly right, than the essay argues. I still do think that there is something to the idea this claim represents, and that it is a matter of the "Apollonian" spirit of inquiry that scientific modernism embodies; but just what that something more precisely is (and that could plausibly be identified as a property not shared by non-analytic varieties of philosophy) remains, I think, still somewhat elusive.

I certainly continue to believe that it is a mistake to think of analytic philosophy, as some of its proponents as well as its attackers have done, as simply, or even chiefly, a *method* of engaging in philosophical tasks of most or all sorts, or as that method plus an (according to some somewhat imperial, not to say imperious) *attitude* to the rest of the approaches to philosophy.

Some features of method are fairly obvious ones: less attention to Great Thinkers and a canon and their interpretation (though analytic philosophy also does history of philosophy), and primary focus on problems and issues and on arguments for and against substantive theses. Perhaps a further step in advancing what analytic philosophy, insofar as it merits being considered as a unitary philosophy, *is*, would be to claim (as have others) that analytic philosophy is, in addition to its distinctive methodology, a continued affirmation of central premises and commitments of the European Enlightenment. This of course simply invites consideration of what the relevant premises and commitments are.

NOTES

1   A test or application of this extensional claim that suggests itself is to consider the 34 philosophers who are subjects of published or currently projected volumes in the distinguished Library of Living Philosophers series, which since 1939 has aimed to highlight the work of the leading living philosophers. Of the 34, 15 seem easily and obviously identifiable as analytic philosophers, and 15 equally easily classifiable as not being analytic philosophers. Of the other four, one is the scientist Einstein, who, inasmuch as he was a philosopher may be classified as an analytic one; Richard Rorty is a "renegade" analytic philosopher; Marjorie Grene is an analytically trained philosopher, primarily working in philosophy of biology, and whose interests shifted to (so-called) "continental themes"; and Arthur Danto is an analytically trained philosopher whose interests have chiefly been cultural and continental.

2   There is increasingly the phenomenon of philosophers whose interests, and published work, cross boundaries and classifications that had once seemed rigid. Understandably, indeed commendably, many philosophers reject the pigeonholing of older disciplinary structures and strictures, and wander and produce results where philosophical passion or curiosity leads them. Brandom, a serious Hegel scholar as well as a philosopher of language, is a representative case; there are numerous others. It seems nonetheless accurate to identify the "crossover" philosophers by their training and background, and the character of the methodology and argumentation of the work they do. (Brandom, accordingly, is

an analytic philosopher with developed interests, and results, in Hegel interpretation; Habermas is a "continental" philosopher with significant interests, and results, in analytic speech act theory; etc.)

3   Michael Dummett, "Can Analytical Philosophy Be Systematic, and Ought It to Be?," in K. Baynes, J. Bohman, T. McCarthy, eds., *After Philosophy* (Cambridge, Mass.: MIT Press, 1987), p. 194.

4   *Origins of Analytical Philosophy,* p. 179.

5   Reprinted in Donald Davidson, *Inquiries into Truth and Interpretation* (Clarendon, 1984).

6   As he argues in his 1946 book *Meaning and Necessity.*

7   Thanks to several members of the Wayne State University philosophy department for helpful comments on an earlier version of this paper, presented in their speakers' series in fall 2001.

8   Scott Soames, *Philosophical Analysis in the Twentieth Century,* 2 vols. (Princeton University Press, 2003).

CHAPTER EIGHT

CONTINGENCY IN

EARLY MODERN PHILOSOPHY

An earlier version of this paper was presented at a conference on Hegel and contingency, held at the University of Guelph, in April 2003. I was asked to make some brief remarks on views of contingency in the early modern period.

We nowadays generally distinguish between what is called (variously) alethic or logical or conceptual or metaphysical modality — necessity, contingency, possibility — and what is called (also variously) causal or natural or physical modality. (The *first* of these two large categories will have, for most philosophers, importantly distinct varieties, which will themselves involve interesting conceptual and historical dimensions.) So, for example, it will be held to be necessary in the latter sense, but not the former, that heavy iron anvils don't travel at 11 times the velocity of light, or that decapitated chickens die. (Differences in the mode of interpreting both, usually styled *de re* and *de dicto* respectively, are also noted — this contrast will play little or no role in my remarks in the present discussion, so I will largely ignore this feature of modality.)

Not all contemporary philosophers *believe in* a genuine or objective natural modality (some philosophers, not necessarily the same ones, profess also not to believe in genuine or objective alethic modality as well). In the 20th- and 21st centuries, positions affirming natural, causal, or physical necessity (possibility, etc.) typically define themselves by reference to a conscious repudiation of Hume's (supposed) *mere regularity* view of the causal structure of the world. More about Hume presently. In any event, we do have now a conceptual location with these two basic kinds of modality, hence, contingency, occupying it.

It is unclear, at least to me, when the differentiation between alethic and natural modality appeared in the history of Western philosophy, though part of my purpose in this chapter is to offer a tentative or speculative suggestion about this. Natural or physical modality is explicitly identified by name in 19th-century philosophy[1]; and what (as I will argue below) may be seen as implicit in the philosophies both of Leibniz and of Hume will make a good case for thinking that constrasting notions of absolute, in principle, contradiction-implying-if-failing-to-obtain necessity, necessity which even an omnipotent agent would not have the capacity to reverse, on the one hand, and necessity-in-accordance-with-the-exceptionless-laws-of-nature on the other, were definite parts of the conceptual and philosophical land-scapes by the last quarter of the 17th century. It seems natural to suppose that if this contrast was in the field, or the background, by that period, it will have entered philosophy considerably before.

Although some scholars—Simo Knuuttila, for example[2]— have seen rather complex and nuanced variations in conceptions of modality over the centuries, I for my part have mostly not seen the case as convincing, or examples from our texts as requiring such complexity. There are, to be sure, interpretive complexities. When the ancient logician Diodorus Cronus holds that a possibility is something true at some time or other, and his opponents Philo of Megara and Chrysippus the Stoic assert that, on the contrary, some possibilities are never realized, and that being possible is not being forbidden or precluded by the content or nature of the thing concerned, are they operating with different senses of possibility, or are they having a disagreement about what things really are possible? (The second seems, in fact, the likelier alternative.) Something close to this pair of views about possibility — with correlative ones about necessity — appear at many subsequent junctures in the history of philosophy.

Likewise, when it is held, as most philosophers since antiquity have held, that it is not possible that the past be altered or reversed, is this a thesis about time and action more than it is about possibility; and in any case, is the relevant possibility the same as the one in which it is said not to be possible that seven be greater than nine, or that something be purple but colourless? There seem importantly distinguishable, from early on, modality in itself and modality *for* (an agent, typically), as well as modality *de dicto* and *de re*; and epistemic and, perhaps, ethical modality (e.g., Luther's "I can do no other"). And, of course, the justifying bases for modal claims, and generalizable results about the character of these claims, are also multiple. Still, it seems to me that there are some relatively simple, or relatively unitary, modal *roots* in human thought, though ones that are at the same time at least a little vague (or underdetermined).

In outline, my own model of the history of modality in Western philosophy is that ancient philosophy has a single not-closely-analyzed conception of the *necessary*, as what is mandated by fate, the gods, or a natural order of the world, and will be unavoidable.[3] Both Aristotle and the Stoics — but especially the latter — developed fragments of what we can plausibly identify as modal logic, and this sharpens somewhat the (folk) conceptions of modality that appear among the earlier philosophers. Cases of logical truth, in addition, of what many philosophers would still claim to be metaphysically necessary truths, and, further, cases of (what we would view as) logical contingencies, appear among the examples they give of things-impossible-not-to-be: some of these states of affairs that seem readily able to be supposed true in some possible worlds and false in others. With necessity follow in their wake possibility and contingency.

As noted, the greatest of the ancient logicians, the Stoic Chrysippus, argued that there are falsehoods that nonetheless have the possibility of being true even though there is no time (past, present, or future) at which they will be so. It seems plausible to think that some deep modal notion — possibility, or necessity, it will not matter which, as they are interdefinable — is something like primitive in human thought, with disputes as to cases a natural and subsequent development. It also seems correct that earliest conceptions of modality, perhaps including all of the (often highly sophisticated, and systematic) thinking about the necessary, possible, and contingent expressed in antiquity, never achieved quite sharp or clear boundaries. That is, there seem to have formed, certainly by third- and second-century B.C. philosophy, ideas of what must be so, what can be so, and what isn't but might be the case (or is but might not be), without there necessarily being very definite ideas about what it will mean or be required for these things being the case, or how it will be determined or adjudicated that they are, or what the outer limits or extremes of the cases that will fall under these notions are. And there specifically does not seem to have obtained, in antiquity, any clear or explicit notion of something's being necessary (or possible) in one sense (e.g., a logical or metaphysical one) but not in another — notably, a causal or natural sense — or contrariwise.

I will offer a speculative suggestion, which more detailed historical and textual investigation than I undertake here would be needed to confirm (or refute): that the bifurcation between alethic and natural modality is most plausibly viewed as a byproduct of the development of philosophically fine-tuned monotheism, in the 9th, 10th, and 11th centuries, chiefly among Islamic as well as Christian thinkers. An absolutely supreme perfect God should be expected to be able to contravene, reverse, or bypass, not just usual regularities of the world — the notion of a miracle may be seen as having, long before, laid the ground for such causal exemptions — but more or less any formulable principle, short of something that would be or imply the contradictory. And yet, alongside such only logically limited power, the sense of a natural and law-like order of the world, implicit in Greek philosophy from its beginnings, and explicitly articulated as causal determinism by the early (not the later) atomists and by Stoicism, will have continued and flowered as medieval philosophy advanced.

I want to proceed directly to the early modern period, and specifically to distinctive articulations of or contributions to modality — and therefore contingency — that may be discerned in Descartes, Spinoza, Leibniz, and Hume. (Nothing like complete accounts of the modal theories of the four philosophers could be offered in this brief exploration, but each has interestingly specific individual ideas that merit special focus.) The first three of these philosophers advanced versions of a — or the — ontological argument for the existence of God; in Spinoza's case, we need to say, for the existence of something he *calls* God, though, as is well known, with contestable entitlement to the term.

At any rate, all three explicitly formulate the idea of God as having *necessary existence*, and this is explicitly contrasted with the *contingent existence* that is had by the rest of the substances, or substance-like things (in Spinoza's case, they are called modes, of the one substance). Hume, for his part, explicitly denies that any such *item* has necessary being. "Whatever *is* may *not be*," he tells us (first *Enquiry*, Part I). The last three of the four philosophers I have named were all explicit determinists. So all three confront the question — it may or may not be a challenge, or objection — how there can be contingent being in a deterministic world.

Descartes does not, it seems, confront this question, since he appears to view the realm of thought, and agency, as not wholly subject to deterministic law. Descartes has, as well, the curious doctrine of the divine creation of the eternal truths. This theory, which Leibniz, as well as many others before and since, have seen as bizarre if not unintelligible, actually gives rise to an unusual and nonstandard system of modal logic, which so far as I know, no one has set out and investigated, though someone perhaps ought to. In this Cartesian system, some or all necessary truths were once contingent, then subsequently, as a consequence of divine decree, necessary. This conception would evidently make an underlying linear time conceptually more basic than anything modal — save for the necessity of the being of the necessary being.

Well before 1700, this Cartesian theory seems to have become only a historical, and mostly ignored, curiosity.

Spinoza's asseverations in the fields of modality pose their own challenges. God — the world — exists of necessity for him. As also already mentioned, whatever occurs in the world does so also through necessity, at least in the sense of having been causally determined. Spinoza can seem to be what might be called a modal throwback: a philosopher who is collapsing alethic and natural modality into each other. There is a small minority of contemporary philosophers who are prepared to defend something of this kind — philosophers, that is, for whom there are no possible worlds (to use that Leibnizian idiom) in which, say, copper never expands when heated, or decapitated chickens revive. In fact, Leibniz aside, a deep current in Western philosophy from its beginnings is precisely an idea that contingency is mere appearance — that its seeming to be possible that things be other than they in fact are (including a proposition's having a truth value other than the one it has) is a reflection just of our ignorance, and that could we know the full principles and workings of nature we would see that the supposed contingencies are all really necessities.

This *may* be the sort of thing that Spinoza thinks. On the other hand he may, like Aristotle, mean the term *cause* to cover, disjunctively and synoptically, the reasons, principles, and explanations of things, whatever their type or kind. I won't attempt to decide this here. If he does intend, or his system allows, alethic/natural modal bifurcation, he in fact *can* avail himself of a way for his world to be both deterministic and contingent; the causal regularities will be naturally but not alethically necessary. Actually, even if they were both, the antecedent conditions in any time slice of the world need not — should not — be *themselves* necessary, naturally or alethically. If that is right, then there will be indefinitely many alternative Spinozistic possible worlds, in addition to the actual one, where different things happen and exist, even if all of them are subject to and constrained by a single set of natural laws (which might or might not also be alethically necessary).

A last modal complexity in Spinoza to mention is his apparent adoption of the late Stoic conception of agent freedom as a not-causally-determined power to have one rather than another *attitude* towards the rest of what happens, (all of) which *is* causally determined. This is the sort of theory we find in Epictetus. The latter's, as well as Spinoza's, claims otherwise, it is difficult or impossible to see how this *can* be a fully truly deterministic view. On the latter, our attitudes should be as determined as everything else.

I will go on in these sketchy remarks to speak of Leibniz and Hume, the two greatest philosophers, in my view, who lived between Chrysippus and Kant—arguably, between Aristotle and Hegel. Both seem to have reached (Hume certainly did) the idea of a genuine, indeed, a radical, contingency of or in the world. *This* really could have preceded, followed, caused, been caused by, *that*, whatever states or events *this* or *that* may be; and it is not just our limited knowledge that may lead us so to think.

Although Leibniz seems also to have come to such a conception, it is difficult to see how he is entitled to it. God, the necessary, and necessarily rational, perfect being, exists of necessity for him, and—in spite of his claims otherwise—it is hard to see how he really can be free in the sense of having genuine alternatives. Rational beings, for Leibniz, never act on whims or with shrugs; so God's actions, including his creations, seem to need to issue from his nature as remorselessly as his existence does. Leibniz *may* not actually mind this; it will be enough, perhaps, for him, that God's, like other agents', acts will be done for reasons, even if they haven't alternatives. In any case, Leibniz does seem definitely to have escaped from the (theoretical) yoke of *natural* necessity, in the sense that, as for Hume, the causal regularities of the world are just patterned conjunctions, with divine *thoughts*, at least, that include indefinitely many variations on and breakings of those patterns.

Hume it is who has the full, clear, explicit idea of the radical contingency of the world, in all its parts, and in it totality. It *happens* to be thus and so, and as we find it. And of course, at the same time, how we do find it to be, how all of it, including our own states and behaviour, is, is fully law-like and patterned.

How much of this background may Hegel have known or been properly impressed by? Certainly he was well-grounded in the thought of the major rationalist philosophers, and his own system deeply involves argumentative reflection on freedom and nature, and on the respective spheres and claims of each. In their essay "Hegel on Modalities and Monadology,"[4] Martin Kusch and Juha Manninen bring together a number of Hegel's comments on modal themes in his predecessors, especially Spinoza and Leibniz, and fashion an interesting and largely persuasive account of Hegel's own confrontations with causality, determinism, and the prospects of freedom. It is not clear whether Hegel will have altogether appreciated, or been concerned about, such — relatively — fine-grained views as contrasts between inherent-(natural-)modality and mere regularity views of the causal order; or whether, if one did adopt the latter, Humean sort of line, doing so might (or might not) vitiate, or at least interestingly complicate, concerns about abridgments of or challenges to the freedom of rational agents posed by nature and the extent of its writ. Hegel, amazingly encyclopaedic though he was, still cannot be expected to have covered everything, or at least everything in every respect.

NOTES

1   Apparently Cournot may be the first to use the relevant vocabulary. See Pascal Engel, "Plenitude and Contingency: Modal Concepts in Nineteenth-Century French Philosophy," in Simo Knuuttila, ed., *Modern Modalities* (Kluwer, 1988).
2   See Simo Knuuttila, *Modalities in Medieval Philosophy* (Routledge, 1993), and the editor's introduction, and the first selection (by Lilli Alanen and Knuuttila) in Simo Knuuttila, ed., *Modern Modalities* (Kluwer, 1988).
3   Though this last term is itself of course modal, signifying what is necessarily not avoided.
4   Martin Kusch and Juha Manninen, "Hegel on Modalities and Monadology," in Simo Knuuttila, ed., *Modern Modalities* (Kluwer, 1988).

CHAPTER NINE

CHARLES W. HENDEL AND HUME
A Review and Reconsideration

An earlier version of this paper was presented as part of a panel session at the Hume Society meetings at the University of Nevada, Las Vegas, in July 2003.

It is in many ways quite salutary to explore the secondary literature on a major philosophical thinker that was done in a significantly earlier time. This is superbly illustrated with the exploration of Hume scholarship of the 1920s and 1930s. As readers will be aware, the Hume literature is immense, and growing weekly. Few — certainly not I — have a detailed, comprehensive command of it, or even a broad, general sense of its contours and play of notes, thematically or diachronically.

It is important, though, to try, and to do what one can; otherwise there is too much risk of re-inventing the wheel, and regarding as a novelty or a breakthrough what was already a familiar item on the table 40 years ago — or 80. It is also valuable to try, by noting respects in which Hume scholarship of an earlier time may look to reflect philosophical and other cultural currents of that time, to hold up the mirror upon ourselves and the thematic and other preoccupations we bring to current Hume research, and thereby disclose and probe what may be some of that research's limitations as well as its successes.

Charles W. Hendel (1890–1982) was an American philosophical scholar of significant stature in his time. A brief review of his career and primary writings may be useful. Born in Reading, Pennsylvania, Hendel graduated from Princeton in 1913, with subsequent study at Marburg in Germany, and in Paris, before returning to America, where he received his Ph.D. from Princeton in 1917. He then taught at Williams College for two years, returning to his alma mater Princeton for the nine-year span 1920–1929. Then followed a Canadian stint, which as a Canadian I will specially note. The years 1929–1940 Hendel spent at McGill University, where he was a professor of moral philosophy, then dean of the faculty of arts and science. In 1940 Hendel left Montreal for New Haven, spending the rest of his academic career at Yale, as Clark Professor of Moral philosophy and Metaphysics and chairman of the philosophy department, retiring in 1963. He made a number of pedagogical innovations at Yale, among them the small-seminar system he had himself experienced as a student at Princeton. It may also be noted that among Hendel's students at Yale was Richard H. Popkin. Other career notes of honour were terms as President of the Eastern Division of the American Philosophical Association and President of the American Society of Political and Legal Philosophy; he also gave the Gifford Lectures at the University of Glasgow in 1962–1963.

Our own focus is on Hendel as Hume scholar, as will be most of my remarks that will follow. In addition to his work on Hume, Hendel was also a Rousseau specialist, with two volumes of work — one of them an edited collection of letters — on that dark and troubling spirit; dark and troubling, of course, both in the careers of the Enlightenment in general and Hume in particular. Hendel also wrote extensively on religion and value, one of his monographs being called *Civilization and Religion: An Argument about Values in Human Life* (1948). Other publications were on Dewey, Kant, and philosophy of education.

Hendel produced five volumes of Hume work: editions of both *Enquiries*, a collection of Hume selections, a selective edition of Hume's *Political Essays*, and his own *Studies in the Philosophy of David Hume*. The latter is the object of primary attention in the rest of this chapter. The work appeared in two, importantly differing, editions; the original in 1925, then the second, long after the first had gone out of print, and in fact after Hendel had himself retired in 1963. A third edition, edited by Lewis White Beck, was published posthumously, in 1983. There were no significant changes in this final edition, and my chief focus here will be on the two editions that appeared during Hendel's lifetime.

The second of these makes a contribution to what we may call recent Hume scholarship — the literature on Hume of the last 40 years. The primary change the 1963 edition involves includes a very useful survey Hendel provides of Hume scholarship over the years since the 1925 edition. The last work cited in this survey dates from 1960; while the centre of gravity in its focus may be said to be on scholarly contributions of the 1920s and 1930s, much attention is given to still more recent work, including that of Von Wright, Flew, and others. Hendel's good command of French and German is also shown in his attention to the Hume scholarship 1920–1960 in both of those languages.

The 1963 edition of the *Studies* also deletes one of the original edition's chapters, on space and time, and adds 130 new pages: a "Supplement" — "On Atomism: A Critique of Hume's First Principles and Method" — and four appendices, chiefly replying to critics, including corrections of what Hendel himself sees as his own earlier errors. The Supplement "On Atomism" is in my view a particularly successful, in places brilliant, defence of Hume against numerous opponents.

Throughout the *Studies*, for Hendel, the primary voice and presence in Hume scholarship is Norman Kemp Smith. Hendel met Kemp Smith at Princeton in 1911, when Hendel was still an undergraduate there. Hendel's own words regarding their connections thereafter may be usefully quoted:

> The association developed into one of almost daily personal meeting until one day in 1916, when I assisted Kemp Smith and his wife and daughter in their embarkation at New York for Britain, where he proposed to enlist himself in some kind

of war work. The separation during the war in which I was also involved as a soldier in the United States Army did not loosen ties which had already been firmly knit. He himself initiated and maintained a steady correspondence. And thereafter we kept in touch with each other through letters and sometimes through visits until within a few months of his death, on September 3, 1958, when he was in his eighty-sixth year. During the forty-seven years of such enduring friendship I graduated from being an apprentice under his direction to the stage where, as he generously expressed it in a letter of June 1913, we were engaged in "common labours," and from that stage to the relationship of a colleague in the study of Hume when we exchanged criticisms of each other's work. It was from Kemp Smith that I learned most, not only about Hume but about philosophy, and vastly more, too, than it is possible even at this late date to acknowledge adequately.

Studies in the Philosophy of David Hume gives an account of most of Hume's philosophical work, tracing its development chronologically and biographically, noting, in detail (if in some cases — perhaps especially, that of Locke — selectively) influences and sources Hume has drawn on. Hendel is particularly valuable in this regard in showing the unmistakable presence in the Humean background of Malebranche, in spite of the obvious wide divergences between the overall philosophies of the two thinkers. Still another thinker whose importance for understanding Hume Hendel was one of the first to discern, and give content, is Cicero. Others to whom Hendel gives significant attention in the prefiguring background are Montaigne and Butler.

It may be noted as well that Hendel is of the party that accords, as of course did Hume himself, greater merit to the first *Enquiry* than to the *Treatise*. Hendel's account of Hume's philosophy is extremely thorough, detailed, and closely textual. He sees Hume as impressively consistent. The philosophical portrait is optimistic and synoptic — too anodyne, it might be held.

But though Hendel sometimes reads perhaps a little too much between Hume's lines, he is virtually always a useful, insightful commentator and source on basic, especially epistemological and metaphysical topics.

Beyond the delineation of the idea-bank that Hume's reading provided him with and the close detailed account Hendel gives on its basis of Hume's classic views in epistemology, Hendel has a particularly central focus on and interest in the *Dialogues Concerning Natural Religion*, and more broadly on Hume's views on theism. In fact, this does not quite adequately convey the thrust of that focus, since, for Hendel, Hume's views on theism, and preoccupations with religion, provide the key to understanding and interpreting Hume's major views in philosophy as a whole. This is particularly true in his first, 1925 edition of the *Studies*; Hendel qualifies and modifies this part of his treatment of Hume somewhat in the later 1963 edition.

At any rate, Hendel sees the youthful Hume's earnest wrestling with proofs of the existence of God, and the viability of a teleological and specifically theistic understanding of the world, as having continued throughout his life, and informing most if not all stages and topics of his philosophical publications, even where this might least be suspected. For Hendel, Humean philosophy is an extended continuation of the discussions presented in Cicero's *De Natura Deorum*, where ancient hypotheses as to the reality of the divine and the latter's explanatory plausibility, or otherwise a Democritean/Epicurean naturalism, vie with each other unendingly, tempered or leavened by notes of extreme or radical Pyrrhonian skepticism or the more moderate Academic skepticism, to which Hume's hero Cicero is regularly (if intermittently) drawn, as is Hume himself. This model is captured microcosmically with Hendel's conviction that the real mouthpiece of Hume in the *Dialogues* is actually the youth Pamphilus, who witnesses and is impressed and moved by the philosophical stances, sometimes the pyrotechnics of the others—especially, of course Philo—but in the end formally, or even informally, embraces none of them, although retaining, apparently, a fideistic commitment to the "naturalness" of theistic belief and its probable, even if unjustifiable, truth.

Hendel thinks, in fact, that Hume's attention to causality has wholly, or principally, theistic roots, or roots in Hume's theistic preoccupations. For Hendel, Berkeley plays a key role in the transition to Hume's conclusion that the causal principle is not a necessary truth; indeed, not a justifiable truth (even if, as Hendel supposes, it is for Hume nonetheless an — exceptionless — *truth*).

By doubting whether our perceptions must, or do, have causes in an exterior physical world, but insisting that they must nonetheless have a cause independent of us (for Berkeley that cause being God), Berkeley is seen as having awakened for Hume the idea that something fundamental — for Hume, the world — might not have a cause at all; then, if the world can lack a cause, the ubiquity of causality being dissolved by a single case, the absence of a need for a cause in *any* instance becomes thinkable, then plausible.

Hendel has, of course, much more to say on the matter than just this, and some qualifications or at least elaborations would be requisite to do his historical and thematic views full justice. Space limitations prevent me providing that justice. I want, nonetheless, to register dissent with much in the general Hendel approach — particularly, though not exclusively, in its emphasis on theistic parameters for understanding Hume. A number of critics of his own day — Laird, Lamprecht, and above all, Kemp Smith himself — also were less than fully persuaded of that approach, even while acknowledging the breadth of Hendel's scholarship and at least some considerable merit in its results.

I myself have argued, as have a number of others, for the sometimes neglected importance of the ancients in Hume's philosophical work, and quite particularly the very real ongoing presence of Cicero in that work and Hume's valuational understanding of the project of inquiry. Hume was a strong Latinist, and he tells us himself that he was from his early years drawn powerfully both to literary and to scientific and philosophical study. If he were an undergraduate today, by these disclosures we may suppose that Hume would have wrestled with whether to major in English or Philosophy — the draw in the first case to Literary Theory, in the second to analytic/empiricist work. It is also clear that Hume had personal, internal, preoccupations with religion and theism, earnest — indeed wrenching — in his teenage years, and of force and moment thereafter. Much of this was without doubt Ciceronian and philosophical. Much also was occasioned by, and focused on, the Scottish Calvinism of his own cultural setting, and that figured in his personal and interpersonal life.

It seems to me, then, that there is some truth in Hendel's portrait and interpretation of Hume, even if, as his own early critics of the 1920s noted, there is a notable absence of documentary *evidence* to support the extent of theism-inspired generation of Hume's arguments and conclusions outside the philosophy of religion, that Hendel supposes. At the same time, there is something quite wrong, and amiss, in the portrait and the interpretation.

Hume — at any rate, as I interpret him — is much more a "scientific modernist," if I may use that phrase, than Hendel sees. He is a child of the Enlightenment, as well as one of its primary flowers and avatars. He emerges in, and is shaped by, the intellectual world engendered by the 17th-century scientific revolution, and really does seek to contribute to endeavours that would apply "mechanical philosophy" to human beings and their doings — to the creation, that is to say, of at least selected parts of *social science*. This is not just a matter of "influences" — of whom Hume has read, and from whom he has drawn nuggets of theory and argument (or more than just nuggets, in some cases). (I will pause to make a parenthetical plug for one of those influences who I think is not sufficiently appreciated currently, even if he is acknowledged: Hobbes.)

Hendel is not entirely unaware of the more "naturalist" or "Newtonian" construal of Hume than his own, it should be noted; and where it is considered in the *Studies*, he rejects it. Thus, for example, a footnote (p. 100) citing H. C. Warren's *A*

History of the Association Psychology remarks that Warren "very properly excludes Hume from legitimate membership in the 'Associationist' school." Such membership will, of course, be a matter of just how that "school" is understood or defined. But, at any rate as I read Hume, there is no question of his commitments to a "mechanical" analysis of human nature, along approximately Hobbesian lines, even if more sophisticated, and involving a much greater role or place for mutualist interactive process—sympathy and its cognates—than Hobbes would have acknowledged.

As for theism, Christian or philosophical, Hume *is*, I would say, preoccupied, even in fact sometimes "haunted," by it. Like many a young person, before and since the 18th century, growing up in a cultural environment heavily dominated by Christianity, Hume was mightily concerned about its claims and their import, for oneself viscerally and personally as well as in more abstract terms. He became a hater of organized religion, glad to see its power diminished and to contribute, himself, to that cause, as he did, powerfully and creatively. These biographical facts alone would lessen the persuasiveness of Hendel's notion of Hume as ultimately a fideist Christian Ciceronian, or the nearest intellectual cousin to one. Hume *is* Philo, not Pamphilus. He is not on a theistic fence, nor, certainly, on a Christian theistic one.

But in any case, Hume, however youthfully preoccupied, has with his adulthood put aside childish things. Even as he draws inspiration, or a prompting to or the kernel of an idea, from many, many sources, including bits and segments independently in many of those sources, and they include Christian theistic forerunners such as Malebranche and Berkeley (and of course also, and hugely, the deeply Christian Locke), Hume is first and last true to the lodestone of the ideal of bringing "the application of experimental philosophy to moral subjects" (*Treatise*, Introduction). I would take this to imply that Humean insights, or convictions, about the contingency of causality reflect Hume's fundamental Democritean naturalist perspective more than anything stemming from impulses from Christian thinkers, Berkeley or any other.

Hendel's work is definitely worth returning to. His wide command of sources, primary and secondary, is impressive. And making acquaintance with his prose, and through it with the interpretive climate of an earlier time in Hume scholarship, including as it will, seeing how many of the debates and issues we may have thought innovations of our own current Hume inquiries, is instructive—indeed, properly humbling. Hendel's own philosophical style is of what I will call, I hope not derisively or unsympathetically, the "Will Durant" school: philosophy as an edifying adornment of our culture, Great Books, Great Thinkers, Great Ideas from whom we all, including those who will become clergymen and supreme court justices, as well as others of humbler station, can and should drink, and learn. Hume is placed in that company and mode. This misses, I would say (as I believe do other more recent presentations of Hume not of "Will Durant" cast), Hume as lifelong "enfant terrible," "emmerdeur," prototype of Reichenbach, Ayer, Richard Dawkins, as also (they are not, of course, unrelated, psychologically at least) ancestor in spirit as well as much content of behaviourist, connectionist, logical empiricist, sociobiological, reductionist philosophical thought.

But there is so much in the fertile genius of Hume; and for helping resituate him in a setting of his background creative influences, including presences that may not always be evident on his pages but which scholarship of the impressive character that Hendel brings to the examination of those pages, Hendel's is a voice deserving continuing, and revived, attending to.

CHAPTER TEN

THE SINGULARITY OF

THE SCIENTIFIC REVOLUTION

Fred Wilson's Defence of the Early Modern
Achievement in Philosophy and the Sciences

An earlier version of this paper was presented as part of a panel session at the Canadian Philosophical Association meetings, at the University of Manitoba, in May 2004.

Fred Wilson's award-winning book *The Logic and Methodology of Science in Early Modern Thought* takes an important place both in intellectual history and in the continuing analysis of fundamental canons of investigating the world. Wilson's achievement in this volume consists in restating, indeed, reinstating, the older view of the scientific revolution as a genuine conceptual and theoretical, as well as methodological and technological, revolution. Wilson argues convincingly that the conceptions of the logic, the modal parameters, and the goals of the explanation of the phenomena of the natural world that were launched above all by Galileo and Bacon differed radically from the Aristotelian models they repudiated and displaced. A project of restoring an orthodoxy, partly dislodged in the "science studies" approaches of Kuhnians and other intellectual historians of recent decades, is in many ways a thankless task; and all the more deserving of commendation and celebration for that fact.

Wilson does not merely reaffirm singularity and innovation in the age of Galileo, Newton, and Hume; he provides close, detailed, textual support for that stature, examining not merely the novelties of the new work, but the texts, perspectives, and theoretical models and methodologies of the ancient and medieval work it displaced and whose inadequacies for serious empirical science are too seldom seen critically and at arm's length. Wilson is not neutral in his probing of these texts and the inferences to be drawn from them. He is celebratory of the insights and the detail of the specific theoretical and methodological contributions, above all of the great empiricist figures: Bacon, Hobbes, Boyle, Newton, Locke, and, supremely, Hume. Wilson is thorough, and a continued or revived case for revisionism in these territories will need to respond to the detail of his account.

Wilson's book consists of seven studies of aspects of the scientific revolution and its contrasts with the prior Aristotelian period. Some of the studies, or parts of them, are devoted to features of Aristotelian logic that prompted or hindered the formulation of a contingent empirical methodology for the new science. Others are devoted to specific conceptual and methodological contributions of Hobbes and Hume, and to the role of Descartes as part-architect and also as an unsuccessful Hans Brinker with a finger in the dyke against the rising tide of modernity. This chapter focuses on selected aspects of Wilson's central thesis. While I share the broad view Wilson defends, and salute his contribution in bringing it, in the detailed way that he does, to the awareness of philosophers and historians of science, I find ground to dissent from, or at least to modify, particular arguments or analyses.

The general burden of my response to Fred Wilson's book is as follows. I think that on the whole, the book's central theses are sound, important, and extremely well-documented and well-argued for. Wilson makes an impressive and mostly convincing case that the received view with regard to the scientific revolution is correct, viz., that notwithstanding partial anticipations of elements of that revolution, a quite new ensemble of methodology, theory, and practice came into the world in the early years of the 17th century, that its primary philosophical or conceptual architects were Galileo and Bacon, and to a lesser and importantly qualified extent, Descartes, and that other significant contributions to the development and articulation of their innovations (especially the theoretical and philosophical ones) were made by Arnauld, Hobbes, and Boyle.

As Wilson sees it, again largely reaffirming the received view, a significant fissure is to be discerned in the responses to the Aristotelian heritage, which the revolutionaries repudiated, in streams appropriately identifiable as rationalist and empiricist. Wilson contends that with qualifications (more, in this case, that I would make than that Wilson does), where they differ, the empiricist fork of this revolutionary stream on almost all issues pertinent to the development of modern science is right and the rationalist fork is wrong. Further, Wilson argues, a fullest creative articulation and some genuinely and importantly new contributions to the development and success of the scientific revolution were due to Hume. The final summary pillar of this reasserted orthodoxy is that one rightly discerns a single evolving conceptual flower, *modern science*, from Galileo and Bacon to the present day.

I have, however, some reservations or qualifications — some of them border on being objections. For Wilson's project as a whole they are minor notes of dissent. Some may contribute to a larger picture of which his is a principal, well-focused part. To formulate them again at a high or summary plane: I think Wilson's case is strongest and soundest with respect to the logic and methodology of science, and more specifically, with regard to the aims and the logic of empirical explanation. Aspects at least of the work and legacy of Aristotle and his followers can, though, I think, be understood in a mode more readily assimilable to what we find in the 17th-century revolutionaries than Wilson allows for. It is possible, with some degree of Procrustean stretching, to see the Aristotelian forerunners as aiming to study the natural world with mostly empty results because of the methodology and the observational technology with which they were saddled. I don't think Wilson might disagree with this; indeed, it mostly restates a central part of his thesis. Yet he writes sometimes as though the Aristotelian scheme and that of Galileo and Bacon are profoundly differing systems, almost incommensurable paradigms, to use Kuhnian jargon. This seems wrong.

Aristotle's focus on, and quest for, *natures*, should be understood as prompted in the first instance by a *biological* model. His paradigm cases of individual substances are living things, grasped or grouped by species: dogs, cats, humans, tulips, mosquitoes, etc. There would seem to be nothing alien, or at odds with modern science or its 17th-century inauguration, in wanting to explore what is distinctive about overtly self-presenting species of animals and plants. Indeed, this is precisely what Linnaean taxonomical inquiry was to develop in a high systematic way in the 18th century. It is true that Aristotle generalizes beyond living things in the quest for natures, that his account of natures is teleological, contrary to a modern perspective, and that he utilizes non-observable states or properties — like having a soul, or potentialities of various sorts — in the account of a nature he favours. But the basic queries — e.g., what is it about the common domestic dog that differentiates it from other kinds of creatures (including some very different, and some rather similar, such as wolves), and by virtue of which we can understand and explain the appearance and the behaviour of the animal? — are properly scientific, in a modern sense, and deserve (indeed, receive) properly scientific answers. None of this, it seems clear, would Wilson deny. The qualification, or complaint, is that he makes Aristotle seem a little more alien or weird, scientifically speaking, than he is.

A second qualification has to do with a key (though not the only) part of Wilson's differentiation between empiricist and rationalist scientific modernism. According to Wilson, the empiricist stream eschewed and rejected, not only teleology, *a priorism* and top-down deductive explanation search via natures, but any presence of rational activity in the science that it endorsed and to which it sought to contribute, seeking all results in contingent matter-of-fact exceptionless regularities. Specifically, while empiricism and rationalism are seen as at one in rejecting teleology in nature and explanations that would allow for exceptions, rationalism is viewed as remaining in the Aristotelian camp in respect of commitments to deductive *a priorism*, natures, and a role for active agency, more precisely, the active agency of God, in the science hailed and supported for the modern age and its advances.

In fact, I think this overstates, and does not adequately correspond to, the historical record. With the slightly complicating or qualifying exceptions of Hobbes and Spinoza, about whom I will make some brief remarks presently, all of the early modern scientist philosophers prior to Hume were committed theists; indeed, almost all were wholly orthodox, and intellectually active, Christians. Newton was the major exception, and even he was an Arian or Anti-trinitarian Christian. All of them — Bacon, Galileo, Descartes, Boyle, Locke, Newton, Berkeley, and lesser figures — thought closely and intently about God, the requirements of faith, and the formation of a world view that would include the deity in the new scientific framework for which they were revolutionary advocates.

A pair of Wilsonian sentences — several others might have been used — will illustrate what I am claiming to be hyperbole in Wilson's statement of very wide contrast between rationalist or Aristotelian otherworldliness and wholly secular humanist empiricist this-worldliness. Wilson is referring to Locke and Huet, the most interesting formulator of a radical skepticism more radical than that of Descartes. "For Aristotle and Descartes,... humankind is semi-divine, split between a heavenly rational part and a sensible corporeal part. Locke and Huet attack this idea of humankind, insisting that humans are thoroughly of *this* world" (p. 122).

But Locke and Huet were both of them committed sincere Christians (as Aristotle — on the other side of the matter — was not). Locke offers what he thinks is a decisive *proof* of God's existence in the *Essay*, and elsewhere vigorously defends his own Anglican Christian orthodoxy, which will imply, as he knows and affirms, human personal survival and judgment after the extinction of the this-worldly body. And Huet, for his part, was a Catholic *bishop*; more fideist than strictly orthodox, it seems, but no less committed to personal salvation, and damnation, in a life to come. It is true that God's role is underplayed in the scientific and philosophical writings of Bacon and Galileo, the twin primary founding fathers in the tale that Wilson (and others) tell. But, notably, both Newton and Locke, in their chief scientific works (the *Principia* [in the General Scholium] and the *Essay*, as already noted, respectively), offer proofs of God's existence, and plainly see the possibilities of his reality as a critical part of the explanatory edifice each adopts and advocates.

The cases of Hobbes and Spinoza may or may not be anomalous. They are interestingly parallel philosophers in a great number of respects — empiricist and rationalist respectively, in Wilson's terms, and unqualified devotees of — in fact, of course, significant contributors to — the scientific revolution. I have held for some time that Spinoza's system is a structure the articulation of which in *The Ethics* is best viewed as being in effect in a sort of code, the key to its unravelling being found in taking the *definitions* of the work literally and synoptically.[1] When decoded, the result is seeing that Spinoza is, indeed, as Hume (and others) asserted, an atheist.

However, an alternative take on this very approach and Spinoza's system is to see Spinoza as aspiring to deliver the straight goods, the best and most that can and should be meant, by others' talk and writing on large philosophical, ethical, and theological topics. He is showing (as he supposes) the real character and nature of God, and what it is to worship him adequately; i.e., with *God* and *worship* understood as they ought to be understood. So he is a *sort* of theist, as well as being, in more or less everyone else's literal sense, an atheist. I have recently come to think that Hobbes's somewhat puzzling relationship to God, theism, and the faith of his fathers, should most plausibly be viewed as essentially similar to Spinoza's.

Hobbes's burden is somewhat heavier that Spinoza's. As a materialist who sincerely thinks that immaterial substances are not merely irrealia or lacking adequate evidential support, but actually incoherent pseudo-postulates, he is endeavouring to do right by theism — indeed, *Christian* theism — without rejecting it.

The result, in the final section of *Leviathan*, is a curious, almost proto-*Mormon*, theology, to which Hobbes seems sincerely committed and that he sees as allowing him to be a genuine Christian (the only sort, indeed, that it is rationally possible to be, he thinks).

At any rate, I think that Wilson understates the degree of interpenetration of theology, in fact, *religion*, and the new science—at least, the new science as it was actually conceived and practiced at the time (even if it contained from the beginning the embryonic seed of a starker, sparer, more purely secular and empiricist future); and that this understatement helps make it possible for him to see greater distance (only *somewhat* greater distance, I hasten to add) between Aristotelian pre-modern Christians and rationalist and empiricist scientific modernists than is warranted. It is certainly true that *after* the period of Newton and Locke, with essentially eccentric (if brilliant) exceptions such as Leibniz (who of course also overlaps the *Principia* and Locke, chronologically) and Berkeley, God rather drops out of the picture in modern science. He is simply absent, as the several sciences flower and advance. It is, as Laplace said to Napoleon, that they "have no need of that hypothesis." However, the great age of scientific revolution, the 17th century, is one rather more of *transition*, in respect of theistic matters (and their serious role in scientific explanation), than Wilson allows.

Perhaps the single greatest difficulty or limitation in Wilson's account, conceptually and historically, is its almost complete omission of the ancient naturalist/materialist/empiricist philosophies; namely, the theories (and schools) of Democritus and Epicurus. The ancient atomists developed the prototypes for much of the theory of the scientific revolution. They are the intellectual ancestors of the "scientific philosophy" represented by many of Wilson's central figures—Bacon, Galileo, Hobbes, Hume—and carried onwards subsequently by La Mettrie, Holbach, Mill, Russell, Reichenbach, Quine, Dennett, and Dretske (to name only particularly prominent examplars).

It is particularly important to bring this conceptual genealogy out, I think, because not only is it historically sound, and
significant, but its key features were also things the medieval
and Renaissance thinkers, as well as those of the 17th and 18th
centuries, were aware of. Ancient, and Cartesian-Humean radical
skepticism, which Wilson does discuss, partly to raise problems
for alleged Aristotelian goals of incorrigible certainty, are an
altogether separate matter, one might almost say a red herring,
from this point of view.

Much more significant are the atomist materialist/
rationalist philosophies, of which the Christian thinkers had
good knowledge, and which they saw sometimes as bogeymen,
certainly as conceptual and philosophical rivals to their own
views, which were firmly to be rejected. Aristotle's philosophy
may, in fact, be viewed as a (partly self-conscious and deliberate)
attempt to mediate between the naturalist, materialist, and
determinist philosophy of Democritus, and the "other-worldly"
abstractionist and spiritualizing philosophy of Plato. Part of
the appeal and success of Aristotelianism within a Christian
philosophical setting will have been its seeming both to be of and
for this world and our embodied selves, and at the same time
allowing for (arguably, actually requiring) both our ensoulment
and a divine artisan of the world.

One of the most important features of the scientific revolution
in philosophical and world-historical terms is that it represented,
and continues to represent, the triumphant return of the spirit
and legacy of Democritus; initially, incrementally, then from the
early 18th century to the present day, completely and entirely.
Even if current physics is indeterminist, and the Democritean
conception is determinist—rejecting the Aristotelian nomic
pattern of "almost or mostly" that Wilson rightly decries—science
in all branches after 1700 has rejected teleology and sought
exceptionless generalization from the plane of observation,
experiment, and postulation where the latter two and the
mathematics their patterns generate and instantiate warrant.[2]
All of the sciences also conceive themselves, whether or not

maintaining a strong unity of science thesis, as parts or branches of a single, broadly unitary enterprise or house, confronting a single, broadly unitary causally interconnected world. This too was very much the conception of Democritus and the Epicurean atomists who succeeded him.

Although Democritus is a determinist and Epicurus is not, the latter's random atomic swerves intended to account both for atomic collisions—hence combinations, dissolutions, and recombinations—as well as for free will, there is fundamental overall unity in the two philosophers' outlooks, outcomes, goals, and methodologies, over and above the shared atomism and materialism. For both, the world is on automatic pilot, so to speak, and the aim and mission of philosophy, natural and moral, is to study and learn the structures and patterns of the world and to explain the observed phenomena of the world: the nature of things. The actual explanations ancient atomism reached are not, for the most part, very impressive—Lucretius's *De Rerum Natura* is filled with cases, very specific and particular, as well as general large-picture hypotheses. But the entire focus is on the observable natural world of physical phenomena, and phenomena (like mind) not obviously physical but argued also to be physical nonetheless, behind appearances. The goal of the philosophical/scientific enterprise is to arrive at explanatory matter-of-fact generalizations, of how nature has in the actual circumstances, this time around (for the atomic systems conceive the world to be infinite in time and space, and subject to long-cycle rearrangement of the component parts), comported itself.

And, again, the medievals and early moderns were very aware of these facts. In fact, we find in the texts of the revolutionaries themselves some most interesting affirmations of these claims and analyses. From Bacon himself (*Novum Organon*, Bk. 1, aphorism 51): "The human understanding is of its own nature prone to abstractions, and gives a substance and reality to things which are fleeting. But to resolve nature into abstractions is less to our purpose than to dissect her into parts; as did the school of Democritus, which went further into nature than the rest." (Bacon is less praising elsewhere, though again shows manifest familiarity with the ancient school. In aphorism 57, he complains of over-focus "in the school of Leucippus and Democritus" on detail, and the particular.) Subsequently, in aphorism 65, Bacon asserts that Anaxagoras, Parmenides, Empedocles, and Heraclitus, as well as Leucippus and Democritus, were all far better at and more usefully contributory to natural philosophy than was Aristotle. Bacon imagines that Democritus, whom he clearly conceives as an iconic ally, would have welcomed and shared in the new science. Thus (Book 2, aphorism 38): "… the microscope… is only available for minute objects; so that if Democritus had seen one, he would perhaps have leaped for joy, thinking a way was now discovered of discerning the atom which he had declared to be altogether invisible." Bacon is not unique among the 17th-century revolutionaries in referring to Democritus, nor in citing him with approval. So also does Boyle.

Likewise, Democritus is a very important figure in the development of the theories, scientific and philosophical, of Galileo, and was so recognized by his contemporaries, adversarial and otherwise. This is brought out emphatically in the secondary literature. Pietro Redondi, assessing the significance and impact of Galileo's 1623 masterwork, *The Assayer*, says of it: "This was the rejection of a philosophy—one that was inextricably connected with the Catholic religion and the reigning mentality. It was also the re-evaluation of marginal, condemned, rejected ideas… [B]esides the refutation of *On the Soul* [i.e., Aristotle's *De Anima*]—that is to say, the sacred text of Scholastic university philosophy—*The Assayer* immediately summoned up before contemporary eyes two names: Democritus and Ockham… [W]hen reading Galileo's very famous passage about the book of the universe, one cannot help but think automatically of Democritus."[3] Redondi subsequently augments this judgment extensively.

Bacon also cites Lucretius, as do Hobbes (who considers Lucretian arguments and explanations at some length), Berkeley (who, addressing a supposed modern scientific materialist in

Alciphron, speaks of "that renowned philosopher Lucretius, who, on other points, is so much admired and followed by those of your sect"), and Hume (his references are almost all to Lucretius as poet and stylist). Even more widely cited than either is Epicurus. The early moderns were, of course, generally extremely well-read in the classical texts.

What is evident, though, is that they also saw the theories, ideas, and some of the arguments developed in the new science as kindred in type to those of the ancient atomists. Even where they disagree with the latter, family resemblance is acknowledged. Thus, Hobbes, distinguishing his own views from those of Gassendi and Digby, which an opponent had assimilated to those of Hobbes: "… for Gassendus, and Sir Kenelm Digby, it is manifest by their writings, that their opinions are not different from that of Epicurus, which is very different from mine."[4] No one, of course, would have imputed, even mistakenly, theories of Plato or Aristotle to Hobbes. Cudworth we find referring to "that antient atomical Philosophy, so successfully revived of late by Cartesius."

Henry More, likewise, asserted that the Cartesian philosophy was "in a manner the same with that of Democritus."[5] Descartes, of course, would have none of this. (Section 202 of Part IV of *The Principles of Philosophy* is explicitly headed: "That the Philosophy of Democritus differs as much from ours as from the generally accepted one." Since Democritus was well-known as having been a materialist anti-theistic and anti-teleological determinist, Descartes may have been being, in part, theologically prudent, as we know that he quite reasonably—in the age of Bruno, Galileo, and Vanini—was on other occasions.) He jealously guarded his own originality in virtually all matters, uniting this spirited guardianship with a professed indifference to and ignorance of the history of philosophy (which modern scholarship has shown not warranted by the actual evidence).

Scholarly remarks and comments on the ancient atomists, and their relationships with the 17th-century figures, made then and since are often clouded by over-focus specifically on atomism, i.e., on the particulars of the atomic theories of Democritus and Epicurus, and how early modern versions of atomism (whether accepted or rejected) were similar or different. (This is largely true of the references to Democritus and Epicurus in Hans Reichenbach's enduring classic *The Rise of Scientific Philosophy* [University of California Press, 1951], a volume to which Fred Wilson's book is an excellent sequel and companion.) A more important part of the theories of Democritus and Epicurus in the present context is that both rejected teleology, a role for a god or gods in the natural and causal order, and advocated an infinite unitary spatio-temporal materialist world, law-governed, for Democritus, at least, entirely by deterministic physical laws. These, along with the adoption of a studious and invariant methodology of eliminative induction, are the key features Wilson identifies as the empiricist scientific modernist departures from prior prevailing Aristotelian natural philosophy.

It bears noting that the early modern period involved *very* considerable acquaintance with ancient atomism, particularly in the Epicurean version presented by Lucretius. "There appeared in Europe no less than thirty-eight printed editions of *De rerum natura* between 1473 and 1626."[6] There may have been an Aristotelian intellectual hegemony, even exclusive monopoly, in natural philosophy in the later medieval period, which survived in schools, universities, and textbooks well after 1600. But the humanist new age, from well before Copernicus, was wide open, at any rate, to the whole of the surviving legacy of classical antiquity. And even before the dawn of the Renaissance, it is interesting to note that both Democritus and Epicurus show up in Dante's *Inferno*. Curiously, Democritus—the determinist—is placed, with Aristotle and a small group of others, as distinguished pagan philosophers in the mild first circle of hell, whereas Epicurus—the indeterminist—is housed in the lower, darker sixth circle (for denying the soul's immortality, Dante says).

Many complex historical and conceptual issues are posed in these territories, of course. For Wilson, the central battle is whether the scientific revolution is a genuinely new and groundbreaking set of developments, or whether such claims are mistaken, and a continuity from earlier prevailing theories and practices a more accurate view — continuists versus discontinuists, one might say, with Wilson firmly in the discontinuist camp. So, mostly, am I. Even if ancient atomism provided certain prototypes and models, it was a minority voice in surviving old texts, and its actual explanations of natural phenomena were generally miserably wrong. The ancients didn't have microscopes or telescopes, as Bacon says, nor a practice of grubby hands-on experimental work, nor any developed mathematics beyond geometry. All of those things made big differences, especially when utilized by the very smart, and energetic, people for whom they were available.

Further, Wilson may want, not entirely unreasonably, to say that he was simply not addressing possible continuities between ancient atomism and the new science, but exclusively alleged continuities between the prevailing Aristotelian natural philosophy and the new science. But — the presence of Democritus and Epicurus, especially the first, deserves inclusion in the story Wilson tells, even highlighted inclusion. It won't change the fundamental accuracy of that story, even if it may lengthen and complicate it.

I proceed to some remarks on logic, the ideas of a logic of truth and a logic of consistency, and formal and non-formal necessities. Again, I think that while the general burden of Wilson's analysis of the history is sound — and often deeply illuminating and instructive, let me add — he exaggerates differences and smooths over complexities.

Let us take as a useful example the conditional "if it is red, then it has a colour." I submit that this expresses a non-formal necessity, and one that no empiricist, or anyone else, would argue to be a non-necessity. Twentieth-century empiricists did sometimes seek ways to show that conditionals of this sort are actually disguised or implicit formal necessities; but it isn't obvious that they are, and most empiricists have honestly acknowledged that it takes work to render cases of this type *formally* necessary, even if it can be done. It is not true that modern Russellian logic rejects non-formal necessities, as Wilson — several times — explicitly claims. What it does is *fail to discern* them. Its nets don't capture or express them. Thus, for example, "Fa⊃Fa" is a suitable substitution instance of "p⊃q," and the former is *necessary — formally* valid, as it happens — even though the propositional form of which it is an instance is not; and other substitution instances will be of the red-implying-colour kind. There is nothing about the *logic* developed by Boole, Peirce, Frege, and Russell that rules out propositional structures and relationships that will be, in fact, strictly necessarily true — synthetic *a priori* necessary truths, indeed. The logic is simply silent as to whether there are such items. It has no mechanisms for capturing, identifying, or expressing them, if there are any. But that is not at all the same thing as *rejecting* such cases.

A further note of dissent. This one will attach specifically to Wilson's critique of Aristotelian models and their repudiation above all by the empiricist thinkers. Even more specifically, this concern will focus on features of the philosophy of Hume, the supreme exemplar — indeed, hero — of the story of the emergence and triumph of modern scientific philosophy as Wilson tells it (indeed, again, mostly quite rightly tells it, as I and many others also suppose).

As the tale is told, the displaced and repudiated Aristotelian natural philosophy seeks to discover and disclose *natures*, the necessary and enduring cores of character and trait of individual substances, aggregable into kinds and species, and which will *explain* the properties of all of the rest of nature, though these natures are themselves left not further resolved or explained. They just *are*, the final residuum of theory and analysis. By contrast, the successor empiricist, and in paramount version Humean, scientific modernist natural philosophy abandons and rejects natures of substances in favour of observable events and states that it studies individually then in aggregation, looking for exceptionless contingent matter-of-fact regularities, *these* to be the final residuum of the scientific quest.

What one finds in Hume, though, seems to tell a more complicating story, even if most of the latter is also there. Hume's cognitive psychological theory identifies the causal mainsprings of our human behaviour as a set of principles of mental association — three, precisely. One thought will succeed another by virtue of resemblance, contiguity, or cause-and-effect linkages (or supposed linkages) between objects (or supposed objects) of the thoughts. Hume famously (or infamously; or at any rate, unsuccessfully, for some) seeks to explain all of our mental lives as reducible to operations and applications of the three principles of association.

My focus here is on the three principles themselves. *Why* are we psychological-association-driven creatures, for Hume, and what, for him, explains the fact that it is these three, and no other possible psychological principles of association, that operate for us? Is not the answer — intimated by Hume's own assertions, in different contexts, of his versions of the idea that explanations come to an end somewhere — that *it is just so*? That is how it is with us human beings, that is what we find when we probe; and there's no more to be said about it. Is this not a nature? And, indeed, isn't the *theoretical stance* Hume is shown here to be taking, one according to which human creatures *have* permanent and enduring natures; namely, propensities to apply the three principles (laws) of association in all circumstances? And does not Hume's theoretical stance — i.e., is it not at the centre of the theory of (this part of) nature he is advocating — that all else in the domain of inquiry is to be explained by reduction to this nature of ours? This sounds rather more complicatingly Aristotelian than one might have supposed.

It is augmented by what one finds as Hume's own response to radical skepticism. Radical skepticism is, as we have noted, another theme given central significance in Wilson's book, as part of showing the superiority of empiricist to rationalist scientific modernism. Hume's own treatment of the matter may have a different lesson. Hume says that radical skepticism is rationally invincible and unanswerable. Its real and proper defeat is to be found in the fact that we humans are unable—psychologically unable—to sustain credence in any conclusions its arguments may validly lead to; indeed, in the even stronger fact that we have unconquerable propensities to believe in an external world, other minds, the general veracity and reliability of memory, and perhaps other philosophical claims and common-sense beliefs. We just can't help but believe in these things, whatever Pyrrhonians among us may bring to our tables. (An apt query on the side, which Hume seems never to ask himself: how does Hume know that these things are so and that they are true of us, or, if so, will remain so?) In any case, this surely tells us still more about our permanent and enduring, and causally efficacious and explanatorily significant, *natures*.

Finally, I think that some of Wilson's Hume interpretations are unpersuasive. Specifically, the view that Hume identifies thought with language, or, at any rate, sees (human) thought as essentially linguistic, seems anachronistic and wrong—even if there is one sentence in one of Hume's letters (which Wilson quotes) that may be marshalled for Wilson's claim. Hume does not actually have a great deal to say about language, one way or the other. Passages from Hume's published work that Wilson cites as making linguistic or semantic claims, or having linguistic or semantic implications, just do not seem to *say* what Wilson finds in them.

I will quote one case, with Wilson's comment, and the reader can make up his or her own mind about the case. " 'Tis impossible to reason justly, without understanding perfectly the idea concerning which we reason; and 'tis impossible perfectly to understand any idea, without tracing it up to its origin, and examining that primary impression, from which it arises' (T 74-5). What this means is that...the new scientific view of humankind developed by Hume and Hartley requires one to *turn outward*, to the world that language, through its syntactical and semantical conventions, tries to describe. For Hume, we must examine not the fit of our language to our ideas but the fit of our language to the world" (p. 131f.; Wilson's emphasis).

If Hume had really held so bold and innovative a view as the thought as language conception that Wilson attributes to Hume, one would expect it to have more highlighted attention in Hume's texts. Further, and I think damningly, Hume's interesting and important (and deeply naturalistic) discussions of the psychology of the non-human animals, and of fundamental commonalities between their thought processes and ours,[7] wouldn't seem to make sense or have the significance Hume clearly seems to attach to them, if our thought wasn't notably conceptually separable from our speech and our language, since the beasts have neither.

And with these comments, queries, and qualifications of what I think is, in general respects, an exceptionally fine and important, book, I close.

NOTES

1   See Peter Loptson, "Spinozist Monism," *Philosophia*, vol. 18, no. 1, Apr. 1988.
2   Biology will seem to some to constitute an exception to this emphatic claim. "Teleological" or functional biological systems, though, are never given a *theoretical* rationale that is at odds with Darwinian natural selection, which in spirit and aspiration is wholly mechanistic.
3   Pietro Redondi, *Galileo Heretic* (Princeton, N.J.: Princeton University Press, 1987), p. 59.
4   *The English Works of Thomas Hobbes*, W. Molesworth, ed. (London, 1845), vol. vii "Of Manners", p. 340f.
5   Cited in D. Garber, J. Henry, L. Joy, and A. Gabbey, "New Doctrines of Body and Its Powers, Place, and Space," in D. Garber and M. Ayers, eds., *The Cambridge History of Seventeenth-Century Philosophy*, vol. I (Cambridge, 1998), p. 588.
6   Garber, Henry, Joy, Gabbey, *op. cit.*, p. 570.
7   *A Treatise of Human Nature*, Book 1, Part 3, Section 16 "Of the reason of animals".

CHAPTER ELEVEN

ENLIGHTENMENT, THE PHILOSOPHERS, AND RACE

Some Reconsiderations

An earlier version of this paper was presented at a conference of the Canadian Society for Eighteenth-Century Studies, hosted by the University of British Columbia, in October 2003.

Emmanuel Chukwudi Eze's useful and instructive (even if not always satisfactorily scholarly) collection *Race and the Enlightenment*[1] contains classic pieces by Linnaeus, Buffon, Hume, Kant, Herder, Hegel, and other 18th-century writers who had things to say about race and ethnicity, and especially about Black or Negro humanity. Eze includes two short encyclopaedia articles, one from the great *Encyclopédie*, the other from the first, 1798 American edition of the *Encyclopædia Britannica*. Nearly all of these selections show a highly valorized racial or ethnic taxonomy in which White Old World Europeans are the most advanced, intelligent, and beautiful of humans; usually, also, the basal or original humans, the other varieties representing departures — typically degenerative departures. The only exceptions to this pattern, among the texts, are the pieces by Beattie, who criticizes Hume for his views of non-Whites; and Herder, who affirms incommensurable differences between historical cultures, each with its own special character and merit.

This chapter undertakes, especially, a re-presentation and reconsideration of Hume and Kant and their published comments on race and ethnicity. It will be important, in order to understand and assess those comments, to situate both against a broader historical backdrop—indeed, not just in the European Enlightenment, but in times and places both before and since.

Hume and Kant are, of course, among the supreme figures in the pantheon of Western philosophers. In standard assessments, they are two of the perhaps five, ten at most, greatest, most important and original and still influential philosophers who ever lived. In epistemology and in moral theory they are bright, still-shining jewels of the European Enlightenment, their work also seminal for metaphysics and philosophy of science. Hume's contribution to themes of race comprised one short footnote—one now notorious short footnote—in one of his many essays on public themes and issues. Kant's writings on race are considerably more extensive, part of a body of lectures and essays on physical and cultural anthropology—also now notorious. Kant lectured on anthropology annually from 1772 to 1796, but his writings touching on race and ethnicity almost entirely date from the 1770s;[2] that is, from the period prior to the creation and publication of the so-called critical philosophy, inaugurated with the first edition of the *Critique of Pure Reason* in 1781. Interestingly, this is also the period during which Hume produced the final version of his "racial" footnote; the two philosophers seem, then, to have been in approximately similar evidentiary positions, as European intellectuals and proto-anthropologists, certainly chronologically.

As intimated, the "racial" writings of Hume and Kant comprise, at least by most reckonings, minor or peripheral or non-central parts of huge bodies of written work. Nonetheless, this material has now received quite a volume of attention, most of it convicting one or both philosophers of being racists.[3] In this regard, Hume and Kant join other philosophers of the canon some of whose writings, or activities outside their philosophical writing, have been seen as racist, or, in some cases, sexist—notably Aristotle, Locke, Rousseau, Schopenhauer, Nietzsche, Frege, and Heidegger.[4] That consequence will then, typically, now, result in a verdict that this material can and should be noted, deplored, and then relegated to an appropriately minor, secondary, and marginal place; or given highlighted attention, for larger, wider issues in the history of ideas, or the subsequent theoretical views, and the practices, of Europeans who read and were influenced by the philosopher in question. Still another view has been that while Hume and Kant were Eurocentric racists, so were most of the rest of their intellectual — and non-intellectual — colleagues and congeners, during the 18th century, and at least most periods since; so that the subject — of *their* Eurocentric racism — is or ought to be of only extremely modest interest, the more important issue being larger and more general patterns of Eurocentric ideology and practice, the impact they have had, and the resistance they have met with from their victims. Finally, some interpreters do argue that Hume's or Kant's putative racism actually does derive from, or at least find parallel in, their theories of mind or of human nature.

In this chapter I want to provide argument that is meant to unsettle at least parts of the foregoing. Some of this unsettling will be on high or large terrain, i.e., without special reference to Hume or Kant. And the remainder of my remarks are intended to provide qualified defences, of a sort, of both the great philosophers, perhaps especially Hume — not of views on human "races" that either thinker held, but rather a qualified defence that makes a plea for a degree of historically contextualized understanding of the setting in which those views emerged and the aims that prompted them.

Although this chapter does not undertake to develop either view in detail, I will suggest that Hume's brief writings in this area reflect his conviction that origins and hidden powers are unknowable, and science, including social science, must proceed on the basis of seeking (cautious) generalizations from warranted observations; and that Kant, like Hume, is engaged in an attempt to be scientific about people, and is prepared to explore origins and the inner workings of nature in ways that Hume is not, and likewise to accord Judeo-Christian, hence Biblical, accounts of human cultural development at least some degree of warrant

(Hume accords them none at all). Both thinkers, I will suggest, do still merit inclusion in the reckoning of achievement, not only in pure philosophy, but in contributions to early stages of serious, and indeed (some of their deplorable conclusions notwithstanding) honourable, anthropology.

I also offer reflections whose import will be in part that it can be to an important degree anachronistic, or otherwise problematic, now, with emphatic and censuring precision, to view earlier thinkers through the prisms of considerably later categories that came to have much sharper, and much more consequential, sense, scientifically, politically, and ethically; specifically, in the cases at hand, much sharper senses, and resting on a considerably wider base of empirical data than obtained before ca. 1775. I do not mean by this to claim that it is not justifiable in an abundance of circumstances to censure morally benighted views, expressed by philosophers as much as by anyone else, in other times or places than one's own; or indeed to subject positions and advocacies to normative scrutiny, just as they will meet appropriately with other sorts of evaluations. There are, nonetheless, horizons of what it is reasonable to have held, or not, in particular times and places; and correlatively, complexity in the application of highly nuanced contemporary terminology to settings at a significant cultural or epistemic distance from ourselves.

Our own age (and culture) frequently forgets that prior to, say, 1945 (perhaps the best-chosen date might be slightly earlier, or considerably later, than that year), it was usual, and common, to classify and assess humanity by type, group, and kind; widely, freely, and more or less unblushingly. Certain limited features of courtesy — public, social, interpersonal, or individual — or considerations of seeking to be scientific, may have imposed some constraints on such habits and practices, in particular circumstances. But such patterns otherwise were ubiquitous, manifesting themselves in public and written as well as private and verbal discourse. They were certainly not confined to White Anglo-Saxon Protestant males, or Europeans; indeed, every one of the preceding sequence can be replaced with its complement and the generalization will stand.

Nor were kind-classifications and accompanying valorizing judgment, positive or negative, limited to matters of skin colour or sex. Social and economic class, age, occupation, religious denomination, nation, region within a nation, individual family or lineage, and sundry others afforded people bases on which to classify and characterize, to praise, and to condemn—at any rate, to judge. (An excellent literary expression of just such attitudes is found in Charles Lamb's 1823 essay "Imperfect Sympathies."[5]) It will be clear that some instances of these (positive or negative) "kind-valorizations" will have played significant roles leading to the unfair (and sometimes quite extreme) advantaging or disadvantaging of many of the kinds concerned, or their individual members. It is also clear that the normative groupings and assessings referred to do not only appear within the "long" 18th century. Indeed, in the specific matter of the characterization of sub-Saharan black Africans, it is instructive to compare two editions of the *Encyclopedia Britannica*, the 1798 edition from which Eze quotes, and the celebrated 1911 11th edition, for some still the finest and highest achievement of all the Britannica editions. The latter's article on "The Negro" is more sophisticated than the 1798 version, and much more replete with data; still, the overall depiction may reasonably be seen to be not markedly dissimilar.

Nor are inegalitarian accounts and assessments of black Africans only to be met with in European texts. It may be of special importance to bring this out with a highlighted attention, since the claim that racism and racial stereotyping are distinctively and peculiarly European conceptions, developed in the centuries that follow Columbus, is so frequently made. A neglected classic of universal history is the 1377 Arabic treatise *The Muqaddimah*, of Ibn Khaldûn. It is a very impressive attempt to provide an explanatory account of human societies and institutions, within the framework of a philosophical history, giving special attention, as the Enlightenment anthropologists were to do, to the role of geographical conditions. Nonetheless, its (Tunisian) author has this to say about Blacks: "We have seen that Negroes are in general characterized by levity, excitability, and great emotionalism. They are found eager to dance whenever they hear a melody. They are everywhere described as stupid."[6] Ibn Khaldûn then proceeds to offer climatological explanations of why these things would be so.

Ubiquity does not validate or justify; and few will deny, I think, that we live in a better world than formerly obtained in respect of the care, sensitivity, and tolerance—and the ability to appreciate differences—with which we group and publicly (even, often, privately) assess each other in our several sorts and kinds. This is a case, I would say, of just the sort of progress that the Enlightenment so often affirmed to be, if not inevitable, probable.

Still, it may reasonably be said, of the context in European intellectual history that we are exploring, that we have to do not merely with free and loose speech that sometimes involved rude, unkind, and inegalitarian characterizations of other humans, by ethnicity and other classifications. The west European societies of the long 18th-century—and before, and after—were, in their colonial empires, slave societies. Furthermore, the European slave trade—concretely, the European acquisition of Black sub-Saharan Africans, as slaves transported to European colonies in the so-called New World, beginning soon after 1492 and finally ending only in 1888 (in Brazil)—had from its inception a rationale, economic and ethical, that was at least related to the same sort of kind-thinking I have been referring to. That is to say, people—European people—weren't simply free and loose with what they thought and said about this, that, and the other kind of people; they thought that it was reasonable and appropriate that *certain* such kinds—specifically, *one* such kind—be bought and sold and utilized as a form of human livestock.[7]

Concretely—again—Hume, Kant, and the rest of the Enlightenment thinkers who wrote about race specifically, all of them included in the Eze volume, knew perfectly well that the European colonies were slave states and territories, where a unique variety of human being was a slave. Several of the

Enlightenment thinkers are on record as having held that slavery was wrong and indefensible, among them both Hume and Kant. None seems to have expressed the view that, if slavery was to exist — or so long as it might exist — non-Blacks (more specifically, White Europeans) should also be candidates for the status of slave. That, of course, was a feature of ancient Greek and Roman slavery, as our thinkers will also have been fully aware; as they will also have been that White Europeans, of their own period, were captured and consigned to slavery in considerable numbers in the Muslim world. The role of Black chattel slavery in the west European expansion into the New World is itself a fundamental aspect of world history 1500–1800. Many have argued, persuasively, that it is difficult to believe that the colonial empires of the Spanish, Portuguese, British, Dutch, and French could have come into being, or at least have had anything like the shape and substance they had, without the ideology of a polarity between an allegedly superior civilized Christian White domain and a (putatively) inferior savage pagan Black one, and of course the technological and logistical power of the first to control and utilize the second.

I proceed from these cursory reflections on the European slave trade, the institution of slavery, and the conceptual or historical conditions that made the west European empires possible, and sustained them, to the question of what we should make of features of *racial anthropology* in the writings of two very famous 18th-century philosophers, both of whom penned the texts concerned long after the imperial systems had been instituted.

Hume's infamous footnote appeared in two versions, in the 1751 — and subsequent — editions, and then, in the revised version, in the (posthumous)1777 edition of his *Essays Moral, Political, and Literary*, in the essay "Of National Characters."[8] Hume begins the essay by noting that though people are prone to universalize national traits, in fact all behavioural characteristics show up in all populations; it is rather, he says, that *proportions* of them differ. He then proceeds to the central question that the essay addresses, namely, what the several national typologies are due to. We are used to nature versus nurture disputes in accounting for human nature or human behaviour. For Hume, the burning query is whether the primary and central causes of how we find people to be are purely physical—for Hume, this means chiefly matters of climate, and varieties and quantities of food and drink—or socio-cultural (Hume's term is "moral"). Interestingly, neither of these causal options is biological; though Hume does clearly suppose that the *effect* to be explained is something that has developed as a deep and not readily alterable or eradicable pattern. Throughout the essay, Hume argues that the latter—the socio-cultural option—is overwhelmingly primary, humanity being explicitly contrasted in this regard with the other animals.[9]

For Hume—this is widely and repeatedly evidenced in his writings, including the *Treatise of Human Nature*, and both *Enquiries*—human character and behaviour is formed more importantly socially than individually. There is, to be sure, a necessary foundation in individual sets of impressions and ideas. But selves, such as they are, are cross-products of social forces. There will, then, be a reinforcing interplay among individual selves where the same social forces are operative, creating types that are distinctive, and that may—will, with enough time, relative isolation, and reinforcement—go deep. They will not be exceptionless typologies within the communities or groups concerned—they are not group "essences" (in at least one sense of that term)—but they will be distinctive, probabilistic clusters of trait, manner, and disposition.

Although Hume resists and opposes the alternative account of why human groups differ as they do, or at least as he and others think they do, in terms of geography and diet, interestingly, he feels the pull and force of that mostly rejected alternative most strongly in the case of the planet's primary latitudinal zones. In this Hume is of like mind with most of the 18th-century anthropological analysts, including Kant. Virtually all of them think that the frozen zone –the regions north of the Arctic Circle and south of the Antarctic Circle–and the so-called torrid zone, the tropics–the region between the tropic of Cancer and the tropic of Capricorn–are just too cold, and hot, respectively, for anything significantly or impressively creative, or active, to emerge in either.[10] Hume has comparable views regarding extreme poverty and over-hard labour. As he will see things, those condemned to such conditions are largely without hope or prospect; they will be, as Hume styles them, "inferior." Those able to participate in, and contribute to, full human life, perforce were formed in and (normally) inhabit the earth's temperate zones, where they live lives not ground down in circumstances of endless and mindless labour and poverty, which prevent education, and have leisure to think and promote gentler manners.

Within those parameters, socio-cultural conditions are everything, and they include contingencies that may be largely accidental: the historical role of individuals who may just happen to have had particular sorts of character and interest, for example, and who were in key influential culture-forming locations at key times.

A little confusingly, two north-south contrasts figure in Hume's (as, also, in Kant's) anthropological discussions. One is the north of the temperate and Arctic zone, contrasting with a south that is the tropics. The other is a north-south distinction within the (northern) temperate zone. This is a northern versus Mediterranean Europe that has a prominent place in European cultural reflections from at least the 17th century. Phlegmatic Germans and passionate Sicilians: that sort of thing. Here, though Hume thinks there is merit and substance to this (as well as to the previous) north-south distinction, he energetically insists that the differences are wholly (or almost wholly) to be understood and explained in socio-cultural, not in geographical or biological, terms.

Given that emphasis, it may not be surprising to see Hume giving, as he does, lengthy attention in the essay not just to national, ethnic, and racial groups, but also to occupations. He thinks that soldiers, priests, and other occupants of distinctive socio-economic niches have their own typologies, which transcend national boundaries. They too are characterological and go deep. Russian and Spanish soldiers will have more in common with each other than either has with the priests of the nation concerned, etc.

With this backdrop, we may proceed to Hume's racial footnote. As mentioned, it appears in two versions in editions of the *Essays*. Hume was an inveterate tinkerer with his own texts, constantly making changes, major and minor, in successive editions of his works. The first version of the footnote says that every significant contribution to civilization is due to Whites, and that Whites are the superior variety of humanity; it also says that Blacks are an inferior variety — strictly, that Hume is apt to suspect this, not that he is sure that this is so:

> I am apt to suspect the negroes, and in general all the other species of men (for there are four or five different kinds) to be naturally inferior to the Whites. There never was a civilized nation of any other complexion than White, nor even any individual eminent either in action or speculation. No ingenious manufactures amongst them, no arts, no sciences. On the other hand, the most rude and barbarous of the Whites, such as the ancient GERMANS, the present TARTARS, have still something eminent about them, in their valour, form of government, or some other particular. Such a uniform and constant difference could not happen, in so many countries and ages, if nature had not made an original distinction betwixt these breeds of men. Not to mention our colonies, there are NEGROE slaves dispersed all over EUROPE, of which none ever discovered any symptoms of ingenuity; tho' low people, without education, will start up amongst us, and distinguish themselves in every profession. In JAMAICA indeed they talk of one negroe as a man of parts and learning; but 'tis likely he is admired for very slender accomplishments, like a parrot, who speaks a few words plainly.[11]

The second version keeps the denigration of the Blacks, but does not claim White superiority to all other varieties of humans:

> I am apt to suspect the negroes to be naturally inferior to the Whites. There scarcely ever was a civilized nation of that complexion, nor even any individual eminent either in action or speculation. No ingenious manufactures amongst them, no arts, no sciences. On the other hand, the most rude and barbarous of the Whites, such as the ancient GERMANS, the present TARTARS, have still something eminent about them, in their valour, form of government, or some other particular. Such a uniform and constant difference could not happen, in so many countries and ages, if nature had not made an original distinction between these breeds of men. Not to mention our colonies, there are NEGROE slaves dispersed all over EUROPE, of whom none ever discovered any symptoms of ingenuity; though low people, without education, will start up amongst us, and distinguish themselves in every profession. In JAMAICA, indeed, they talk of one negro as a man of parts and learning; but it is likely he is admired for slender accomplishments, like a parrot, who speaks a few words plainly.[12]

Between the two versions Hume will have read the criticisms of his opponent Beattie, and possibly received other input, and decided that there was no adequate case for White superiority over, e.g., east Asians or Amerindians. Beattie had compared Hume to Aristotle, linking Hume's denigration of non-Whites to Aristotle's claims that Greeks were intellectually and otherwise superior to non-Greeks, and that many of the latter had the natures of slaves and were appropriately consigned to that condition. Beattie also argued that civilization takes time—and literacy and metallurgy. The lack of these material conditions will be sufficient, he argues, to account for the absence of high civilization, and technological prowess, in non-White sectors of the globe where they obtain. *Pace* Hume, Beattie continues, some non-White societies, notably Amerindian ones in Mexico and Peru, did develop advanced culture. Finally, Beattie argues that creative innovation is never the work of a people or a society, but of an individual or small group within a society; accordingly, claims of superiority will attach at best and at most to those individuals (or, Beattie adds, their lineal descendants), not their wider cultures.

Clearly, with the second version of the footnote, Hume has accepted the case for significant and impressive cultural achievement in non-White societies. He has also deleted the claim that there are four or five "species" or kinds of humans. This deletion may reflect the impress of the work of Buffon on the Scottish proto-anthropologists, Hume among them. Whether or not Hume had thought of species in a literally biological sense when he wrote the original version of the footnote, awareness of the tighter, more scientific sense of the term that Buffon's work highlights will have been a factor in leading Hume to delete the term as at least potentially misleading. What he does not revise, Beattie's criticisms notwithstanding, is his low view of Blacks — i.e., sub-Saharan Africans. (North Africans were viewed, by all of the 18th-century "proto-anthropologists," as Whites.)

As intimated, Hume makes it clear that his judgments of relative superiority and inferiority are based on what he takes to be creative contributions to civilization: achievements in the sciences, engineering, technology, or the arts, whose making a difference for general human well-being would be, he would suppose, more or less manifest and objective.[13] If a "people" made few or no such contributions, that would be grounds for judging them inferior; if they made many, they will be held to be superior.

Might adverse circumstances prevent or impede such contributions—e.g., abject poverty, systematic suppression, bondage, or servitude? Yes, Hume plainly allows this. Still, he notes that creative merit — of the sort he affirms — does sometimes arise even where circumstances have been extremely adverse. The odds will be heavily against such achievement, but it will sometimes occur anyway.[14] If a "people" are being judged, in these scales, if such rising against odds never, or more or less never, occurs, that will be reason to impute deficiencies to *them*. Hume thinks the available evidence shows more or less no such rising against odds in Black populations; and he indicates that he thinks there has been a sufficient length of time for relevant observations to have occurred, and a sufficient diversity of circumstance, including the many contexts in which Blacks are found in Europe as well as in the new world, and Africa. Hume does not say so explicitly, but it seems clear that he has considered but rejected the claim that with more time, or a diffusion of literacy or metallurgy, Black populations would manifest individuals of technological or other cultural innovative genius.

Is Hume a racist? There are complexities in what may be meant by racism, and they are exacerbated in the 18th-century setting. We have seen that Hume thinks that what is distinctive, and difference-producing within the species, about humans is not significantly physical, but rather socio-cultural. Some early moderns considered or affirmed notions of more than one human species, with different creations of each: the so-called polygenesis view.[15] Richard Popkin in fact assigns this view, quite implausibly, I think, to Hume.[16] There is no textual evidence at all that Hume held the polygenesis theory.[17] It is true that in the 1751 version of the footnote, Hume uses the term "species"; it does not appear in the 1777 version, and in the earlier text it most likely means something no more precise in sense than "variety" or "kind."[18] Those exploring or advocating the polygenic theory seem especially to have been drawn to it by Biblical reasons, when put into conjunction with growing anthropological knowledge.[19] Can *these* (allegedly) outlandish human creatures really be descendants of Noah and his wife, the flood a mere four thousand or so years ago?, such speculators seem to have been asking themselves.[20] Hume will have had no comparable scriptural commitments or concerns. Of course, acquitting Hume of the charge of advocacy of the polygenesis view will by no means suffice to absolve him of the charge of racism. Nineteenth-century and subsequent racist positions only rarely adopted explicit polygenesist stances. (They are more typically grounded in Lamarckian biological conceptions.)

Hume in fact thinks, as we know well from his primary and most famous texts, that there are severe limits to human knowledge. There is ever so much—he thinks—that we would love to know, but do not, cannot, and never will. We are condemned, he thinks, to limit knowledge—science—to observations we may note and generalizing hypotheses we may mount on them. We may hypothesize "hidden powers" in many areas of natural investigation, but cannot really discover or fathom them. He makes it clear also that he regards Biblical authority as dubious in the extreme, our most securely reliable relatively old data sources being texts of classical antiquity.

Hume's real view of human origins and prehistory will have been that both are a mystery. We find ourselves as we are in our several tribes and groups, in the several parts of the world; thus and so, with commonalities sufficient that there is a definite human nature, which—Hume is adamant—remains unchanged in all times and places, and also real local differences. Some of the latter, he thinks, go deep. They aren't easily alterable, in some cases evidently not alterable at all. But their causes, Hume makes plain, will be socio-cultural adaptations—if we may use that term—to time, place, and wholly contingent circumstance.

There is no question that Hume does not evince admiration for Black humans. He is rude about them. He is rude also about some other varieties of human in this essay—and about none so rude as he is in the essay about clergymen, and their natures and personalities. A Black person, then or since, reading Hume's words, could not read Hume as a friend. Hume has, it is plain, at least a *prejudice* against Blacks. More pointedly, and theoretically, it is plain from the footnote, in both versions, that Hume regards the Black characteristics that, as he supposes, consign them to an inferior status, as features and matters of nature.[21]

Nonetheless, it seems justified to resist calling Hume's footnote racist. A racist, we may think, should be someone who *should have known better* (than to make the comment, or have the view, which they express), given the facts available to them; and it is not clear that Hume had such facts. Further, Hume is insufficiently biologistic for the racist label to seem apt. Hume has made it abundantly clear in the essay the footnote appears in that he regards the chief determinants of national and ethnic traits as socio-cultural; hence, the "nature" operative in this as in other cases will be a matter of socio-cultural factors that have coalesced and concretized over time. Presumably were different socio-cultural factors operative over comparable periods of time, coincident, possibly, with appropriately fortuitous geography — *but by no means needing to involve changes in skin colour, body morphology, or any other purely physical traits* — quite different "natures" would manifest themselves. Broadly, Hume makes it clear in several places in his writings, there is a single shared human nature, which all human beings participate in, even if there may be local variations of one sort or other.

> Stature and force of body, length of life, even courage and extent of genius, seem hitherto to have been naturally, in all ages, pretty much the same. The arts and sciences, indeed, have flourished in one period, and have decayed in another: But we may observe, that, at the time when they rose to greatest perfection among one people, they were perhaps totally unknown to all the neighbouring nations; and though they universally decayed in one age, yet in a succeeding generation they again revived, and diffused themselves over the world. As far, therefore, as observation reaches, there is no universal difference discernible in the human species….[22]

Hume in the footnote is being Humean. He is going by what he thinks is reasonable observational evidence, and he is being — to use his own distinction — the anatomist, not the painter, of human valorizable traits.[23] The stance is, to be sure, cold-blooded. And he may be held not adequately to ask himself whether the condition of slavery *will not have been an impediment of kind*, unlike and not comparable to the condition of abject poverty and obscurity from which some nonetheless, among their own people, rise to those scientific or technological achievements. Hume might specially have asked himself this in the knowledge, which every Black slave will have had, that, at least in the Christian parts of the world, only Blacks were slaves.

It is to be noted in addition that Hume was a strong opponent of slavery as an institution. Hume's remarks on slavery are in fact unusually vehement, and explicitly directed at the New World institutions of slavery of the European empires.

> As much as submission to a petty prince, whose dominions extend not beyond a single city, is more grievous than obedience to a great monarch; so much is domestic slavery more cruel and oppressive than any civil subjection whatsoever.... The remains which are found of domestic slavery, in the American colonies, and among some European nations, would never create a desire of rendering it more universal. The little humanity, commonly observed in persons, accustomed, from their infancy, to exercise so great authority over their fellow-creatures, and to trample upon human nature, were sufficient alone to disgust us with that unbounded dominion.[24]

Accordingly, Hume's judgments of Blacks are not components of a case that they are "well-suited" to the condition and institution of slavery (still less, of course, that, as some scripturalists held, they merited that fate because of Noah's curse on the descendants of Ham). Hume's view is, in fact, that of the 11th — the 1911 — edition of Britannica, which is also unequivocally, in fact quite passionately, opposed to the evils of slavery.

Some other methodological, and some additional empirical, comments are appropriate to make. There was no such thing in Hume's day as a controlled psychological or social experiment. Social and historical data primarily existed only in crude form, and most such empirical data derived from pooled comment and reflection, at best reasonably carefully observationally based, and wide reading, in ancient and modern sources, including travellers' and explorers' accounts. Perhaps no one should have said anything until really modern techniques and results had arrived; on the other hand, if the proto-social scientists of whom Hume is in many respects an outstanding case, had remained silent, no such techniques or results would have arrived.

Some factual considerations also merit mention. It is only very recently — within the past few decades, some results being only a few years old — that it has become knowledge, and not merely one of a number of speculations in palaeoanthropology, that all living humans descend from a tiny group (in fact, a single male and a single female, though not partnered with each other) living a mere 190,000 years ago or so. Almost all pairs of living humans will have at least one common ancestor who will have lived much more recently even than that. All humans are, in fact, very closely related genetically. But this is not and was not knowable *a priori*. It was not even a good common-sensical piece of near-obvious folk observation or intuition. Many scientists had supposed that human differentiations into so-called racial groupings had occurred long before this.

It could well have turned out that some such view was true; just as it could perfectly well have been the case that other hominid species than ours have survived to the present. It deserves reflection, and accompanying imaginative projection into the evidential shoes of European proto-social scientists of two and a half centuries ago, that there could well have survived tribes — communities — of unevolved *Homo habilis* or *Australopithecus afarensis* individuals, in different parts of the globe. If there had, they would have posed for us, it seems reasonable to believe, complex issues of description and of norms of interaction and treatment. In this regard, Linnaeus, in a passage also anthologized in Eze's book, initially classified anthropoid apes as human beings.[25] This was subsequently withdrawn,[26] and almost all of the Enlightenment thinkers were of monogenesis persuasion, on the ground (at least) that, as they knew, all so-called human races can and do interbreed with fertile offspring resulting. It still would not follow that distinct human varieties might not be quite distant from each other biologically. We learned, only recently, and for many, including many biologists, it came as a surprise, that all humans are, as it were, close cousins. The moral I draw from this is that it is the truth, only, that can set us free, and the truth is only gradually acquired; it is not there for us on a platter. Progress on this front, it may be said, is *not* to be seen in a hope that human beings might be caused to become (so to speak) "*kind-blind*"; but rather that they will acquire broadly accurate "kind" knowledge, which will in turn teach us how little there is in such "kind" differences, and how little they matter.

Although Kant's anthropological writings, and more specifically the things he has to say about race and ethnicity, are lengthier and more developed than Hume's, they may reasonably, in fact, receive a much briefer and more cursory treatment here.

Kant makes it clear that humanity is a single species, divided, he supposes, into four races. Interestingly, this is exactly the number latest evolutionary prehistorical studies assign. Two of Kant's four are in the current reckoning—Whites and Negroes; a third, which Kant calls "the Hunnic (Mongolian or Kalmuck) race," are approximately east Asians (except that for him Chinese are a mixed case), but his fourth—"the Hindu or Hindustanic race"—does not correspond to modern taxonomical classification.

At any rate, Kant takes what we may now see as familiar positions. Whites are the best, and the closest to original humanity; the other races being departures, with Blacks the most distant, and all departures negative in character. With Teutonic precision, Kant sees the creative cradle of humanity as the zone "between the 31st and 52nd parallels in the Old World." It may be noted that the latter parallel of latitude is below Berlin, and well below Kant's own Königsberg—so he certainly cannot be accused of specially favouring his own home territory. (Also excluded from the Edenic palm will be all of Britain north of London, as well as northern Germany and all of Scandinavia.) At the other extreme, the 31st north parallel just manages to include Alexandria, in Egypt, and most of Israel, i.e., of the Holy Land, and virtually all of the early centres of civilization in Mesopotamia (Iraq). It will be reasonable to surmise that for a thinker even as (relatively) sophisticated and "modernist" as Kant, the Biblical account of human origins—which locates those origins *somewhere* in the general area of Iraq, Iran, or countries adjacent to their east—should turn out to be at least approximately right. That is to say, that Whites will be the "basal" humans, and human beginnings and protypes found in a Biblically mandated "zone" on the earth's surface, is not *merely* (culturally) self-serving in Kant. It would no doubt have come as a great surprise to Kant to learn that (modern) humans actually originated in sub-Saharan Africa,[27] and *long* before the time implied by the Book of Genesis.[28]

Kant, unlike Hume, appears to see the causes of racial foundations and maintenance as primarily and essentially geographical—matters above all, Kant says, of "air and sun."

What judgment to make of Kant's racial anthropology? Not very much, in my view. It is more developed, more thorough, than its 18th-century predecessors; but not particularly original otherwise. It is surprising, therefore, to find a recent writer assigning to this Kantian work the origin of the very *concept* of race.[29] Not merely surprising: preposterous, it seems to me. As always, of course, it depends what may be meant by, or imposed on, the relevant idea. The concept of something like races, within the human species, is locatable in Aristotle; it figures also in the universal history of Ibn Khaldûn.[30]

In fact, the concept of race, before the 19th century, when a genuinely scientific biology begins to emerge, seems plausibly identifiable as a folk concept that will have been formed along the lines of a *breed*, for example, of pigeon or dog.[31] Semantically, these are reasonable cases of (so-called) *natural kind* terms, now most persuasively understood with a referential semantics. Collies are *those* sorts of dogs (and Shetland ponies *those* sorts of horses, etc.), with the salient physical and behavioural traits that we observe, and whatever inner machinery, causal history, and relations (including relations of genetic propinquity) that they in fact have, some of which we may know and some not. Likewise with beagles, basset hounds, etc.

In fact, the analogy may contribute still more to the present case. *Wolves*, *jackals*, and other apparently canine wild creatures can seem to some simply to be wild varieties — breeds — of dog, and to other observers to be quite distinct species of animal, only somewhat superficially resembling *Canis familiaris*. As it turns out, of course, the latter, not the former, is the more nearly right view. In other cases, two putatively distinct breeds of dog can turn out really to be just varieties of a single breed. (Teacup poodles and standard poodles differ rather dramatically in size, and typical coloration, for example; both are regularly deemed poodles, though we can imagine canine observers who might view the differences as great enough to warrant a differentiation of breed.)[32]

Virtually all human groups encounter other human groups that occasion a breed-like conception of self and other. No human groups differ by appearance as much as some distinct breeds of dog do. (In fact, breeds of dog differ in overt or observable characteristics more markedly than do varieties or breeds of any other species of animal.) However, one of the things noted — significantly — about the human visual system is that we have an extraordinary capacity to distinguish individual human faces, many of which differ extremely slightly. Most normally sighted adult humans can recognize and distinguish thousands of such individuals. With cognitive/visual systems of such subtlety, it is hardly surprising that humans would register difference by kind and group as well as by individual. As well as the groups that will seem, whether or not justifiably, to be clearly and definitely of distinct "breed" from themselves, most human groups, particularly since the early modern period, encounter also human "breeds" that they find difficult to place or classify with confidence. Are those people of the same "breed" as us, or a different one, or a cross between us and a definitely other them?

And then along comes the 18th century, with a bunch of European investigators wanting to bring Newtonian scientific precision to these matters — to sort out, and clarify, such folk views as may be warranted, or not, and to give causal explanations of these evident facts of human "breeds" that Europeans, Arabs, and everybody else have long noted. The Enlightenment is above all the foundational period for the human and social sciences, and these efforts, the efforts in particular in this regard of Hume and Kant, are a part—just a part—of this endeavour. And like other founders, they get various things wrong as well as some right, and they make some self-serving and own-group-vaunting theoretical choices, as well as some that are more disinterested.

Perhaps we should nonetheless throw stones at Hume and Kant. Views of the sorts they expressed were and are cruelly exclusionary of basic and sizeable parts of the human family. But those who would do so might perhaps ask themselves whether they could realistically expect a foundational matrix that might have been significantly otherwise.[33]

NOTES

1   Emmanuel Chukwudi Eze, ed., *Race and the Enlightenment: A Reader* (Blackwell, 1997).

2   They include passages in *Observations on the Feeling of the Beautiful and the Sublime*, which appeared in 1764, an essay "On the different races of man" from 1775, and passages from Kant's *Physical Geography*, written in the 1770s and published posthumously. All are included in the Eze volume. The 1775 essay (titled in this translation "Of the Different Human Races") appears also in Robert Bernasconi and Tommy L. Lott, eds., *The Idea of Race* (Hackett, 2000).

3   Among the contributions to this literature, some of it focusing on just one of the philosophers, some on both: Meg Armstrong, " 'The Effects of Blackness': Gender, Race, and the Sublime in Aesthetic Theories of Burke and Kant," *The Journal of Aesthetics and Art Criticism*, vol. 54, no. 3, Summer 1996, pp. 213–236; Robert Bernasconi, "Who Invented the Concept of Race? Kant's Role in the Enlightenment Construction of Race," in Robert Bernasconi, ed., *Race* (Blackwell, 2001), pp. 11–36; Christopher J. Berry, *Hume, Hegel and Human Nature* (Martinus Nijhoff Publishers, 1982), pp. 107f.; Paul E. Chamley, "The Conflict between Montesquieu and Hume: A Study of the Origins of Adam Smith's Universalism," in Andrew S. Skinner and Thomas Wilson, eds., *Essays on Adam Smith* (Oxford University Press, 1975), pp. 274–305; Emmanuel Chukwudi Eze, "The Color of Reason: The Idea of 'Race' in Kant's Anthropology," in Katherine M. Faull, ed., *Anthropology and the German Enlightenment: Perspectives on Humanity*

(Bucknell University Press and Associated University Presses, 1995); Emmanuel C. Eze, "Hume, Race, and Human Nature," *Journal of the History of Ideas*, vol. 61, no. 4, 2000, pp. 691–698; Arnold Farr, "Can a Philosophy of Race Afford to Abandon the Kantian Categorical Imperative?," *Journal of Social Philosophy*, vol. 33, no. 1, Spring 2002, pp. 17–32; Aaron Garrett, "Hume's Revised Racism Revisited," *Hume Studies*, vol. xxvi, no. 1, April 2000; Aaron Garrett, "Hume's 'Original Difference': Race, National Character, and the Human Sciences," *Eighteenth-Century Thought*, vol. 2, 2004, pp. 127–152; Lewis R. Gordon, *Bad Faith and Antiblack Racism* (Humanities Press, 1995); Ivan Hannaford, *Race: The History of an Idea in the West* (The Woodrow Wilson Center Press and the Johns Hopkins University Press, 1996), especially pp. 214–224; Marvin Harris, *The Rise of Anthropological Theory* (HarperCollins Publishers, 1968), pp. 85–88; John Immerwahr, "Hume's Revised Racism," *Journal of the History of Ideas*, vol. 53, no. 3, 1992, pp. 481–486; Eric Mark Kramer and Lonnie Johnson, Jr., "A Brief Archaeology of Intelligence," in Eric Mark Kramer, ed., *Postmodernism and Race* (Praeger, 1997), p. 37; Eric Morton, "Race and Racism in the Works of David Hume," *Journal on African Philosophy*, vol. 1, no. 1, 2002, pp. 1–27; Robert Palter, "Hume and Prejudice," *Hume Studies*, vol. xxi, no. 1, April 1995; Richard H. Popkin, "Hume's Racism," in Richard H. Popkin, *The High Road to Pyrrhonism* (Austin Hill Press, 1980); Richard H. Popkin, "Hume's Racism Reconsidered," in Richard H. Popkin, *The Third Force in Seventeenth Century Thought* (E. J. Brill, 1992); Silvia Sebastiani, "Progress, National Characters, and Race in the Scottish Enlightenment," *Eighteenth-Century Scotland*, no. 14, Spring 2000, pp. 11–15; Silvia Sebastiani, "Race and National Characters in Eighteenth-century Scotland: The Polygenetic Discourses of Kames and Pinkerton," *Cromohs*, vol. 8, 2003, pp. 1–14; Eric Voegelin, *The History of the Race Idea From Ray to Carus* (Louisiana State University Press, 1998) (originally published in German in 1933); Naomi Zack, *Philosophy of Science and Race* (Routledge, 2002), especially ch. 1 ("Philosophical Racial Essentialism: Hume and Kant"); John H.Zammito, *Kant,Herder, and the Birth of Anthropology* (University of Chicago Press, 2002).

4   Their numbers would likely prove easy to add to. Voltaire, for example, makes remarks on black intelligence (in "Of the Different Races of Men," in his *The Philosophy of History*; and in "The Negro," *Short Studies in English and American Subjects*) that are closely similar to the views of Hume and Kant on the same subject, except that

Voltaire was an explicit *polygenesist* (advocate of the view that there were distinct biological species of humans), unlike (as will be argued), Hume or Kant.

5   In *Essays of Elia*.

6   Ibn Khaldûn, *The Muqaddimah: An Introduction to History* (Franz Rosenthal, trans. from the Arabic; abridged and edited by N. J. Dawood), (Princeton University Press, Bollingen Series, 1967), p. 63.

7   Strictly, this overstates, neglecting, as it does, the fact that native Aboriginal populations had been enslaved by the Spaniards and Portuguese in the early stages of European presence in the New World. They had died in such numbers, or were otherwise deemed not suitable as slaves, that New World slavery became entirely an institution involving sub-Saharan African Blacks.

8   David Hume, "Of National Characters," in David Hume, *Essays Moral, Political, and Literary* (Eugene F. Miller, ed.), Liberty Fund, 1985. It deserves mentioning that it is only in this edition that the change in the footnote — Hume's revision — was explicitly noted in a scholarly text of Hume's work. Thanks to Silvia Sebastiani for pointing this out to me.

9   The "geographical" accounting for human differences was most prominently associated in the 18th-century context within which Hume was writing, with Montesquieu. Indeed, Hume's essay seems to have been conceived, and couched, consciously as a kind of dialogical engagement with Montesquieu.

10 Geographical conceptions of differential bases of human diversity, including variations involving intelligence, appear long before the European Renaissance. One such source is, interestingly, one of Hume's favourite classical authors, Cicero. In the latter's *De Natura Deorum* (ii.xvi) we find the following: "[I]t may be observed that the inhabitants of those countries in which the air is pure and rarefied have keener wits and greater powers of understanding than persons who live in a dense and heavy climate; moreover the substance employed as food is also believed to have some influence on mental acuteness…." (H. Rackham, trans.)

11 Miller edition of *Essays Moral, Political, and Literary*, p. 629.

12 Miller edition of *Essays Moral, Political, and Literary*, p. 208.

13 Hume's criteria for such achievements are the people's constituting "a civilized nation" with "arts" and "sciences," and with individuals eminent "in action or speculation" or who are "ingenious manufacturers." Civilization, it is plain, for Hume, implies literacy.

14 "[L]ow people, without education, will start up amongst us, and distinguish themselves in every profession" (p. 208 of Miller edition of *Essays Moral, Political, and Literary*)..

15 The polygenesis view was articulated in a developed way especially by Isaac La Peyrère, in his *Praeadamitae* (1655).

16 Richard H. Popkin, "Hume's Racism," in Richard H. Popkin, *The High Road to Pyrrhonism* (Austin Hill Press, 1980).

17 In the *Enquiry Concerning the Principles of Morals*, Hume refers to the European maltreatment of Indians as pretended by its perpetrators to have involved one human species subduing another. He makes it clear that this pretence was, in his own view, baseless, and the actions it produced violations of principles of justice, and humanity. Interestingly, he couples that subjugation with the still more widespread subordination of women by men, which Hume also plainly condemns. (See David Hume, *Enquiries Concerning the Human Understanding and Concerning the Principles of Morals* [Selby-Bigge, 2nd ed. (Clarendon, 1902)], p. 191.)

18 Sir William Petty, in a paper evidently written about 1686, calls three distinct settlement groups in Ireland in the medieval and early modern period "species," where there is clearly no question that simply groups or communities of people are meant (Marquis of Lansdowne, ed., *The Petty Papers*, vol. I [Constable and Houghton Mifflin, 1927], p. 57). This has an added significance, since Petty, in another of his unpublished (until 1927) papers, "The Scale of Animals," says, "That of man itself there seems to bee severall species" (*The Petty Papers*, vol. II, p. 30). He goes on to speak of "Races and generations" of men, the phrasing evidently intended to be synonymous with "species." Petty then gives examples to illustrate the conception he has in mind — of distinct "species" of humans — with parallel cases of distinct breeds or varieties of dogs, horses, and ducks. Again, then, there seems no notion here of literally distinct biological species, i.e., of the polygenesis view.

19 There are exceptions — i.e., non-Christian defenders of the poly-genesis view. Voltaire was one. Another advocate of polygenesis was Hume's relative and sometimes-hectoring mentor, Lord Kames (who appears to have been significantly influenced by Voltaire). Hume clearly dissented regularly from the views of the opinionated Kames. There is no particular reason, nor any biographical evidence, to suggest that he shared this Kamesian view. We know as well that while Hume found Voltaire's work entertaining, he did not hold Voltaire in high regard intellectually. "I know that Author cannot be depended on with regard to Facts," Hume says in a letter of 1760

(J. Y. T. Greig, ed., *The Letters of David Hume*, vol. I [Clarendon Press, 1932], p. 326.)

20 A polygenesist of Christian or Biblically grounded convictions will presumably have held (and many may be presumed explicitly to have thought about the matter, and concluded) that when Noah loaded the ark with pairs of all of the animal species living at the time of the deluge, he will have led on board a pair of each species of human other than Noah's own.

21 And, it is to be noted, Hume's strong opposition to New World slavery notwithstanding, his denigration of Blacks was to be cited, in the period after his death, by proponents of slavery in the long polemical battles that preceded the abolition of slavery in the British Empire. (See Iain Whyte, *Scotland and the Abolition of Black Slavery, 1756–1838* [University of Edinburgh Press, 2006].)

22 "Of the Populousness of Ancient Nations," in Miller, p. 378.

23 Robert Palter points out ("Hume and Prejudice," p. 7), drawing on historical studies by Keith A. Sandiford and Peter Fryer, that "it seems that really impressive instances of individual Negro intellectual achievement in England [likewise significant Black leadership or antislavery protest] did not appear until the 1780s" — i.e., well after Hume's death. Beyond Britain and her empire there were cases of Black achievement that an educated European might readily have known of, during Hume's lifetime. One such individual was Peter the Great's general, administrator, and military engineer Gannibal (noted subsequently as Pushkin's great-grandfather). Interestingly, one of Hume's last intellectual activities was the preparation of an advertisement for an English translation of the memoirs of Baron Manstein, covering Russia during the period of Gannibal's participation in Russian affairs of state. Manstein, unfortunately, doesn't mention Gannibal. It is unclear whether Hume will have known of him from other sources.

24 "Of the Populousness of Ancient Nations," in Miller, p. 383f. The essay is replete with impassioned observations on the degrading and deplorable character of slavery in all times and places, and its bad effects on owners as well as, more obviously, on the slaves themselves.

25 In the 1735 edition of *The System of Nature*. Linnaeus there itemizes five alleged varieties of human: American, European, Asian, Negro, and the "wild man." It may be plausible to see the 1754 version of Hume's "racial" footnote's reference to "species of men (for there are four or five different kinds)" — this is one of the deletions made for the later version — as reflecting or derived from Linnaeus's

classification. One should note the caution taken by both Linnaeus and Hume. In 1735 Linnaeus does not identify his five sorts of humans under a label of any kind.

In subsequent editions of the *Systema Naturae* they are called *varietates*—"varieties"—which will imply that they are *not*, for Linnaeus, distinct species. Hume may be following Linnaeus's lead.

26 The 1756 edition of *Systema Naturae*, published in Holland, with (occasional) French annotations, has reduced the original five human varieties to four (American, European, Asian, Negro).

27 Probably in Ethiopia, possibly in South Africa, but certainly within the east African region between and including these two countries.

28 In these respects we may see Hume as more sophisticated or scientific-modernist than Kant. Hume eschews *any* knowledge of the circumstances of human beginning, and explicitly mistrusts and repudiates the Biblical narrative as even a crude or approximate guide to what will turn out to be the correct story of these remote and arcane matters.

29 See Robert Bernasconi, "Who Invented the Concept of Race? Kant's Role in the Enlightenment Construction of Race," in Robert Bernasconi, ed., *Race* (Blackwell, 2001). Bernasconi notes that others have made similar claims, of a Kantian role in the formation of the concept of race, among them Walter Scheidt, in 1924, and Wilhelm A. Mühlmann, in 1948. Another earlier writer who assigns Kant an especially creative part in the development of a theory of race is Eric Voegelin. See his *The History of the Race Idea* in *The Collected Works of Eric Voegelin*, vol. 3 (Louisiana State University Press, 1998), p. 6 and passim (the original German text was published in 1933).

30 And something along the lines of the idea continues significantly non-normatively today. The University of California, Berkeley *Wellness Letter*, vol. 20, no. 1, October 2003, p. 8, providing medical advice on diabetes, informs its readers that "many people with diabetes have no symptoms. Thus, everyone age 45 and older should get a blood test for diabetes every three years. Those at high risk (Blacks, Hispanics, Asians, native Americans, obese and/or sedentary people, and those with a strong family history of the disease) need more frequent screening, starting at age 30." Presumably even in a nonracist utopia, it would be hoped that 35-year-olds who were neither obese, sedentary, nor with a family history of diabetes might be in a position to determine, as might observers, whether they should have screening for diabetes more frequently than every three years, or not.

31 Cf. Sir William Petty's usage of "species" and its characterization via breeds, cited above. It is interesting to note that Hume, in both texts of his footnote, characterizes the so-called races as "breeds of men." Voltaire, earlier (in "The Negro," 1733), asserts that "[t]he negro race is a species of men as different from ours as the breed of spaniels is from that of greyhounds." This is, of course, not altogether helpfully clarifying, as Voltaire was of polygenesis persuasion and as, of course, spaniels and greyhounds are members of a single species.

32 It is instructive in this regard to reread Ch. VII ("On the Races of Man") of Darwin's *The Descent of Man* (originally published in 1871). Darwin imagines an investigating naturalist trying to decide whether humans comprise one or more than one species, and giving a wealth of physiological data favouring one, then the other hypothesis, and finally showing that the evidence actually shows overwhelmingly that all humans are of a single species, the several significantly distinguishable groups or kinds constituting "varieties or races."

33 Thanks to Roger Emerson, Jean-Pierre Schachter, Silvia Sebastiani, and Catherine Wilson for comments on earlier drafts of this paper.

CHAPTER TWELVE

KANT, CHRISTIANITY,
AND A KINGDOM OF ENDS

A shorter version of this paper was presented at a conference on Kant held at the University of Auckland, in July 2004.

It may seem an odd enterprise (even, perhaps, for some, a cold-blooded or cruel one) for an atheist naturalist to attempt, as a philosophical exercise or endeavour, to set out what seems to him the most intelligent version of Christianity. It may also seem quite pointless—why bother? Or else to express unresolved features of one's personal history; or a subliminal wish to reconstitute oneself as Christian; or as a rather shoddy way to try to impress some friends, some of them believing Christians. Perhaps some creative pyrotechnics might come up with something; or again they might not. One will declare there to be unassimilable core features of any Christian conception of reality, and then perhaps the exercise was again one of ultimate triumphalism, reaffirmed self-vindication.

A partial answer to these queries and ruminations will affirm that, just as the God of medieval Latin Christendom really is a hugely fecund conceptual postulate—philosophy was enriched by good minds focused in those directions—so is there synoptic conceptual wealth in what can be made of the Christian deity, and a conception of the universe in which he figures centrally, from what may be held (no doubt pretentiously, certainly precariously) to be a matured late-day perspective. The proof in this regard will, to be sure, be in the pudding.

This chapter is not intended to offer even tentative or inductive argument for Christianity, or for theism in any form. Kant rejected all of the traditional arguments for God's existence, showing crippling flaws in each of them. He replaced them with a so-called moral argument that he himself claimed was hypothetical or conditional. I think that that argument too was unsuccessful, and indeed that no argument ever produced by anyone gives any substantial reason to believe in the reality of gods of any kind. Nor am I able to see a plausible basis for a completely fideist stance in respect of theism; indeed, the very idea of belief that something is true where there is acknowledged to be no ground or warrant for that belief, not just according to others', or publicly affirmed standards or criteria, but even according to any of one's own, private and inner in addition to public, seems to me of doubtful coherence.

Still, many sane, rational—indeed, highly intelligent—people do have theistic beliefs and commitments, and I for my part, though I do not myself share them, am prepared to accord them some variety of Jamesian "will to believe" rationality: I would see them as cases where the evidence does not forbid or preclude the conviction, and where a coherent theistic system of the world may be formulable, with evidence that underdetermines the theism but that can be given a theistic role and plausibility.

In any case, the whole focus and thrust of the present endeavour is not to provide even modest support for any variety of theism. It starts, rather, from the cold and abstract fact that there are cases in the history of empirical investigation—indeed, in recent history of science— where, in the absence of final and decisive confirming evidence, there has been a set of rival explanatory hypotheses, each with advocates among specialists, some one or two (or three) among this set being regarded and acknowledged as the hypothesis that would turn out to be the right one (or the likeliest two, or three, among a larger group), and—surprisingly—still another in the set, regarded as not particularly likely, a long shot, turned out to be the one that was right, when final, crucial, deciding data at length came in.

When something along these lines happens, everyone (in the relevant category of specialists) is surprised; but things also, typically, fall into place. One sees that (even though this hadn't been anticipated, at least by most observers), or *how*, relevant data in the relevant field of inquiry fit and configure. They needn't have done, but… they do. *That* is how the world turned out to be, and to work, in that domain.

It is within this — somewhat austere, or abstract — framework, and against this background of methodology, that this chapter proceeds. It asks: suppose this particular long shot did turn out, surprisingly, and against odds (indeed, with what seemed to most disinterested observers rather strong contra-indications), to be correct, how might salient data be interpreted, or understood, in light of the supposed surprise outcome? How could the world — the world as we *know* it — be made sense of in a Christian theistic way, if *in addition* to (and not replacing) the knowledge we have of the world, we had also knowledge that some version of Christian theism was true? What might that version most plausibly be expected to be like, and how would it, or might it best, cohere with the world as we know it?

I note at the outset of these explorations that their object is specifically *Christian* theism, and not theism as such, or even the intersection of the three great "religions of the book" (Judaism, Christianity, Islam). I think that it is quite often, by philosophers as well as by non-philosophers, not adequately appreciated how *little* mere theism, as such, does or would give the inquirer, just by itself. (This is one — just one — of the deep insights achieved by Hume's *Dialogues Concerning Natural Religion*.) It would be perfectly possible that intelligent activity — very impressive intelligence, and very impressive activity — had had something to do with creating and/or designing our galaxy, our universe among the set of multiverses (if there is such a set), or the whole of the "natural" order, and this intelligent activity still have (now, or ever) nothing much of significance at all to do with the minutiae of terrestrial life — with me, or you, or us.

The bare fact of theism, as such, if it were a fact (and known to be), would, rationally, be little more than something of interest to persons with the right sort of physical and metaphysical imaginations, and no one else (or to no one on any other basis). It is only a personal God, and one with the powers to know and care about *me*, that will make for a theism that could matter. Among the "personal" great monotheistic religions, Christianity, I would argue — though shall not do so here — is pre-eminent if not unique in its developed conception of a personal, existentially serious, and universal structure of human–God realities and relationships; if, at least, any of the three are.

Obviously, for the purposes of this project, not only will Christian theism, in some version or form, be regarded as not logically or conceptually or metaphysically impossible or incoherent — as some would contend — but also as having at least a moral or serious possibility of being true. Moral or serious modality is a somewhat tricky or elusive matter, and I do not have an analysis, or truth conditions, for it to offer. Yet I think that many, perhaps most, philosophers would be prepared (many indeed would be eager) to accord it content, substance, even importance.

Examples seem best to bring out the idea, at least approximately. Although it is evidently *logically* possible that in the interior of the moon there is a lake filled with orange juice, or that Ralph Nader will be elected president of Singapore, or that Einstein was the real author of the novels of D. H. Lawrence, none of these things is morally or seriously possible. We know that they are not the case, and only radical skeptical hypotheses could accord them even a moment of our attention. Indeed, many much more prosaic, logically possible options are presumably not morally or seriously possible ones. It is not *really* — sometimes people use that adverb in lieu of *morally* or *seriously* — possible that the physical universe, or the human species, be only as old as Old Testament chronology seems to imply that it is, or that smoking actually causes intelligent growth in squirrels, or that human space travel to a neighbouring galaxy will occur before the present century has ended—to involve all three temporalities in the picture.

On the positive side of the ledger, it may be said that there is a moral possibility that there was a real Robin Hood, that eating hamburgers can cause Alzheimer's, and that humanity will be destroyed in a nuclear war within the next 35 years. It may be that moral or serious possibility is just a matter of falling within a certain range of probability (with various background assumptions of reliable evidence). Or something else may be involved, not readily allowing assignments of anything that quantitative. Moral or serious possibility may be the same as what is called epistemic possibility, perhaps with some additional qualifications. At any rate, I will assume that we are working with an idea of content in this instance, and that it is reasonably and appropriately brought to bear on the case at hand.

Part of why moral or serious possibility is reasonable and important to apply to Christianity is because that religion makes central parts of its claims on historical grounds, or by reference to alleged historical events and alleged historical human beings (most notably, just one of them) acting in history. To rest on history is to give hostages to fortune.

Some scholars have seriously questioned whether, or denied that, there even was a historical Jesus. His story is extremely close, some think implausibly too close, to that of a whole set of other Near Eastern saviour gods of the half-millennium preceding his supposed life. It may seem somewhat unlikely, though, that writings affirming his life and death—the first epistles of Paul—would have appeared a mere 20 years or so after his alleged death, if he had never existed; and the general outline of the story of Jesus's career, claimed Messiahship, and execution at the hands of a known Roman governor, has a historical plausibility and fit in first-century Palestine. (Jesus's brother, and other family members, are also attested as still living in the Jerusalem area after Paul had begun to write.)

In any case, theological clarity as to what Jesus supposed himself to be and was regarded as being by his followers then, and in decades and eventually centuries afterwards, is hard to achieve. The Jewish Messiah does not seem, ever, to have been regarded as a literally divine figure; rather, as someone with a divine *mandate* and purpose. Be that as it may, Jesus became, in Christian conception, a divine being, one "person" of a divine Trinity — whatever that theory is supposed to mean, or can be construed as meaning. This idea seems definitely absent from the first three, the so-called synoptic Gospels, but at least partly formed and present in the fourth Gospel, and parts of the Pauline epistolary body. In fully articulated later Christian orthodoxy, Jesus — Christ — is God on earth, and Mary, his mother, the Mother of God. He is also a human being. The way in which his two "natures"are united during his terrestrial journey was to give rise to acrimonious theological dispute, culminating in schism.

For my purposes in this chapter, the precise nature of Christ is mostly secondary, though I will offer some remarks under this head in a later corollary context. Christ does, though, play a more direct and important role than deciding theological — Christological — arcana might suggest.

Summarizing the preceding, then, there are objections as to whether Christian theism really has a moral or serious possibility of being true. Some of the objections are historical, others have to do with the psychological and anthropological credibility of the theory, others with theological details and their apparent implications. I am going to assume that these objections (as to Christianity's moral or serious *possibility*) are answerable. I do not assume that Christianity has any high degree of probability of being true (nor do I in fact believe that it does); just that its probability is not zero, and high enough that the theory may be regarded (as *many* other theories incompatible with it also will be) as a contender for being true.

In what follows I will try to set out what I will presume to call a most intelligent Christianity — understood as what should be viewed as a Christian theory that is as close as possible to orthodox and received Christian views, but modified where dictated, arguably, by considerations of ethical and existential seriousness. The ground, and central part of the rationale, for this Christian picture is chiefly due to Kant.[1] He professed an orthodox Christianity; but also denied the possibility of his, or anyone's, rationally defending it. So I claim that though he might decline to follow where I think argument will lead, Kantian rationality will offer no resistance to that argument, and indeed the spirit of his own views will accompany the journey.

Part of the preceding should perhaps be elaborated upon, with appropriate emphasis. Kant gives ·no indication, ever, of favouring departure from a generally orthodox, and, indeed, a generally Lutheran orthodox, interpretive Christian theological line, albeit within an Enlightenment framework, including opposition to or distaste for enthusiasm, mysticism, and superstition. Some articles of the faith he defends, some he thinks he can more or less prove, others are left as mysteries of faith that nevertheless are never doubted or left outside an integrated edifice or unity of Christian affirmed doctrine; Kant never suggests that theological revisionism would be warranted. Certainly, departures from theological orthodoxy will have been conceptually available to him, and well-known, even if publicly or politically inconvenient, or worse, to pursue, especially after the accession of the theologically rigid, and zealous, king Frederick William II, in 1786.

Newton was of course an Arian, or Unitarian, as were Priestley and others (including German theological writers of Kant's day); and Socinianism added to Anti-Trinitarianism a focus on Christian ethical thought that might have been thought congenial to the Kantian Christianity I will be advancing.

During the long reign of Frederick the Great, through which most of Kant's work and thought were formed, religious pluralism, even skepticism, flourished in Prussia, yet Kant, though latitudinarian, seems never to have been a freethinker. Kant does, consistently and emphatically, argue not merely for the conceptual, but also the ethical autonomy of ethics from theology (which will be a key consideration in the Christian theory that will be developed in what follows), i.e., of the autonomy of the idea of the Good from that of the idea of God; something allowed by, though not required for, received Christian orthodoxy. (For some, this is an objection to, or at least a qualification upon, Kant's being taken as a sound or optimal exemplar of Christan thought.) Further, he argues, in *Religion Within the Bounds of Reason Alone*, that the highest ethical mode, involving the inwardness of conscience and development toward Christ-like perfection, are given full expression in the role and teaching of Christ in the Gospel narratives.

In the account to follow, departure from Christian orthodoxy will not, or need not, occur in the treatment, role, or indeed central significance for a kingdom of ends, of the figure of Christ. Departures for which I will argue — and argue both that they make for a better and more plausible Christianity, as well as being prompted by and in the spirit of Kant's conception of a kingdom of ends — will involve the divine nature, and the creation.

The dialectic I will use will seek to formulate the Kantian Christianity I propose by way of, or in the company of, objections or resistances to particular Christian themes and tenets. In such a crucible, I think, can best be achieved and articulated a Christianity that an intelligent, and serious philosopher (including, importantly in this context, one not antecedently committed to Christianity) might entertain as *possibly* right, the best-bet version of Christian theism should it happen to turn out — as it might — to be true.

One of the central philosophical insights that may be assigned to Kant is the idea of a duality of philosophical foundations: that the world, indeed every philosophical object, project, and topic, may be (and must be) approached in itself and as itself, and that it, and they, may and must be approached from a perspective and angle of vision that can only be *mine*. The item — whatever it be — as it may and must be on its own, as theory from-no-perspective finds or determines it to be, and the item for me, inasmuch as it figures — cognitively, affectively, or ontologically — in a logical space whose radial centre is me. It is not always appreciated,

I think, that Kant *had* this insight, or that it plays as central a foundational and methodological role in his philosophy as I believe it does. If this were conceived as a more textually focused and historical paper than it is in fact intended to be, I would try to justify this Kantian interpretive view, and its importance in Kant, more extensively than I will.

Like other great insights—and I think that the irreducible-duality Kantian insight is a profoundly great and important one, moreover one that is *sound* and *true*—there will be reason to see partial anticipations and articulations of it prior to its appearance in the work of its major creative author. That too is matter for scholarship that will not be significantly engaged here.

The subsequent descent, and history, of Kant's insight—which might be dubbed *foundational dualism*—is also complex, and opaque. One can discern it, slightly tilted, in Schopenhauer's bifurcation of the world as will and the world also as representation, and in the Kantian-Schopenhauerian doctrine of the world as all that is the case, and the world also as my world, that appears in Wittgenstein's *Tractatus*. The idea appears also more prosaically, or concretely, in discussions in analytic metaphysics and semantics of the eliminability, or otherwise, of *indexicality*. John Perry's (and others') arguments for the ineliminability of indexical terms and concepts—which Russell had appropriately called *egocentric particulars* (well, his use of the term *particulars* in this context is confusing)—make the case, in a different vocabulary, for Kant's visionary discovery.

I once came to the view that of all of the philosophers of the canon, none grasped as clearly how the world looks from God's point of view, insofar as we could hope to divine it, as Leibniz. No one else, I insouciantly concluded, knew as well what it would *feel* like, phenomenologically, to be God, as did Leibniz. I now think that *Kant* has still stronger claim to these offices and achievements. Kant, of course, stands to a considerable degree on Leibniz's shoulders. Not only did he know his work, there is a line of philosophical descent from Leibniz, through Wolff, to Kant. Indeed, there is a good case for a kind of parallelism in the fundamental relations between Leibniz and Kant, and those subtending between Locke and Hume. In both cases, it may be argued, there is an almost Freudian repudiation, and honouring, of the father. Jealously denigrating that father, who is nonetheless covertly respected and seen as anchor and reference point, the later philosopher will cover, in both cases, the same terrain as the earlier, only this time do it right.

At any rate, Leibniz, although he *does* have each substance as a primitive ego, a *moi*, representing the whole of the world to itself—and Kant's foundational dualism perhaps could never have been formulated had he not discerned this in Leibniz—this does not quite reach Kant's conception, which is of something profoundly individual, outside theory and system (so to speak), and (in the Sartrean and post-Sartrean sense) *existential*. I am alive, and conscious, and find myself with these spatio-temporally structured horizons of possibility, within which are facts, for me, some evident, some not, and facing alternatives of action, among which I must choose from bases and principles as they seem warranted to me. That others are in like case is itself a piece of *theory*, very well-grounded theory as it may be, that is on the *other* fork of the foundational duality. *One* of those others, for whom, also, the world is *their* world, in the manner in which it is for me my world, is (if he is real) God.

Beginning to put some of the foregoing fragmentary thoughts together, it may be noted that typical concern focused on evils and deficiencies of the world attends to particular cases. *This* unnecessary throbbing toothache, that pointless death, either through malevolent agency or cruelly uncaring impersonal nature, individual cases of suffering, pain, and the extinction of a conscious life, easily present themselves in experience, and easily aggregate. Cases where good is achieved by them, that could not, in principle, have been achieved less painfully, are few and far between in this easily enlarged aggregation; if indeed there are any at all. Arguments that any impressive range of them are an unavoidable consequence of the great good of free will, or that they play a part, in a causal or aesthetic network, on which the overall coherence, value, or merit of the whole ineluctably depends, are profoundly unconvincing. Anyone who is intellectually honest will acknowledge, not just at the beginning, but at middle stages and at the end of their inquiries, that theodicy is a steeply uphill enterprise. (As Kant himself certainly saw, and affirmed. "[T]heodicy," he concluded, in "On the Failure of all Philosophical Attempts at Theodicy," "is not a task of science but is a matter of faith."[2]) I will be offering only partial, and oblique, contribution to that enterprise with anything that I will have to say as the present investigation proceeds.

Were *I* in a position to foresee and prevent some palpably unnecessary evil — a case of pointless suffering, say — I would do so; so goes many a response, voiced or unvoiced, to the problem of evil. God, of course, is not supposed just to foresee and have the power to prevent the world's evils; he is supposed to have designed that world, in all its detail, diachronic and sequential as well as at any given time, indeed to have willed that it should be precisely and exactly this very world, in all that detail. Thus the gravity of the problem of evil. How *could* a being do *that* and be a good or just being, someone to whom humans could appropriately give ethical allegiance?

Leibniz tries directly to step imaginatively into the divine shoes, so to speak: to conceive of a perfect being in the circumstance of making a world actual, confronting his alternatives, and having a rational decision procedure for opting among them. Leibniz thinks of distinct vectors that would in their conjoint operation dictate that just one world — our actual world — would ensue. One of these vectors is amplitude of being. A rich, teeming, varied, pluralistic cornucopia of possibilities, a world crammed with objects and events of a huge range of sorts and kinds will be dictated by this parameter. The Leibnizian ontological plenum will, indeed, allow — may actually encourage — the idea of a vast array of *subworlds* (mutually independent and incommensurable) structures of individuals, states, and events, all housed within the single created and actual world; so impelling might the ontological amplitude vector be. With so much able to be made conjointly real, at least some of that teeming jungle will inescapably be unpleasant. Another vector constrains and marshals the preceding one. This is a coordinate of order and simplicity. The world is to be a rational place, elegant and beautiful in the structure of the laws and principles that govern it. And it is to be the expression of perfections that are moral as well as of other sorts. There is then an ethical vector, which modifies or colours the preceding two. The cross-product of these three parameters is our world.

How much of the high Leibnizian rationalism of the preceding Kant accepts or incorporates is unclear. There is for him, though, a more highly valorized central focus on the idea of the person. Free rational agency is the *nec plus ultra* of what a world can contain of value. That is indeed the core component of God's nature, and perfection. To be a self, with an inner conscious life, prospects of communication with other selves, and projects for acting in the world, is not just of inherent value and worth; it is of supreme value and worth, that without which nothing else can have value or worth. The degree of ethical and ontological centrality personhood has for Kant, and its partial anticipations in the *moi*-hood of Leibnizian monads, may or may not be partly attributable to Kant's, and Leibniz's, shared Lutheran Protestant heritage. Hegel, who shared that heritage and a variant of that ethical and ontological understanding, was to discern a special philosophical lineage originatively embodied (from Christian roots) in the world-historical figure of Luther.

If one were God, then, one would want that the universe should contain *persons*, indeed a community of persons; a kingdom of ends, in Kant's phrase. Just how many such persons there would be, with what *other* natures, attributes, skills, and locations in the world, is unclear, nor need be addressed. It makes sense — it may or may not be *ethical* sense — that there should be a pluralistic divergence and range of kinds and sorts of persons. This is a great-chain-of-being sort of notion, whose detail, and alternative possible versions and forms, need not detain us. It does — somehow — seem clear that even if it were possible, a world all of whose persons were as perfect as God, or nearly as perfect as he, would lack something of deep value that a world not only consisting of "demi-gods," but also of lesser, frailer persons, would have; and it is not just the greater diversity that lesser persons would provide.

Supposing then that a perfect and holy will, seeking to do maximal good — to create what will have maximum value — undertakes, out of the deep sense of its unsurpassable value, and, perhaps deeply impelled by *love* (that specially Christian component of divine perfection) to create a universe with other persons, and that a best such world will have an array or span of *kinds* of persons, including some with sorts of powers and aptitudes (especially conscious and free-agency sorts of powers and aptitudes) such as we find in ourselves, what *otherwise* will be a suitable setting and content for the universe? A mere *club* or *clubhouse* of persons seems plausibly *not* adequate or sufficient, not *serious* or *existential* as a terrain within which free conscious personhood can obtain and develop. It may seem persuasive and convincing — I do not say that Kant himself will have thought this through in quite this way, only that so thinking will converge on or merge with what, and how, he does think — that a genuinely serious and existential *housing* for personhood will not only not be a clubhouse (by which I mean a setting that *doesn't matter*, that can be any sort of shell or space within which persons, and the universe, can be altogether focused on *personhood*); it will also not be a *home fit for heroes*, in the idealistic phrasing coined and politically motivating after World War I. Rather, it will be a *natural* world, within which personhood is to be found, but rather as a rare and rough gem, surrounded by and immersed in, and indeed a part of, a vastly larger order of non-personal, indeed mostly quite impersonal forces and states and facts, going on and proceeding on their own and as themselves.

This last claim is, in fact, quite a critical one for the overall aim of the present paper. My own view — also that of many, perhaps most other philosophers, and most, possibly nearly all scientists — is that the observed and experienced universe is, top to bottom, through and through, a wholly natural place, a place that natural science can address and study. Even if there *might* be something ineluctably special about consciousness, or culture, or normativity, which might defy forever and in principle reduction to or expression as something that physics textbooks, or tomes of scientific psychology, might capture, this would be, if true, anomalousness within a broad setting of law and system of an altogether natural, regular, and law-governed kind. There might or might not be rational prospects for a version of theism, even Christian theism. If there were, this would presumably involve a formally non-naturalist component in the world as a whole (that is, encompassing both God and the universe he creates). There are no prospects at all for reincarnation, astrology, precognition, or miraculous healing. God, if real, and active, works in and through nature. Haldane famously said, a little mockingly, that if there is a God he has an extraordinary fondness for beetles, since there are so amazingly many distinct species of them.

I am proposing turning Haldane, to some extent, and in a certain way, on his head. The bullet *must* be bit, as I see it: this *is* a natural world. A virtue can, and arguably should, be made of this necessity, that is, by he and she who would seek to formulate the most intelligent Christianity possible. God, if real, has willed that this be a natural world; by which I mean that he will have willed that the world operate (possibly not *totally* exceptionlessly) on its own, according to laws and principles that will configure in ways, and with results, that are independent of specificities of willed outcomes. The further, existential claim—which seems to me implicit, at least, in Kant's theological, ethical, and psychological vision—is that a better, a more genuinely valuable, and *serious*, world will be one with persons, of different stages and formed-out-of-nature sets of attributes and dispositions, and whose outcomes (natural and moral) will have been let go of, by the creator. It would seem very difficult to suppose that this could occur in a genuinely serious way if the deity preserves literal omniscience; i.e., including advance knowledge of *everything* that happens, is chosen, and is done. There *might* be some way to secure the latter; I don't insist that there couldn't, only affirm my own inability to see how it could be had.

The difficulty is not one posed by determinism and alleged conflicts that that has with free agency. I am myself (at least, six days out of seven) a compatibilist, hence see no problem with free choices that were predetermined and knowable millions of years before their agents' existence. The problem, rather, is with the existential and ethical challenge of the world's seeming—if a God knows in advance all of the detail of its content, and orders that it *be*, with all of that detail—to be a mere play, a charade, something not merely not serious, but a cruel façade. One may recall Russell's summary portrait and judgment of the divinely created cosmos in "A Free Man's Worship."[3] Or, if Russell's ethical strictures could somehow be evaded, and an orthodox picture of a God of the "omni-s," and creation, be ethically defensible, still, it is arguable, a better, higher, more serious, more existential, conception will be one that departs from orthodoxy in these respects.

The nearest thing achievable as a rational Christianity, or indeed, in this case, a rational monotheism of any sort, would, I am suggesting, have to depart from Christian orthodoxy in a certain respect—although arguably it might be held or made to conform—and see the divine creator as having willed, or launched, radical contingency. By this I mean that "the whole world in his hands" idea should be abandoned. God should be seen as a serious being, in an existential sense; and scripting a cosmic play that one is then having performed is not a serious act, or at any rate not as serious an act as a truly serious being would be capable of and would prefer. A scheme of things must be seen as having been set in motion that was allowed or willed to spin out of the divine hands, as it were, to unfold and elaborate itself in ways that would never have God—or hardly ever, only incredibly seldom, and then because God simply could not bear not to—intervene.

Literal total prescience could be allowed to go hang if necessary. God should be seen as quite wonderfully, masterfully anticipatory, able to figure and to follow the future any present will be pregnant with; but not with it guaranteed by magic, or logic. There would be a way he would figure, a mechanism or methodology. He would be, rather, more like Laplace's master cognizer in this respect. Let it be effortless, and more or less instantaneous, but some variety or cousin of computation should be imputed to him. And the conception should be able to handle the idea or the possibility of God willing that there should be intrinsic randomnesses—as in quantum mechanics, for example—that he would intend that he himself wouldn't be able to track the precise outcomes of, anticipatorily.

For it really would be better, and greater, that one should want that there be other persons, with dignity and autonomy; that one will to refrain from being the author of all. There is greater love in this too. And part of what this seriousness, and this love, would imply is that the world, once launched, be left to be the world. It is not only humans who should not "play God" with the world; God should not play God either. Of course, he could not but be the ultimate author of all being, at any rate all other than his own. Creation and love are what define *his* high seriousness and high intelligence.

Three difficulties—at least—pose themselves before the line of thinking being developed here. They may reasonably be confronted right away, as each might be fatal to any plausibility the general approach might at least initially be thought to have. All three are traditional or familiar parts of the dialectic surrounding the problem of evil and the argument from the problem of evil it gives rise to.

First is the consideration that even with the slightly limited omniscience we are supposing, the deity would have been able to tell in broad terms at least how things would turn out, and they include horrors that a god worthy of the name would not will or tolerate. The second is that with whatever resolve of non-intervention, some of the directions things have taken could not, morally, see divine power sitting idly by. If the overall model is supposed to be approximately parental, and we have been supposing, above, that mature creativity, and love, would wish that the world should contain *other adults*, and not merely beings who would remain always, at most, adolescents overseen by God; still, what parent who is *there* and *observing* could see its offspring in some of the extremities of pain or viciousness that humans are quite often in without doing something to help, if it could?

(I will say parenthetically that, to me, at least, the idea that God *does* sometimes intervene and help, in oblique occasional ways, is altogether unpersuasive, a non-starter; for, quite apart from the fact that there is no actual *evidence* of such intervention, the occasions that might be so construed introduce *caprice*, or *whimsy*, into the workings of the world — why this time, rather than those eight million other equally appropriate occasions when he did nothing? — at odds with the overriding idea of a sensible Christianity. But my allegedly sensible Christianity still won't formally rule out occasional divine interventions, on grounds inscrutable to us.)

The third difficulty is that it seems clear that there are better alternative (possible) *natural* worlds than ours. That is, we can conceive a universe launched, to spin as it will, i.e., in accord with deterministic and/or indeterministic principles, that would in fact come out, predictably, as a more impressive piece of divine workmanship — with adult autonomous free agents in it, and anything else we think significant or valuable in our universe — than the one we've got.

We may hope at least partly to address these difficulties by restating, and further advancing, the argument that has preceded. A perfectly good omnipotent being would, out of his goodness and not out of loneliness (or other lacks), will that there be other persons. Their numbers, locations on hierarchical scales of cognitive or other powers, and what diversity of them by kinds (of all manner of sorts), are questions that need not be entertained in this context. The perfect being would will that there be other persons in a Kantian sense, i.e., rational agents with inner consciousness, autonomy, and self-direction. Moreover, the perfect being would will that there be such persons with what we may call adulthood — and in this case, an adulthood that would necessarily attach to the creator as well as the created. Adulthood is not being under even the reserve constraint or control of another person. One person could in fact cause the existence of another where the fate — the life experiences — of the created person remained always subject to modifying intervention from the creator. We may describe such continued capacity for modifying intervention as the creator's being and remaining *parens aut in locus parentis* to the created person. Such creation is not the creation of adults. A creator might seek such a role, and such a power, in relation to a person it had created; and such a role and power might be prompted by a certain kind of love. But — "if you really love him/her, you set him/her free" — you want autonomous adulthood for that other, such that you not merely would not, but also could not, step in, modifyingly, at any subsequent stage. If you valued rational personhood enough, you would abridge your powers, such that no capacity of modifying interference would remain to you.

Note that the idea that a "serious," more existentially elevated world will require the creation of "adult" persons is entirely independent of levels and judgments of good and bad for our world or other worlds. That is to say, the case that an optimal world will have adult persons will apply to worlds otherwise ethically impressive just as to ones not spectacularly so. Accordingly, it does not contribute to addressing the problem of evil or the ethical status we may think the actual world has, except to the extent that our world may be held to have genuinely adult persons in it.

Again, some questions need not be pursued; in this case, the could-God-make-a-stone-so-heavy-that-he-couldn't-lift-it sort of question. We do not need to consider whether somehow divine power could have (or be argued to have) a reserve beyond operational reserve; or whether the sort of loving person-creating-and-respecting envisaged would have to imply the perfect being literally rendering himself no longer omnipotent. Morally adult parents of morally (as well as physically) adult children *cannot* intervene guidingly, correctively in the latter's lives. The "cannot" is not merely moral: that is, it is not simply that they will themselves to no longer intervene as they formerly did. They are (something like) psychologically incapable of so intervening. It is not logically or conceptually possible that a relationship of adult "co-personhood" be sustained if they did, and the logic of creating adult persons implies that the *option range* for interaction with the created person now excludes such interventions. They are no longer "thinkable." They are no longer (in some sense) *possible*.

But if this is so, its logic will imply further that the setting within which the created person lives and functions is immune, or beyond the possibility, of subsequent "doctoring" also. I do not play invisible helping stranger to those I truly have adult co-personal relationship with, modifying the environment such persons will occupy (for individual occasions or longer stretches), any more than I step in later to modify their minds. They will have a world that has become *theirs*, because I have given it to them and abandoned proprietary claim to it. If I cannot "play God" with persons I respect, whom I treat as ends, then neither can God.

A perfectly good creating will might be expected nonetheless to create a structured environment for persons it created that would systematically "take care of" their needs, and the situations that would or might arise for them, with an advance completeness; setting out the salt, the fruit bowl, and the flowers—as it were—for those "guests" in the home that will be provided for them, to every degree and for every possible and actual eventuality. This is something like what Leibniz envisages.

However it is arguable—I here argue—that a truly serious, rational consciousness, imbued with adulthood and the desire that there be other truly adult rational consciousnesses, would aim higher and more seriously than this: it would will for its created persons a *natural world*.

A natural world is a world that flows from a (relatively) small stock of conditions or states in accordance with causal laws, deterministic or probabilistic; with no *dei ex machina* (at any rate normally, usually, or systematically); that is, with no interventions or interferences from agencies outside that world. It will be — again, possibly excepting quite extraordinary occasions — a world that sustains itself.

Some natural worlds are straightforwardly simple, deterministic, and predictable. Others, however, are complex beyond all possibility, not merely of detailed foreknowability by finite intelligences, but also by anything we can describe or conceive — in detail — as an infinite intelligence. Thus, a natural world where a rational finite agent decides to choose one alternative action rather than others according as a quantum randomizing device indicates, will have — certainly may have — outcomes that were not in any trackable sense predictable.

Of course, it may be insisted that an infinite mind is conceivable who will just know — somehow — whatever is to be, and that that is what is envisaged for God. I am proposing that the perfect being, willing the reality of a world with adult ends in themselves that *he* respects, to be set in a "serious" adult environment, not a cosmic experimental lab or "Globe theatre," would will that, so far as he could do this, the world of these created persons would be significantly not "trackable" by him, in advance. Usual theologies will insist that God cannot help but know, everything, in advance. Again, then, the view argued here is that a genuinely "holy" will, a God *worthy* of being God, would find a way to limit his capacities insofar as doing so would be required by genuine respect for other persons than himself.

Actually, we need to consider the two descriptive hypotheses, viz., that an omniscient/omnipotent God somehow manages to limit or diminish his omnipotence and omniscience in the interests of having the world contain genuinely adult created persons, as we have understood the latter idea; and that a creator God has those limitations all along.[4] Both pose complexity. If the first is supposed, we apparently need to think of a being who once knew what he knows no longer, and once could do what he subsequently cannot. On the other hand, some of the limitation we have supposed not genuine, because some things may not be knowable in advance, in principle. However, even if this is so, we are conceiving of respecting another's adulthood as implying at least some cases where the honouring or respecting party *could* physically and psychologically intervene, but will not, out of respect for the autonomy/adulthood of the other. Also, if in these and other cases the omniscience was as total as it could have been, then we seem back in the state of things, prior to the self-diminishing, which all on its own seemed contra-optimific. In that earlier state, or at that earlier stage, God in relation to the world — specifically, its created person component — will be just as "bad," or sub-optimal, as in the original more Leibnizian supposition.

So we seem to need to conceive a world where God was "limited," along lines indicated, all along. This may make for a better total universe, but it seems to problematize the nature of God himself, who will now appear to be less perfect — because less powerful and knowing — than he might have been.

But perhaps this may just point to, and help establish, that *good* and *perfect* have relational as well as intrinsic components; and justify the idea that a more truly perfect being will have limitations that another possible being — a less perfect being — would not have.

We may still ask about the case of the truly omnipotent and omniscient (and wholly good) being, supposed as possible even if not actual. Such a being *could not help* but know everything future that was metaphysically knowable. It would seem, then, that this being would not be able to create genuinely adult limited persons. If we suppose that the latter are real, we ourselves among them, we will have reason to infer that there does not exist an absolutely omnipotent, omniscient, wholly good being: not a loss, we may suppose, if the total state of the universe (God plus everything else that is real) is better than if there were.

In spite of the theologies of the most acute of the Christian metaphysical philosophers from Augustine to Leibniz, it is quite clear that the conception in the original Christian scheme of things does not include a literally omniscient God. The idea of the incarnation all by itself shows this (other features of the Biblical narrative, or the logic that underlies it, also do). "God so loved the world that he gave his only begotten son...," the text says (John 3:16). The love, the gift, the redemption, make no sense, and are morally empty, if a state of affairs has not come to pass that was not altogether anticipated. If all times are present to God, literally and co-equally, then the incarnation is a charade, mere robotic automatism, the merry-go-round having come now (*then*) to this, God having known from eternity that it would. (One might compare the Leibnizian picture with that of Vonnegut's *Slaughterhouse Five*.) This is not something intelligible as love, or as a gift painful to the giver, called forth by love; at any rate, not in or for a mind of high moral seriousness. So, at least, it seems to me.

Considerable accommodation to the classical theologies is possible. As with God and the stone (the one too heavy for him to lift), the sensible account is to declare that God has only such powers as are consistent with his being, and remaining, perfect (understanding the latter, as we may now do, as involving relational states as well as intrinsic ones); and to *argue*, in this case, as we have done, that this will require creating a world, and persons contained in it, made beyond the full cognitive power and reach of the creator. An alternative route is also possible, viz., arguing that free will *as such* makes logically (conceptually) impossible full anticipation of its employments; so that God's knowing in advance all human choices (hence all of their consequences) would be like his making a square circle. Neither omniscience nor omnipotence are, of course, sensibly constrained by the conceptually or logically impossible.

As a compatibilist, I cannot take this alternative path. I see no logical difficulty with foreknowledge, in principle, of all free choices. But I believe without claiming to know that compatibilism is true. In any case, the first option — the "Kantian" option (where there is much in the future that God really doesn't know) — seems to me inherently plausible on its own. Neither alternative, it should be stressed, nor what is implicit in Biblical claims, requires a future that is a blank slate for God, even in respect of the cases of freedom. Much can be probabilistically anticipated with deep rational confidence, about people and what they will do, without compromising freedom or existential "seriousness."

As well as involving community, or its possibility, personhood is separateness, and a reality of a self's inner space and distinctive station. Nor can the moral and ontological significance of a kingdom of ends preclude differences by kind, or tribe, of person that may make for chasms of separateness between one kind of person and another, as between one individual person and another, whatever their tribal sort. One is alone in one's separate selfhood, just as one is in potential interactive and moral communion with all other selves, and — perhaps — in one species or other of special relationship with other selves of one or more of the kinds one is part of, and — perhaps — in one species or other of special relationship with particular individual others one has bonds with.

These generalities applying to all persons apply also to God, if there is or were a God. Together with other parts of postulates of a theology grounded in classical Christianity and — modifiable — classical Christian theology, these generalities will permit, possibly entail, that God is not our "special friend," our personal "Harvey."[5] Rather, God is "the boss," the one in charge, creator and orchestrator of a scheme of things, with a will that is not negotiably opposable. This consideration must inevitably lead to "Freud's objection" to the possibility of a serious or coherent theism. Freud's objection is the claim that no monotheism that large numbers of humans could actually adopt will fail to be a projection of a relation to a (human) father, and only taken up, by anyone, by virtue of that fact. I take this objection to be one of the weightiest, if not *the* weightiest, of the obstacles to a coherent or serious possible (Christian) theism.

I do not propose fully addressing Freud's objection here. I want to remark, though, that the issues — moral and psychological — confronted here are a special instance of whether *hierarchy* is morally and rationally coherent. Others can be smarter, wiser, more knowledgeable — about *everything* about which I have any knowledge — than me; indeed, significantly more so. And though another cannot, perhaps, have just my perspective or take on things, or have my interests — but only, at best, know what my perspective is, or what it is like, and take my interests to heart, or know what is in my interest (whether I see it or not) — they could be so benevolently and reliably disposed on my behalf that I might come, rationally, to trust and conform to their counsel (even where I might not at first see its soundness), finally invariably and unblinkingly. But still, in the end, I must be answerable for and to myself. Another cannot be persuaded for me, nor can another acknowledge that something is in my interest for me. Now, so far at least, at least a Protestant, Lutheran Christianity can accommodate — indeed it affirms — the spirit as well as the letter of these reflections. What is supposed to be *wanted* is the free, unconstrained, reflectively rational assent to Christian truth, not a sheep's subsumption in what one was merely conditioned to, or what comforts.

So far, then, well and good. But it is not clear that Christianity can accommodate what a plausible theory of rational moral autonomy must insist on, viz., the permanent maintenance of the possibility that my interest may diverge from that of anyone else. (How the latter is parsed is critical: it is the permanent maintenance of a possibility, even in the face of what might be a metaphysical impossibility that such divergence should occur.) Even in heaven, as it were, in paradise, at God's court, the morally serious person will — must — sustain indefinitely, is condemned to it, in fact (Sartre-style), practical reason's version of what-it's-like-ness. (The latter, famously, though anachronistically, linked to Nagel, is — we may say in this context *merely* — cognitive and phenomenological.) Can any version of theism allow this, even the most liberal Lutheran Protestantism?

One may respond: yes; if it *must*, then, of course it can. Let heaven be, in that sense, eternally a republic, with a ruler continually reaffirmed, and reconfirmed, in his rule by the rational assent of the ruled, the saints never coming to a terminus of lulled sleep on the bosom of their Lord (as it were).

And will this not be a part of the other side of the coin with which we began? If God is, while another person, still wholly Other, and holy other, he is strange, remote, immense, a much vaster Jupiter who'd not do to us what Jupiter, because he swore, does to Semele; but who could, as we'd know he could. In his station he made the universe, and us, and me, and runs the place, at least in some general sort of way. No such being could be my pal, whatever the degree of his affections. He might require things of me, even as he respected my personhood. And there could always be the possibility of my—rationally—not seeing things his way, even if I were to be invariably, on each successive occasion, persuaded (always ultimately by myself) that I would and did see things his way.

Still: I do not feel sure that this does really, in the end, work. The idea of a serious Christianity cannot be just the idea of a certain metaphysical story for the universe, *this* turning out to be the reality behind appearances: viz., a special sort of constitutional monarchy. The idea of the holy, of the sacred, and species of fear and beauty known in their presence or their contemplation, cannot be reduced merely to metaphysics or philosophy-of-law for the cosmos; and it is strongly arguable that there cannot be religion without those ideas—and arguable in its train that those ideas *are* sublimations of approach to the parental bedroom. This last will seem at first "village Freudism"; but only at first, if one thinks carefully. (It need not be the parental *bedroom*; but rather, to seeing the parent in internal psychological nakedness, that is, sensing at least some of what it feels like to have the thoughts, feelings, attitudes, of the parent, as *they* experience them. God, like Noah, cannot be seen naked by his children, even though—just think about it—there would be such a thing as his *being* naked, there would be such a thing as what it was *like* to be God, *it* would be something, and not blank mystery, ever somewhere else on a horizon, something hidden. It seems clear that for every person, including a divine or infinite person, there would, necessarily, be such a thing as what it would be (like) *to be* that person.)

And again: if it all *were* just metaphysics (a particular theological one) and cosmic philosophy of law (even if the best Kantian one), then why bother about it at all, unless one just happened to be interested in such things, and while one was interested? There'd be no compelling *reason* to be interested, if one just weren't, particularly. (It might, of course, be in one's prudential self-interest to be interested, because of attendant possible benefits and losses; but such considerations as those will be alien to our purposes in this project.)

As already intimated, perhaps the very largest impediment to the possibility of a serious Christianity, as a moral, existential, and ontological vision of the world and the place of humanity within it, is posed by whether Christianity can assign humans a location, condition, and stature that *isn't* essentially an analogue of that of "man's best friend," the dog. In classic versions of Christianity — this will be contentious for some, but it does seem nonetheless incontestably true — a human being is and ought to be to God rather as a dog (especially a "good dog") is and ought to be to a human being. Faithful, loyal, looking up for guidance, comfortable and confident in the direction and the world-ordering of the wise master, who knows, as one oneself cannot, what is for general good and my good, what the plan is, what we should do next; obedient, tail-wagging, fierce in vigilant prosecution of the master's commands, ferocious opponent of *his* enemies, grateful, cheerful, unquestioning, sentimental. This is the Freudian critique of religion — or much of it — and more in addition. Not least of all, more morally. For some quite loathsome individuals have good and loyal dogs. The dog does not discriminate on this plane. A serial killer may have a good and loyal dog, happy basking in the sunshine of this master's rule, and such attention as this master may accord.

God — not to put too fine a point on it — is, if real, a serial killer. He is the Apollo-Artemis of all of our days' ends. He may — unlike human serial killers, we may suppose — have justification in his killings. Maybe. But… he has a lot to answer for. Heavy is his burden, just as is ours. The advocacy of Christian virtue must confront, and ponder, tales like Darwin's tale of the hand-licking loyalty of the tortured dying dog to the man performing vivisection on it.[6]

My point here is only obliquely, and partly, to turn attention again to the problem of evil. It is, rather, to ask whether a Christian view can have humans escape and transcend the moral condition of dogs in their relation to the deity; or find, I suppose, some way of dignifying, elevating, and rendering serious the condition of the dog—though this seems quite impossible. Only, I think, the idea of *adult* personhood, understood as it has been advanced here, offers hope of escape from a merely dog-like, hence a non-serious, estate for us. A subtle triangulation, of ourselves as truly autonomous rational agents, and of a particular, limited, natured *kind* (that "crooked timber of humanity," in the vivid Kantian phrase, which unites with, and frequently bedevils, our transcendent personhood), in relation—potential close community—with other persons, supremely that highest person, who is also "the boss," and also, as all persons are, himself as himself (herself as herself), must be conceived, and found persuasive, if this is to work.

I conclude with two corollary parts of Christian theistic theory: the afterlife idea, and the nature and role of Christ. Both add something, and something Kantian, to the position we have been sketching.

The position with respect to an afterlife that a serious, existential, and maximally plausible Christianity should affirm should be one of utter, abject faith, or hope. An afterlife of *any* kind should be regarded as objectively improbable, on Lucretian and other naturalistic grounds that are accepted as formidable. Not even a formal stance of confident triumphalism should be maintained. Rather the attitude of the Victorian graveyard painting: *Can these Dry Bones Live?*[7] With that attitude there is felt and lived doubt and uncertainty. One does not know, nor think that one knows. Yet there is both hope and faith. The hope is more or less mute, but serious and sincere. The faith is somewhat more vocal, and unites a Biblically grounded innocent's trust

("In my Father's house are many mansions; if it were not so I would have told you."[8]) with Kantian argument: were we not to continue into a state of more direct divine relationship, and a more morally coherent distribution of desert and outcome, or at least condition, we really would have been left in a kind of cosmic lurch; there would be a fundamental coherence and rationality the world would be deficient in.

This attitude, and argument, would not be held, or left, in a condition of petulant demand or expectation, with the ground prepared for a cosmic *ressentiment* were immortality, or an afterlife at all, not accorded. In principle that there might be justice, or reason, in this life alone being our lot, is *thought* and patiently accepted. This might be His will; and the Kantian argument may not have taken account of important, relevant, possibly quite unknown premises. The note, though, remains hope and faith — strong faith.[9]

Yet too intelligent Christianity would not give a great deal of thought, or priority, to heaven. This is not just because one knows, and acknowledges, that one does not really know — neither objectively, nor inwardly — that there is an afterlife at all. It is, and more importantly, because the cosmic *point* of the scheme of things, the Christian scheme of things, if that is what it is, cannot be that I should be preserved: it cannot be the enactment of an exchange, or a contract — that if I do my part (believe, lead a certain kind of life) I will merit, at any rate receive, my cash reward (the cash, of course, in a celestial currency).

Nor is this just a matter of old, mildewed theological issues of works, merit, and grace. The older Christianity is hopelessly egocentric, *childishly* expectative, even when just optatively so; as Kant himself saw, rejecting, for example, the idea of petitionary prayer as "an absurd…delusion," and ritual prayer as "superstitious delusion."[10] Rescue from death can be a desired, hoped-for part of the intelligent Christian conception, and faith that it shall be so also. But that should not be at the centre of why one is in it, why one sees the world in that way. An intelligent Christianity, if there can be one, must be *for*, and live in, this world, this life, this earth, these bodies and minds. Heaven may frame the picture, and the picture may be conceived as incomplete and incomprehensible without that frame, but the content, of theory, practice, thought as well as action, is here and now.

The following Christology—theory as to the nature of Christ—may be formulated and then held up for compatibility with identifiable or plausible assumptions of the three synoptic Gospel narratives; if judged compatible, it may then be asked whether this may be the Christology intended in one or more of those narratives. For this Christology, Jesus Christ is a human being who is miraculously created in a direct divine act. In a biological sense he has no father. In this he is like Adam, who is willed by God into being, fashioned from dust. Unlike Adam, Christ does have a mother. Possibly the latter's maternity of Jesus is intended in Aristotelian or similar manner as an instrumental or "vehicular" maternity, Jesus not receiving an individual human nature or identity even in part from his mother; rather, wholly from God, just as, or like, Adam receiving his individual human nature from and through direct divine volition.

Jesus, on this view, is the second Adam, created to be the world-historical instrument of divine will and purpose. He is only in this sense "son of God" —though it is a plausible and appropriate sense; he is understandably, with comparable symbolism, styled "son of Man." A virgin birth is occasioned for him because he is not son of a human father, and also because the purity of his nature and engendering and role on the earth will require freedom from, independence of, human sexuality.

Just as Jesus' creation will be a divine miracle, so too will his rising from the dead. Again, direct volitional intervention in history on the part of God will be involved, and not a supposed power or capacity on Christ's part to return to life after having died. Strictly, Christ will not have risen from the dead, but have been caused to rise. The miracle will be God's, not his. At the same time, God will have invested Christ with power and capacity to perform miracles while alive—for example, to heal illness and cause to rise from the dead in the case of other humans.

More, perhaps, should be said about Christ's "sonship" (of God), for this interpretive view. We note that the Gospel—e.g., Matthew—says that God has the power to fashion from stones children for Abraham. Were he to do so, those stones—it is implied—will *be* Abraham's children, even though Abraham will not have carried out procreative or generative acts to produce them. This will suggest, in turn, that Mary's being "with child by the Holy Ghost" is not intended to be thought of along the lines of Zeus impregnating Danae, in the form of a shower of gold. Mary becomes pregnant with Jesus, rather, through a divine volition that she should be so. God, in this conception, is and remains immaterial. He does not transform himself into a materiality of any sort, in order to engender Jesus.

The latter may be said to be obvious, and part of any and all broadly Christian views. Yet there is more typically—and it is encouraged (at least) in New Testament texts beyond the Synoptic Gospels—a view that, irrespective of the mechanics of the engendering, Jesus *is* God's son. For the interpretation offered here, this is only metaphorically the case. All men are God's sons, in several Biblical, including Old Testament, passages.

Christ may be seen, for a specially Christian view, as the supreme expression of the community of personhood; as the link or intermediary who symbolizes and in whose terrestrial career is forged and pledged personal relatedness involving both (and all) personal relata, i.e., including God himself, in his own inner life, as well as the rest of the persons. For a more *literal* Christianity, this role will be tied critically to historical facts about Jesus being rather just so (i.e., rather as the Gospel narratives imply); for a more *liberal* Christianity, arguably, this need not significantly be the case.

I will conclude on this—theologically as well as dialectically—inconclusive note. My aim in the foregoing has been to sketch a rationale, and some of the conceptual contours, for a version of Christian theism. If it has any merit at all, it will attest further to the remarkable philosophical acuity, and the integrity, of Kant, whose broad naturalistic vision of the world as we find it and know it is united (not altogether unproblematically, to be sure) with an extraordinarily deep and systematic conception of free, rational, ethical agency, necessarily manifesting itself as a relational structure, a community, of selves that are to be apprehended both from my own location and from that of reality as a whole.

NOTES

1   Kant's primary writings directly focused on religious and theological topics are collected together in A. W. Wood and G. Di Giovanni, trans. and ed., *Religion and Rational Theology* (Cambridge University Press, 1996) (in the Cambridge Edition of the Works of Immanuel Kant). The most important of these works is *Religion within the boundaries of mere reason* (1793). (The latter was in earlier translations called *Religion Within the Limits of Reason Alone*. As the more familiar rendering of the work's title, I have preferred to refer to the work by the latter name.) No adequate or sufficient sense of Kant's religious and theological views, and of their very special character, can, however, be achieved except also by inclusion of the theories and doctrines of the first two *Critiques*; for the purposes of this essay, Kant's ethical writings above all.

2   I have preferred the translation, both of the passage and of the title of the work in which it appears, provided in Howard Caygill, *A Kant Dictionary* (Blackwell, 1995), p. 390. The title given in *Religion and Rational Theology* (in the Cambridge Edition of the Works of Immanuel Kant) is "On the miscarriage of all philosophical trials in theodicy." The passage cited appears on p. 34.

3   See Bertrand Russell, *Mysticism and Logic* (George Allen and Unwin, 1917), p. 40f. The Russell depiction of divine creation, the resulting world, and human nature, is particularly telling, and relevant for the present account, since he too imagines an essentially naturalistic order within which the divine purposes are realized.

4   Thanks to John Bishop for pointing this out to me, and for helpful discussion of the issue.

5   Harvey is a large imaginary rabbit in a popular 1930s film, invisible to all but the character played by James Stewart, with whom the latter has illuminating ongoing friendship and consultations.

6   Charles Darwin, *The Descent of Man* (Princeton University Press, 1981), p. 68.

7   The full title of the painting (by Henry Alexander Bowler) is *The Doubt: "Can these Dry Bones Live?"* (1855). The line quoted in the title is from Ezekiel.37.3; the painting, and the central conception of religious doubt and its fideistic resolution, was inspired by Tennyson's "In Memoriam."

8   John 14:2.

9   A degree of parallelism might be seen between the argument made here and the most plausible assessment to make of the argument for Descartes's *second* major theistic conclusion in the *Meditations:* viz., that God is not a deceiver (and couldn't be, morally, as a perfect being). In fact, Descartes's argument is woefully unsuccessful, as Leibniz seems to have seen (though he puts the matter somewhat opaquely). God, if real, and morally perfect, *might* have all sorts of reasons to be a deceiver, i.e., to allow, or actively cause, human beings to be in deep, profound, and undetectable error about their circumstances, including the reality or nature of physical objects, other selves, or our apprehensions of either. (The philosophy of the monadology might, indeed, be seen as tacitly premised on just such a possibility.) The truth, about these or other matters, might be too painful for us to bear, or greater good be achieved for the world by us (given the natures we have been endowed with) through one sort or other of fundamental error. It isn't obvious that one or other of these isn't the case; and still less obvious that a perfect God would owe it to us to fail to deceive us for any manner of reason that seemed good to him.

10   Both characterizations appear in *Religion Within the Limits of Reason Alone.* (See Wood and Di Giovanni, eds., *Religion and Rational Theology*, pp. 196n and 194 respectively.)

HOMERIC
TOPICS

CHAPTER THIRTEEN

PHILOSOPHICAL REFLECTIONS
ON HOMER

The original version of this paper was delivered at Wilfrid Laurier University, in November 2001, at the request of the late Professor Graham Solomon, then chair of the philosophy department there, and himself a scholar of very wide and well-informed interests.

Philosophers, at least in my experience, have been distinctive often for having major secondary passions in their lives that are at some distance from what they do professionally and academically as philosophers. I am not referring to features of philosophical emotional and domestic lives. In respect of *them*, philosophers are, I suspect, much like other academics broadly speaking.

I refer, rather, to what has struck me as a pattern of passionate interest in and commitment to something other than philosophy, as well as to philosophy, that never rivals philosophy in its claims on ultimate allegiance — indeed subsists always in the shadow of after-hours and leisure time — but that is nonetheless both viscerally involving and far away from what philosophy involves.

Thus, John Pollock, the prominent epistemologist at the University of Arizona, has long also been a serious professional photographer, with a studio, and prizewinning photographs created in it during his leisure time in the summer. Peter Hare, of SUNY Buffalo, is also a serious photographer. Richard Taylor was, I believe, the president of the New York State Beekeepers Association, and very involved in the apiarist's life when not teaching and writing philosophical books and articles. Jan Narveson, of Waterloo, has had a serious, professional-level involvement in classical music production, which has subsisted, separately, in a parallel lesser stream, beside his primary philosophical activities. I know of many other comparable cases. I may be wrong, but I think that—with, undoubtedly, many individual exceptions—no other academic disciplines exhibit this major-minor duality, at least to quite this degree, intensity and conjunct-distance.

I do not know whether this quite qualifies for the pattern I describe, but for many years I have had a very strong, though never philosophy-rivalling, interest in Homer. While involved preoccupation with the poet (or poets) of the *Iliad* and the *Odyssey* may not be quite the same sort of thing, characterologically, as beekeeping or photography or music—it is also, as philosophy is, an academic pursuit, and engaged at least occasionally in a philosophical way—my own central interests in Homer have not in general been particularly philosophical ones. They have been historical (and pre-historical), archaeological, philological, and last but by no means least, literary. My Homeric interests, and activities, have been arcane, language- and passage-specific, pedantic, comparative, and speculative.

They began when I first read the *Iliad,* when I was, I think 13 or 14. It was quickly followed by the *Odyssey*. Both readings were accompanied—indeed, prompted—by Hollywood movies that I had seen and been impressed by: *Helen of Troy,* starring Rossana Podesta in the title role (with a host of illustrious others in cameo roles), and *Ulysses,* with Kirk Douglas as the hero. Neither was great cinema—this may even be too kind a judgment—and, as I soon discovered, neither was a very faithful rendering of Homeric originals. But each had a certain something, imaginatively, and caught—in fact, launched—passionate engagement with things Ilian. So at least it was for me. This passion grew rapidly, and I read voluminously in the secondary literature on the poems, the focus being decidedly on issues connected to history and myth. I was a closet Schliemannite. Heinrich Schliemann, you recall, was the German businessman who had become enthralled with the Homeric stories as a child, then grew up to seek, and find, the Bronze Age sites where the stories' action (some of it "offstage," as it were) had taken place: Mycenae, Tiryns, and Troy itself.

With this passion, it will be appreciated, I went on to study ancient Greek. I came late to it, and made only a certain degree of advance. I had five years of high school Latin, which helped. And there was the accompanying presence of ancient Greek philosophy, which was playing a then minor but not insignificant role in my growing interest and education in philosophy. By the time I got to Pittsburgh as a graduate student in philosophy, my Homer-passion had reached the point that I was enrolled concurrently in a Master's program in Greek, begun after I had arrived at Pittsburgh. I took just two courses in this program, one on the *Odyssey*, the other on Plato's *Symposium*, with a Pittsburgh classicist who was a Pindar specialist. I gave it up because philosophy got too involving, excitingly involving; and because I found I was staying up half the night doing Greek vocabulary lists and wondered if I really wanted to be spending this proportion of my time in this way.

Still, I never abandoned Homer. Indeed, my first academic publication was a short Homer article. It was followed by two others. They are modest, very specific textual pieces. But I remain proud of this little part of my c.v. And I continue to subscribe to *Nestor*, the Mycenaeological bibliographical newsletter, and to read at least some of the ongoing (and gargantuan) secondary Homeric literature, and — of course — to return to the texts of the *Iliad* and the *Odyssey* themselves.

Graham Solomon learned somehow of my Homer interests, and he it was who asked me to give the paper this chapter is based on. Inquiry led to the knowledge that it would be to a chiefly philosophical audience, and that primary interest would be in a *philosopher's* take on Homer or Homeric themes.

I should add to my scattered autobiographical disclosures that I did at length acquire quite considerable interest in ancient Greek philosophy. I have taught the Pre-Socratics several times, and Plato, of course, and Aristotle; also Plotinus. My deepest philosophical interests in antiquity, though, are in the three Hellenistic schools—Stoics, Epicureans, and Skeptics—and especially the Stoics, on whom I have done a considerable amount of work. I have also long been aware that others have had philosophical sorts of things to say about Homer: discussions of his place in the Pre-Socratic background, notably, and (with Homeric references and allusions to cosmic formations and divine governance), as a special case of the speculative cosmological protophilosophy that so many of the world's peoples have produced.

These things noted, I had not myself been primarily, even secondarily, interested in Homer in these ways or for these reasons. I was, rather, probing rival claims to the dating of the Catalogue of Ships part of Book II of the *Iliad,* whether the case for distinct authorship of the two great poems was conclusive, whether the oral epithet-formulae embedded in the poems paralleled traceable evolution of the poetry and the stories in the centuries prior to Homer and going back to a historical Trojan War and earlier, resembling archetypes in Near Eastern mythology and art, which of the Homeric characters should be seen as likely having what sort of origin—purely mythological, coming from cults and rituals that had disappeared, purely fictional, inventions of literary artistry, Homer's or his predecessors, or, in some cases, legendary/historical, going back to once really living individuals. These are, I think, issues that may be no closer to philosophy than are Pollock's photography, Taylor's beekeeping, or Narveson's music.

I am reminded of a claim that Nuel Belnap, who was one of the Pittsburgh philosophers when I was a graduate student and still is, was said to have made. Belnap is said to have claimed—boasted, I guess one may say—that he could be given a group of essays on any subjects (engineering, basket-weaving, Jacobean religious poetry, nuclear physics; whatever), and he would be able to write a preface for a volume publishing them in conjunction that would show their fundamental and unitary interrelatedness. Belnap was being a bit facetious of course; and also, I think, making, or gesturing towards, an interesting philosophical point. All things are interconnected and shed some sort of light on each other, and are parts of larger frames, and stories, cultural and ontological, in which more comprehensive intelligibilities in the nature of things are achievable, and ought sometimes to be aspired to.

This idea has also a certain *existential* significance — and part of the philosophical significance of Homer I will be discussing is of specially existential character. But before entering the plane of specifics, I would say that I think that it is desirable, inwardly, existentially desirable, for each of us as human persons to seek to integrate all of the areas of thought and concern and life that engage and involve us. The unexamined life is not worth living. And neither is the altogether compartmentalized life, even if lots of examination goes on within the separate, hermetically sealed compartments. What matters to me, at all, anywhere in my life, ought — at least in some moments, and they are peculiarly philosophical ones — to be brought into a single, larger integrated frame of mattering and mutual encounter.

Accordingly, I am particularly, deeply grateful to Graham Solomon for causing me to try to integrate, and decompartmentalize, these parts of what has mattered, a lot, for me.

There are two kinds of dimensions to Homer that I want to discuss from what I hope may be seen as a philosophical perspective. One is large and cultural, and the other is more personal, or individual, or existential. I will have a good deal more to say about the second than the first.

The first philosophical dimension to Homer is his importance as, in effect, the Bible — indeed, the King James Bible, so to speak — of the ancient Greeks, including deeply, richly, and thoroughly the philosophical ancient Greeks. Knowledge of the Homeric poems was close, intimate, and all-pervasive in the Greek world, from the sixth century B.C. to after the rise of Christianity to hegemony in the Roman imperial state. Lines, phrasings, and of course all of the individual stories, themes, and characters, even ones we might think of as minor ones, were very familiar and very well-known, and make echoing reverberation throughout the Platonic corpus, in Aristotle, in the fact that the philosophical poems of Parmenides and also of Empedocles were written in dactylic hexameter—i.e., Homeric, epic—verse. You cannot really know any Greek philosophy, it may be said, unless you know, reasonably well, the *Iliad* and the *Odyssey*.

The question of our own relation, culturally, to Homer is itself an interesting and important—and philosophical—one. It is a special case of our cultural relations to the ancient Greeks; and of what what we call Western civilization is, and is for us, whomever "we" are. All claims of global villages, of a ubiquitous multicultural mosaic, and of postmodernist or what I have elsewhere called Californian modalities noted we betray, I believe, only our own lack of self-knowledge if we deny that the West is a diachronic world-historical cultural reality, of depth and grip, and that its substance certainly includes Canada, the U.S., Australia, New Zealand, and all of the Western European national societies, as well, more arguably, as many other parts of the world. I speak not just of demographic majorities, but also of institutions and practices, a *Sittlichkeit* that, while diverse, has deep, broad commonalities extending through time as well as through space. Religious, artistic, and ideological as well as concretely material legacies make up this common substance.

The usual line is that Western civilization begins with the classical Greeks, as Western philosophy does. Usual lines are so typically not for nothing, and so it certainly is in this case. There are direct lines of transmission and development from the ancient Hellenic world to the present, with an uninterrupted possession of literature and projective identifications a succession of peoples and national societies have had, or made, from or in that world. And of course Homer is a central part of that inheritance. There has probably been no single generation since the time of the birth of Aeschylus (said to have been in ca. 525 B.C.) but that dozens, at least, of young male members of that generation living somewhere between Athens and Vancouver have imagined themselves as Achilles, or Hektor, or Odysseus, or all three.

Yet there are also discontinuities to note. The European Dark Ages (especially an approximately 250-year period following the death of Charlemagne, in 814) were very dark indeed, and the Greek inheritance was in any case transmitted, in the West, through a heavily Roman prism. I have sometimes thought that to a certain extent we can deceive ourselves in a projective Hellenism—so to speak—motivated, and animated, by love of the wonderful surviving texts of Grecian antiquity. A number of scholars have argued that the Greeks were more alien and distant from us than we, even a highly educated we, may often suppose. In such skeptical moments, I have sometimes thought that our own Augustans—the writers and thinkers of the Enlightenment—were culturally wiser than us, now, in their Latinized renderings of Greek names: Minerva instead of Athena; Neptune, not Poseidon; Ulysses rather than Odysseus. He is, often, I would say, at least for me, Ulysses (even if the gods do sound now more fittingly rendered—for some unclear reason—in Greek, not Roman, versions).

Returning to antiquity: just why the Homeric poems had *quite* the degree of impact and significance in ancient Greek life that they did is itself a matter of significance, and, in its own way, philosophical significance. The poems are, of course, literary masterpieces. They are cultural foundation texts. Lines in the Catalogue of Ships were used to settle border disputes in classical times.

This does not explain, though, why this would have been the case. The poems themselves recount incidents in the final months of a long war, long before the classical age, and a series of subsequent events in a short period 10 years later, involving the delayed return home of one of the participants in that war. Hardly stuff, one might have thought, to constitute a collective national epic and national charter document. The poems are written, moreover, in an artificial version of Greek, never actually spoken on earth, with fossilized component phrasings and grammatical forms from more than one period in the long ancestry of the Greek language, a great deal of it archaic before the ages of Pericles and Socrates.

One of the secret, or only occasionally disclosed truths about the poems and their appeal, which may contribute more than might have been thought to the question of their prolonged impact in antiquity, and since, is that, as well as being deep and eternal presentations of tragic and other dimensions of the human condition, the *Iliad* and the *Odyssey* are escapist fare for male adolescents.

This will appear more obviously true for the *Odyssey*, which relates the adventures of a man who, as well as being smart and brave and strong, has a series of adventures in exotic locales with monsters, battering storms, and sundry other spills and thrills. Odysseus is, of course, trying to get home to his faithful wife and his faithful son. Obstreperous others get in the way—notably the sea-god Poseidon. It takes him 10 years to get from Troy back to Ithaka. (The two places are, in fact, less than 600 kilometres apart, as the crow flies. Even going round the Peloponnesus, by ship, is a distance of under a thousand kilometres. Even with a few pauses and delays, 10 years is a long time to take to travel a thousand kilometres through the wine-dark sea.) Eight of those 10 years, we duly learn, are spent in idle luxury making love to two beautiful goddesses (Circe and Calypso). We first encounter him in the poem gazing forlornly out to sea, pining away for home and hearth and Penelope, just wishing he could leave Calypso's island, even though he would be made immortal if he stayed with her. We aren't necessarily to suppose that all seven of Odysseus' years with Calypso were quite this miserable.

At any rate, he does duly come back home, to a famous, thrilling revenge on a horde of freeloaders who had been trying to make time with his wife. Again, it is the stuff of high adolescent adventure. Odysseus not only escapes death in numerous near-death episodes, in one of them he even "knows" death—visits the dead, in the underworld—and returns. This last is also a weightier, more philosophical theme, and itself a considerable dimension to the poems and their appeal: they are about death, the ineluctable fact of it, its ungainsayable negativity and bleakness as prospect and as reality.

The *Iliad* is more directly and more obviously about death, since it is about war. It is a war rather pointedly without an obvious justifying cause, and involving much suffering, many deaths, including those of a heroic defender of his homeland—and him a family man and representative of family values—and, in prospect, the death also of his killer, the magnificent barbarian Achilles.

Although the *Odyssey* has probably had greater appeal among readers over the years, I myself, like some others, have always preferred the *Iliad*. It is the deeper work, more tragic, more connected to the large canvas of human reality, even in spite of the great ordinariness of so many of the touches and scenes of the *Odyssey* (and, for that matter, even in spite of the unedifying squalor of so much of the incident, and the characters, in the *Iliad*). Another of Homer's readers who preferred the *Iliad* was Alexander the Great. We see in his enthusiasm for the poem some of the proof of the fact that as well as its depths and heights, the *Iliad*, like the *Odyssey*, is in one of its gleaming facets a piece of adolescent male fantasy.

There have been historians' debates about Alexander, some seeing him as a large-minded cosmopolitan, larger-minded indeed than Aristotle, conceiving and partly implementing a world without distinction between Greek and barbarian, of universal citizenship. The opposing school views Alexander as—not to put too fine a point on it—a psychopathic thug, who just happened concurrently to be a military genius. Robin Lane Fox, in his fine biography of Alexander, catches, I think, a splendid middle ground of portraiture, seeing him as essentially a permanent adolescent, of adolescent enthusiasms and energies and of raw talent, for whom Achilles is prototype and model.[1] (Alexander died, of course, before he was 33.)

Achilles is the original James Dean, the impossibly beautiful, fast, strong young man, who will die young, best of the best, and know imperishable fame. Achilles is a rock star, passionate, intemperate, impulsively cruel, also generous; he is splendid, magnificent, child of a goddess, doomed. He has also a best pal. What friendships are so intense, so feeling, vividly *lived,* as those of young men? So, at least, young men, including young men who read the *Iliad,* suppose.

Another warrior of a later time drawn also to Homer, as Alexander the Great was, was Lawrence of Arabia. At least as strange a man as Achilles, or anyone else in the Homeric poems, Lawrence was a classical scholar and archaeologist in addition to being a desert fighter. In the years following the Great War, he went through a succession of changes of name, and other disguises. In one of these incarnations, as T. E. Shaw, he produced a beautiful translation of the *Odyssey.* Its preface discloses that Lawrence didn't care for Odysseus, that earlier man of destiny. No matter. Homeric verse evoked his own considerable lyric gifts.

I have moved without remarking it to my second philosophical Homeric theme, universalist human typology in the poems. There is, though, an issue or an element in the poems that overlaps the cultural groundingness of Homer in ancient Greek life, including its philosophical parts, and all that issues from it, including ourselves still in the present day, and these several singular human touches in the two works. Homer offers so many things, certainly not only adolescent fantasy.

The cultural *centre of gravity* in the poems, especially the *Iliad* though in fact in both, is curiously, and remarkably, very *communitarian.* The Homeric world is a world of individuals — indeed, of distinctive well-defined individuality of character — but the poems' heroic individualism takes place against a clear background of shared public psycho-socially translucent life. It is a world of family values, but even more of community values — values of the *lawos,* the people or the folk. They are sometimes over-identified, in my view, as aristocratic values.

This world is not, of course, democratic, or egalitarian — anything but that. But it is a web, a network, of interconnection and mutuality, located in the eye and concerns of — so to speak — the common man, in his consciousness of fellow common men. We're all in this together, in this world. One of the standard so-called heroic epithets, the repeated phrasings that accompany the appearance in the verse of the poem's characters, is *poiména lawōn,* "shepherd of the people." Many of the similes in the verse speak to features of common life, and unkingly occupations. But more than this, there is frequent direct appeal to the idea of value in what someone does — in the *Iliad,* of course, this is typically in battlefield situations — when it provides something reliable for "us in general." Great Aias is specially appreciated in this way; so is Odysseus. The psychology of the warrior implied in the lines of the *Iliad* is typically, and frequently, the psychology of the ordinary warrior, the citizen soldier; not, particularly, that of the hero. There are moments of fear as well as of courage, but there is above all a solidaristic conveyance of a centre of life, in a majoritarian set of approvals, disapprovals, aspirations, dreads, and valuation derived from wide community judgment.

There accompanies, indeed, intensifies, this — as in a society, a world where "we" are at home, a world belonging to "us" — a sense of some individuals who are strange, odd, different from us, and opaque in that (some of them, of course, are fellow members of our community). There are indeed characters Homer clearly dislikes. Paris affords a good case of this. Homer plainly disapproves, and represents most of the characters of the *Iliad* as disapproving, of this lover of beauty. Paris is irresponsible and has brought devastation and ruin upon his people by his shameless taking up, and making off, with someone else's wife. Paris is represented above all as flighty, sometimes a brave and resolute fighter, as well as sometimes a skulking coward. Homer *may* have presented a strong warrior Paris some of the time only because his tradition affirmed that Paris killed Achilles, the greatest Acharian warrior, and there needs to have been a doughty warrior to do that.

At any rate, Homer doesn't approve of men who get involved with other men's wives. They upset a social order, and cause wars. Likewise Homer disapproves of other varieties of shamelessness. The Ithakan serving maids who had cavorted with the suitors are all identified by the loyal servants at the end of the *Odyssey*, and summarily hanged. The context makes clear that this was entirely what they deserved, as the poet and his society see things. Throughout the poems, value attaches to those who are hospitable, reliable, consistently honouring of the gods; and disvalue to those who are not.

And then there are the strange ones: notably, Achilles himself. He is not "one of us." He is different; and not just because he is stronger, braver, and handsomer than the rest of us. Out of anger he lets the side down. And when his friend Patroklos is killed, he returns to the war for vengeance, not as a miffed club member rejoining the club. His vengeance is terrible and, apparently, disapproved of by Homer: he abuses Hektor's corpse, and at the funeral of Patroklos he personally slits the throats of 12 Trojan captives to accompany Patroklos in Hades.

Philosophically, Achilles represents a proto-Nietzschean conception of the blond beast beyond good or evil, the magnificent inwardly driven heroic individual. Moderns sometimes have trouble with Achilles because of these qualities — and also with some fellow-feeling for Homer's own societal valuations — together with the fact that, sympathies for Hektor notwithstanding, Achilles really is the hero of the *Iliad*. He truly is "the best." That is the idea, and Homer never really suggests otherwise. Achilles simply marches to higher drummers than the rest, and we, like them, are meant to acknowledge the splendour of his brief presence among us.

And Achilles is not only brutal, strange, and magnificent. Though the greatest warrior in the war, it is Achilles, uniquely, who steps outside the setting of the war launched to restore a wayward wife and, in the process, secure plenty of loot for the restorers' troubles — the poem is quite clear that these are both seen as legitimate war aims — to reflect on the dubiousness of the whole endeavour. "Yet why must the Argives fight with the Trojans?" Achilles asks, rhetorically, of Odysseus and Aias, who have come offering bounteous amends from Agamemon if Achilles will put aside his anger and return to battle; amends Achilles refuses. "And why was it the son of Atreus assembled and led here these people? Was it not for the sake of lovely-haired Helen? Are the sons of Atreus alone among mortal men the ones who love their wives? Since any who is a good man, and careful, loves her who is his own and cares for her...." (*Iliad*, xxiv. 517–551)

Similar notes of reflective detachment appear also in Achilles elsewhere in the poems. Three may specially be noted, two in the *Iliad* and one in the *Odyssey*. The two in the first poem involve Achilles in encounters with a son and his father. Lykaon, yet another of the 50 sons of King Priam of Troy, has the ill luck to run into Achilles in the battle by the river, where he is slaughtering Trojans in revenge for Lykaon's brother Hektor's killing Patroklos. The ensuing scene deserves full presentation. I quote from the Lattimore translation.

And there he came upon a son of Dardanian Priam as he escaped from the river, Lykaon, one whom he himself had taken before and led him unwilling from his father's gardens on a night foray. He with the sharp bronze was cutting young branches from a fig tree, so that they could make him rails for a chariot, when an unlooked-for evil thing came upon him, the brilliant Achilleus, who that time sold him as slave in strong-founded Lemnos carrying him there by ship, and the son of Jason paid for him; from there a guest and friend who paid a great price redeemed him, Eetion of Imbros, and sent him to shining Arisbe; and from there he fled away and came to the house of his father. For eleven days he pleasured his heart with friends and family after he got back from Lemnos, but on the twelfth day once again the god cast him into the hands of Achilleus, who this time was to send him down unwilling on his way to the death god. Now as brilliant swift-footed Achilleus saw him and knew him naked and without helm or shield, and he had no spear left but had thrown all these things on the ground, being weary and sweating with the escape from the river, and his knees were beaten with weariness, disturbed, Achilleus spoke to his own great-hearted spirit: "Can this be? Here is a strange thing that my eyes look on. Now the great-hearted Trojans, even those I have killed already, will stand and rise up again out of the gloom and the darkness as this man has come back and escaped the day without pity though he was sold into sacred Lemnos; but the main of the grey sea could not hold him, though it holds back many who are unwilling. But come now, he must be given a taste of our spearhead so that I may know inside my heart and make certain whether he will come back even from there, or the prospering earth will hold him, she who holds back even the strong man."

So he pondered, waiting, and the other in terror came near him in an agony to catch at his knees, and the wish in his heart was to get away from the evil death and the dark fate. By this brilliant Achilleus held the long spear uplifted above him straining to stab, but he under-ran the stroke and caught him by the knees, bending, and the spear went over his back and stood fast in the ground, for all its desire to tear a man's flesh. Lykaon with one hand had taken him by the knees in supplication and with the other held and would not let go of the edged spear and spoke aloud to him and addressed him in winged words: "Achilleus, I am at your knees. Respect my position, have mercy upon me. I am in the place, illustrious, of a suppliant who must be honoured, for you were the first beside whom I tasted the yield of Demeter on that day you captured me in the strong-laid garden and took me away from my father and those near me, and sold me away into sacred Lemnos, and a hundred oxen I fetched you. My release was ransom three times as great; and this is the twelfth dawn since I came back to Ilion, after much suffering. Now again cursed destiny has put me in your hands; and I think I must be hated by Zeus the father who has given me once more to you, and my mother bore me to a short life, Laothoé, daughter of aged Altes, Altes, lord of the Leleges, whose delight is in battle, and holds headlong Pedasos on the river Satnioeis. His daughter was given to Priam, who had many wives beside her. We are two who were born to her. You will have cut the throats of both, since one you beat down in the forefront of the foot-fighters, Polydoros the godlike, with a cast of the sharp spear. This time the evil shall be mine in this place, since I do not think I shall escape your hands, since divinity drove me against them. Still, put away in your heart this other thing I say to you. Do not kill me. I am not from the same womb as Hektor, he who killed your powerful and kindly companion."

So the glorious son of Priam addressed him, speaking in supplication, but heard in turn the voice without pity: "Poor fool, no longer speak to me of ransom, nor argue it. In the time before Patroklos came to the day of his destiny then it was the way of my heart's choice to be sparing of the Trojans, and many I took alive and disposed of them. Now there is not one who can escape death, if the gods send him against my hands in front of Ilion, not one of all the Trojans and beyond others the children of Priam. So, friend, you die also. Why all this clamour about it? Patroklos also is dead, who was better by far than you are. Do you not see what a man I am, how huge, how splendid and born of a great father, and the mother who bore me immortal? Yet even I have also my death and my strong destiny, and there shall be a dawn or an afternoon or a noontime when some man in the fighting will take the life from me also either with a spearcast or an arrow flown from the bowstring." (*Iliad*, xxi. 34–113)

Achilles then finishes poor Lykaon off. Subsequently, after killing also his brother Hektor, dragging Hektor's body behind his chariot three times round the walls of Troy, Achilles brings the corpse back to the Achaian camp, where it lies unburied. Achilles stages the funeral and funeral games for his beloved Patroklos, where additional Trojans are despatched. Meantime Hektor's loss is mourned mightily in Troy. He was the mainstay of Trojan defence, both militarily and morally. He was a powerful warrior, a symbolically effective battle leader, a figure of virtue—yet also, in the poem, very human. A virtuous husband, and father, esteemed by the gods, as by his parents and worthiest of the 50 sons of Priam. The latter resolves to go to the Achaian camp to beg for the body of Hektor from his killer, Achilles.

What follows is one of the most poignant, and moving, scenes, not only in Homer but in the entirety of the world's literature. It crowns the achievement of the *Iliad* and is its finale. It is better known than the battle scene between Achilles and Lykaon; also lengthier. I refer you to Book XXIV of the *Iliad*, for the full emotional and dramatic richness of this encounter between the aged king and his son's killer. I note here particularly that we again find Achilles rising above the particularities, not only of his ethos and cultural setting, but also of his passions—for he remains still besottedly preoccupied with the lost Patroklos. Achilles feels the humanity of the suppliant Priam, and recognizes both what it has taken to come as Priam has done, and sorrows for him, and for himself in relation to his own aged father, and through both for the lot of the whole of humankind.

> "Ah, unlucky, surely you have had much evil to endure in your spirit. How could you dare to come alone to the ships of the Achaians and before my eyes, when I am one who have killed in such numbers such brave sons of yours? The heart in you is iron. Come, then, and sit down upon this chair, and you and I will even let our sorrows lie still in the heart for all our grieving. There is not any advantage to be won from grim lamentation. Such is the way the gods spun life for unfortunate mortals, that we live in unhappiness, but the gods themselves have no sorrows. There are two urns that stand on the doorsill of Zeus. They are unlike for the gifts they bestow: an urn of evils, an urn of blessings. If Zeus who delights in thunder mingles these and bestows them on man, he shifts, and moves

now in evil, again in good fortune. But when Zeus bestows from the urn of sorrows, he makes a failure of man, and the evil hunger drives him over the shining earth, and he wanders respected neither of gods nor mortals. Such were the shining gifts given by the gods to Peleus from his birth, who outshone all men beside for his riches and pride of possession, and was lord over the Myrmidons. Thereto the gods bestowed an immortal wife on him, who was mortal. But even on him the god piled evil also. There was not any generation of strong sons born to him in his great house but a single all-untimely child he had, and I give him no care as he grows old, since far from the land of my fathers I sit here in Troy, and bring nothing but sorrow to you and your children. And you, old sir, we are told you prospered once; for as much as Lesbos, Makar's hold, confines to the north above it and Phrygia from the north confines, and enormous Hellespont, of these, old sir, you were lord once in your wealth and your children. But now the Uranian gods brought us, an affliction upon you, forever there is fighting about your city, and men killed. But bear up, nor mourn endlessly in your heart, for there is not anything to be gained from grief for your son; you will never bring him back; sooner you must go through yet another sorrow." (*Iliad*, xxiv. 517–551)

The final scene in which Achilles is a kind of existential philosopher unawares is in the *Nekyia* of the *Odyssey*, the episode in Book XI where Odysseus visits the underworld and meets many of the shades of the famous dead, talking to several of them. Among them is the shade of Achilles, who of course has died at Troy not long after the events of the *Iliad*. Odysseus hails Achilles on having achieved such glory, and stature, not only living on the earth but here among the dead. Achilles' brief reply speaks volumes. He says that he would prefer to be alive, living as the most menial servant of an agricultural labourer, than to be lord among the dead. One notes that there is no expression of regret that he had chosen the briefer life of glory over the longer life of obscurity that he could have opted for. There is no regret, just the hungry passion to be alive that is our lot. Interestingly, Achilles then immediately goes on to ask Odysseus about what glory his son Neoptolemos may have achieved back among the living.

The poems' depictions of their female characters, and the whole issue of woman and Homer, is a theme all by itself deserving extended treatment, much of it highly philosophical. The poems are, of course, products and reflections of male-dominated societies. They are testaments of patriarchy. Captured and enslaved women are war loot in both poems, their fate as providers of sexual and domestic service presented and accepted with a casualness that is striking. The war itself, of course, is occasioned by the running off of a royal wife with a foreign prince, her desires or preferences never brought into any reckoning of what either her home or her adoptive people ought to do about it—Helen's being a daughter of Zeus himself mattering little in this regard.

Yet many of the female characters are depicted subtly and sympathetically, Helen herself among them. Helen is soft-hearted, somewhat weak, stunningly beautiful—of course—yet not particularly sexy—that is, sensual or powerful in virtue of sexual magnetism. This fits with Homer's general moralism, his love of family values. Some females in the poems are strong; supremely, of course, some of the female goddesses; outstandingly, Athena, who in both poems is smart, knowing, and *very* physically powerful. Perhaps only Zeus is conceived as stronger. Aphrodite, correlatively, is weak; even a mortal, Diomedes, can take her on and prevail (with the support, to be sure, of Athena). Hera, also, has a real personality: she is an effectively manipulative wife. It is not clear how much, or exactly what, should be made of the divine portraitures in the poems. While the overall tone of the poems is on the whole secular, even humanist, and the gods can appear very flawed, sometimes repugnant or contemptible, many of them had serious, significant, active cults in the wider world of the poems, contemporaneous with their creator or creators. That is, Homer's contemporaries, and presumably

Homer himself, believed in the reality and the causal efficacy of these beings. Some gods, notably Athena and Apollo, *never* lose dignity in the poems, are always formidably powerful, serious agents in human life. This must likely reflect, not Homeric *literary* decisions to represent these gods in these ways, but theological convictions in the poet and his audience.

Goddesses aside, Homeric women are often interesting, three-dimensional, and vivid. This is especially so in the *Odyssey*. Penelope is represented as virtuous and loyal, but also clever, and effective at managing what is after all an extremely difficult situation: 108 unruly and rapacious suitors camped, not at the door, but inside it. She is very much portrayed as having been *worth* returning home to. Helen appears again, when Telemachos, searching for news of his father, journeys to Lakedaimon and the court of Menelaos and his wife. She is gracious, charming, happy to share with her young guest her recollections of strolling round the Trojan Horse with her third husband—Deiphobos, Paris' brother, Paris having been killed—Menelaos, her first and final husband, inside the horse with Telemachos's father, Odysseus. Equally gracious and resourceful, Nausikaa, the Phaiakian princess who finds the waterlogged and battered Odysseus washed up on her country's shores, is especially lifelike and likeable. So much so, that, together with the considerable additional female presence in the *Odyssey*, she led the Victorian writer Samuel Butler to the conclusion that the poem was composed by a woman, Nausikaa a self-portrait of the alleged, Sicilian, author. Robert Graves was to take up and advocate the same idea, writing a novel (called *Homer's Daughter*) to try to give plausible setting and motivation for it. These efforts notwithstanding, it is extremely unlikely that the Butler-Graves thesis is correct—though not impossible: one must recall Sappho. But there is too much else that goes on in the poem that is, or seems to be, overwhelmingly male in orientation.

At any rate, the human depictions in both poems are distinctive, subtle, and sometimes strikingly sophisticated. Probably larger than any other human parameter, in both poems, is the centrality of family ties, especially parent–child ones. The *Iliad* begins, as it ends, with an aged and loving father bringing ransom and entreatment for the release of a much-loved child: Chryses for his daughter Chryseis at the beginning of the poem, and Priam for the body of his dead son Hektor at the end. Many other intergenerational family pairings appear prominently: Odysseus and Telemachos—and at the end of the *Odyssey*, the additional earlier generation as well, with Odysseus' aged father, Laertes; Nestor and his children, including the specially lamented Antilochos, killed at Troy; Achilles in the underworld, wanting above all to learn from Odysseus how things have gone for his son, Neoptolemos. Many, many other cases appear, in brief highlight in the poems, of proud, or grieving, parents, or as with Thetis, divine mother of Achilles, both, the parent–child bond a gleaming rivet in the fabric of the world the poems bring to us.

Other existential notes to remark in Homer, or facets that may be deemed philosophical: a guiding motive for the warrior heroes, something that can prompt the individual and make sense of the world even in the face of inevitable, and rather hopeless, death, is the achievement of glory, *klewe' andrōn*, "fame among men." Such motivation is not unknown even now, and even among philosophers. There is a valuing of intelligence, especially typified in Odysseus. The philosophical substance of this valuation should not be overstated. Odysseus is above all resourceful, not speculative, much more endowed with know-how—knowledge how—rather than knowledge that. He is clever, tough, much-enduring, resilient, a survivor. He does have the philosophical trait of unquenchable curiosity—to explore the homes of monsters, to hear the songs of the Sirens, however maddeningly enthralling they will prove. This note is captured splendidly in Tennyson's poem "Ulysses."

This is again in the more youthful, even if later composed, *Odyssey*. The overwhelmingly dominant note of the *Iliad* is more sombre, frequently almost Schopenhauerian in mood. A heavy weight of the sorrow of things, and the inevitability of the operation of human folly, shadows the poem, and the conception of the world that informs it, and us, as we experience it. That sad note is captured well in Homer's assessment of preoccupations with genealogy, or with pride of ancestry or family. The words are placed in the mouth of Glaukos, who has encountered Diomedes on the field of battle, the Achaian wanting to know who his opponent is, and of what lineage. The reply: "High-hearted son of Tydeus, why ask of my generation? As is the generation of leaves, so is that of humanity. The wind scatters the leaves on the ground, but the live timber burgeons with leaves again in the season of spring, returning. So one generation of men will grow while another dies."

I must conclude. I will give a final Homeric philosophical nod in the direction of Vico. The great Enlightenment Italian philosopher Giambattista Vico, in his *New Science* the founder of philosophical history, gives in his work a particularly central place to Homer, not only in honour but in the conceptual articulation of the human journey and its self-understanding. A chief part of Vico's great work is, in fact, called "The Discovery of the True Homer." Vico was troubled, as Plato had been, by morally challenging elements of plot and character in Homer; but convinced, as Plato was not quite so sure, that there was a central, foundational philosophical message in the poems. Exploring it must be left to be the theme of another occasion.

NOTE

1   See Robin Lane Fox, *Alexander the Great* (E. P. Dutton, 1974).

CHAPTER FOURTEEN

TRADITION, HISTORY, AND

ORAL MEMORY IN EARLY GREEK EPIC

The original version of this paper was presented at a classics conference, on myth and history, at the University of Guelph, in February 2004.

Barry B. Powell, Halls-Bascom Professor of Classics at the University of Wisconsin at Madison, has just brought out a new study of Homer, called *Homer*, in Blackwell's Introductions to the Classical World series.[1] It is, in my view, an exceptionally good, lively introductory study of the poet, or poets, of the *Iliad* and the *Odyssey*. (Powell is of the now-likely-minority view that a single individual composed both). I recommend Powell's book highly, not just for the reader who comes reasonably new to the poems, but for the scholar seeking fresh ideas about the circumstances of creation and transmission of the epics.

Powell has lots of creative ideas, his own and drawn from other scholars; some are surprising, and he makes what I certainly thought an impressive case for most of them. For example, he believes that the poems were composed early, not late, in the eighth century B.C., and that what we have are descendants of texts dictated by the poet in the setting that actually launched the earliest form of the Greek alphabet. That is, Powell thinks that there is a good case for supposing that the alphabet was primarily and originally devised to record the work of a celebrated oral poet. Powell sets this view out in a more detailed and scholarly way in his earlier books *Homer and the Origin of the Greek Alphabet*

(Cambridge, 1991) and *Writing and the Origins of Greek Literature* (Cambridge, 2002); he acknowledges that the idea was mostly anticipated in the work of Wade-Gery, in 1952.[2]

Powell also argues that Homer probably lived, not in Chios or somewhere else nearby on the Ionian coast, but on the island of Euboia, adjacent to the Boiotian mainland. Archeology has evidently shown that Euboia enjoyed a nearly singular degree of material and cultural prosperity in the ninth and eighth centuries—new finds have apparently expanded the picture of that prosperity—and a number of ancillary factors encourage the idea of locating Homer in that (also Ionian-speaking) setting.

I found the idea of a Euboian Homer particularly attractive for a reason that Powell mentions but does not, I think, give quite the weight it deserves. Homer and Hesiod are the earliest known Greek composers of epic. Hesiod is certainly located in Boiotia, as his *Works and Days* autobiographically discloses. What has been puzzling is that Homer and Hesiod compose in essentially the same epic vocabulary and dialect—an artificial dialect, never spoken by living human beings—that has an Ionian core, with fossilized forms from much earlier periods and some presence of Aeolian forms (from a more northerly part of the Aegean world). There are some differences, linguistically, between Homer and Hesiod, some usually held to encourage the idea that Hesiod comes a bit later, but they are relatively minor. Hesiodic poetry also has a special penchant for catalogues—lists of heroes, heroines, places—sometimes very lengthy ones; and these also have a striking occasional presence in Homer, most obviously in the *Iliad*'s Catalogue of Ships and Trojan Catalogue, but elsewhere as well.

Again then, we seem strongly encouraged to see Homer and Hesiod as distinct authors in a single larger poetic tradition, in both cases obviously with lengthy antecedence. But how could this be if Homer is over the Aegean in Chios or Smyrna, and Hesiod is in the interior of Boiotia; and both areas had just emerged from a Dark Age shortly before they composed? A Euboian Homer will place them as reasonably near neighbors, and an early Ionian epic developing as a single thing from long earlier, evidently originally Mycenaean, beginnings, will make sense.[3]

Anyway, much as I have learned from, and admire and recommend, Powell's book, my praise comes to qualification; which will in turn introduce my central topic in this chapter. Among several themes that the study of Homer engages, Powell addresses the issue of "Homer and history." Powell affirms the view, as have Sir Moses Finley, G. S. Kirk, and others before him, that "the world" of the Homeric poems is largely the world of the poet's own day; with even the conscious archaizing that the poems involve mostly extending only somewhat earlier in time. This stance is intended, more or less provocatively, to contrast with views that other, mostly earlier scholars have taken — or are alleged to have taken — according to which the *Iliad* and the *Odyssey* derive from and reflect, even if opaquely and fragmentarily, realities of the 13th-century B.C. Bronze Age.

What I want primarily to explore on the present occasion is what I think are unexamined complexities in the very idea of a, or the relationship between, legendary traditional creative material — of which the *Iliad* and the *Odyssey* are very prominent, but of course by no means the only, instances — and historical realities on which they may be based. I will first point out a fundamental *ambiguity* in the very idea of a relationship between Homer — or the *Nibelungenlied*, the *Song of Roland*, or other legendary /traditional literature — and history. If I am right, quite distinct questions may be posed, as well as distinct ideas of what will count for reaching an affirmative and for reaching a negative response to such questions, in asking about legendary/ traditional literature and history. Someone with one conception in view would seek satisfaction with one sort of answer — if it could be had — and someone with the other would seek it with something quite different.

Suppose one is examining a piece of traditional or legendary literature or other material — or indeed, so far as that goes, a work purporting to be a historical novel or play, or a poem of a literate culture that appears to refer to events anterior to its composition. With reference to a period or periods putatively appearing as the material's setting or locale, a time and a place and cultural environment, with a group of named individuals said or implied to be carrying out actions in real places, one might ask how accurately the time, place, cultural environment, practices, and institutions are. This is Powell's question, as it was Finley's and others'. This question asks how accurately the "world" putatively represented is rendered. Did the poet, storyteller, or creative artist get the mode of organizing society right, the religious and economic arrangements and institutions, methods of warfare, seafaring, styles of costume, burial and other mortuary practices? Or to what degree did they, if — as presumably almost always will be the case — only partial accuracy, at best, is achieved?

In fact, though, there is a quite different "Homer and history" sort of question that can be asked, and that I think is the one motivating more "Homer and history" inquirers than those with the anthropological and social-historical interests of the first constituency. This sort of question is one focused almost entirely on proper names and on individuals and places they purport to refer to in the work in question, and — though, I will argue, to a slightly reduced degree — events and stories bearers of those proper names are said or implied to have enacted or participated in the work. This is the child's question, was there a real King Arthur? An actual Agamemnon? A genuine Trojan War? And just as some children who loved and filled their imaginations with dinosaurs grow up to become adult investigators of dinosaurs, some — Schliemann might readily be taken to be the model or archetypal icon for the phenomenon — who asked at a parental knee whether Troy really fell or Robin Hood actually slew the king's deer in Sherwood Forest grow up to become scholars who want to try to see what light serious scholarly investigation might shed on these issues.

And — it is importantly to be noted — if you want to know whether there was a real Agamemnon who commanded a bunch of Achaian warriors who sailed across the Aegean, lay siege to

Troy and conquered it, you don't necessarily seek to know, or attach primary care to whether, the particular pieces of literature that inspired you to become interested in such questions give even a reasonably or approximately good rendering of how Agamemnon might have dressed, or what the warp and woof of life in general in his cultural setting may have been. You *may* also want to know such things as these. Perhaps the really dedicated and hard-core Schliemannite will hope that, or be interested whether, the *Iliad* and the *Odyssey* are as near to being cultural and historical simulacra of a Bronze Age world as possible. But it is important to discern that we encounter here conceptually distinct kinds of questions.

Interestingly, *philosophy* may help to bring out the contrast I am drawing, and may help to give it conceptual precision. I offer here a bit of interdisciplinarity, whose utility may be of real, if modest, value.

In the philosophy of language there was developed, and is still widely accepted, a theory called the causal theory of proper names. It seeks to identify the semantics, and what in an importantly qualified way may be called the *meaning*, of a proper name. The theory developed out of problems and dissatisfactions with other, earlier theories of the meanings or semantic roles of proper names. According to some of the latter theories, the meaning of a proper name should be thought of as some sort of concept that goes with the name.

Take the name *Aristotle*, for example. Concepts like *the teacher of Alexander the Great*, *the founder of the Lyceum*, *Plato's most important student*, and others, *go with*—certainly are true of—Aristotle, and some argued that some such concept or other, or possibly a disjunction of them, or maybe a cluster of them with only a majority of the members of the cluster being required, could capture and be the meaning of the name *Aristotle*.

But astute philosophers found serious, ultimately crippling, objections to any idea along these lines. First of all, a proper name *as such* doesn't really seem to have a connotative force or internal content. (The name may, of course, have etymological meaning, but that is different and irrelevant. People don't, for example, name a son *Roy* because they believe that their offspring is or will become a king. *Roy* will truly be the boy's name even if he never becomes royal.) Still more critically, it seems clear, on reflection, that the bearer of a proper name could have had a different history than the individual concerned actually has, and still have been that individual. If Aristotle, for example, had been kidnapped by passing extraterrestrials at the age of seven and lived to become the manager of a fuel-supply shop on a distant planet, and not a philosopher or writer or teacher, it would still have been him, Aristotle, to whom these things would have happened.

Anyway, the causal theory of names — developed, by the way, by a philosopher named Saul Kripke — says that we should think of a proper name — a genuine one, at least — as launched with a kind of baptism or dubbing. A person, animal, object, place, etc., is *dubbed*, *named*, such and such ("Aristotle," maybe). Subsequent uses of that name, the theory goes, will continue to *refer* to the individual in question so long as there is a *causal sequence* that proceeds from that first dubbing, with subsequent uses being picked up and prompted from earlier ones, uninterruptedly. You can see how, according to this theory, it will be possible to refer to someone (or some thing) after it has died (or gone out of existence). I can refer, now, to Napoleon, and it will *be* a once-real Napoleon I am referring to, by virtue of my having picked up the name from books, lectures, etc., which in turn got the name from earlier books and occasions, going back eventually to people who were using the name to refer to a flesh-and-blood Napoleon who may have been standing before them or riding by on a horse (and ultimately, of course, to an occasion of literal baptism, when his parents gave him the name in his infancy, in a properly public setting). Crucially, at every stage of the sequence, the name is used with the intention that it refer to the same individual as one supposes is being referred to by the person, book, etc., from whom the name was picked up — whoever the individual being referred to may have been — and where someone might start to get dim, or inaccurate, about some of the details, the context or stories that *go with* the name (or, of course, they might not).

You may note a couple of things about this theory. One is that it doesn't tell you what to say or think about proper names—there at least apparently are many such—that don't, and never did, refer to actual, real individuals: Persephone, Superman, Sherlock Holmes, etc. One will have to have a different or further theory to cover those sorts of cases (and philosophers do offer theories to seek to do this). More positively, the causal theory won't require that for a proper name successfully to be transmitted over time, maybe over many centuries, and possibly long after its original bearer has ceased living, the name need be *spelled* or *pronounced* just as it originally was (if indeed there was an original spelling—illiterate people of course use proper names, just as literate people do).

Also, the same name is of course often given to distinct individuals. The second husband of Jacqueline Onassis, for example, was also named Aristotle. *His* proper name will go back to a dubbing or baptism from his own family, and not earlier. So the idea will be that with a particular proper name in which we may be interested, a causal chain of reference may be conceived of, for *that* name, going back to whatever initial baptism or dubbing *it* may have had. And, of course, with *some* names, at least, with lengthy causal referring chains, there could sometimes be different sorts of mix-up or complexity.

For example—and this will start to lead us back from semantics and the philosophy of language to our central themes—there are references in different versions of the *Nibelungenlied* to a character named Dietrich of Bern. There seems some good reason to believe that *two* individuals in the historic past have been combined in the background of the development of this story: one of them Theodoric I (d. 451), king of the Visigoths, who was killed in the battle of Troyes against Attila the Hun, and the other Theodoric the Great (455–526), king of the Ostrogoths and founder of the Ostrogothic monarchy. Although the former fits the chronology of the *Nibelungenlied* story better and actually fought against Attila (the *Etzel* of that story), it is the latter who seems more fundamentally or centrally the Theodoric, or Dietrich, of the story's references. One might see the blending, or confusion, as easy and natural to occur, since the two original individuals were both actually named Theodoric, and were both prominent Germanic kings operating in the same *approximate* areas and at reasonably approximately related times—even if Theodoric the Great was only *born* four years after Theodoric the Visigoth had died. At any rate, one can see here both how one might think of *applying* the causal theory of proper names to the name *Dietrich* as it shows up in the 13th century textual retellings of the tale of the *Nibelungenlied* (and where, it is to be noted, Dietrich is only a marginal figure, not one of the major heroes, heroines, or villains of the story); and also how, in particular cases, and ways, applying it might involve complication.

Returning to our earlier theme, I think that the sort of thing that the earnest inquirer wants answers to, when he or she asks, was there a real Agamemnon? Odysseus? Helen of Troy? Trojan War? is, even if it is not consciously (or unconsciously) conceived with reference to Kripke's theory, something like: when *I* read my texts of the *Iliad* and the *Odyssey*, in English translation or in Greek, and I encounter the names *Agamemnon, Odysseus*, etc., is there an uninterrupted causal ancestry of my using those names that culminates in once living people and events that will have been actually observed and referred to by earlier versions or forms of those names, leading to the formation of stories in which those individuals and events were intended to be referred to, and that were then passed on, transmitted, coming eventually to my and others' attention?

If this is right, you can see, I think, how different, and from *this* point of view how secondary, the matter of degrees of verisimilitude in cultural fit—how authentic the "world" of the poems—is. We can also see that we might conceivably be able to say: Yes, there was a real Agamemnon, or Herakles, or Helen— or one or more of these individuals might have been real—even if it turned out that the real one was hugely different in all sorts of ways from the way the character is represented in early Greek epic. Of course, it might be additionally interesting, icing on the cake, so to speak, if it were to turn out that not only do references to Aias Telamonios—Ajax of Salamis—go back to a real Ajax, but that the individual in question used a tower shield (as Ajax is several times said to have done in the *Iliad*). (And we do in fact know, from the archaeological record, that some Achaian warriors of the Bronze Age, but not, apparently, later, did use tower shields in battle.)

A particularly interesting, important, and reasonably certain case of the direct causal sequence proper name phenomenon is provided by the hero of ancient Mesopotamian saga, *The Epic of Gilgamesh*. Gilgamesh was, evidently, a real king of Uruk (or Erech) in the 27th century B.C. or thereabouts, and the epic began its long journey in story a few centuries later, intended from that start to refer to the historical king.[4] The example is of strong relevance to my purposes, because there is a serious possibility—without more intermediary data it can be only that—that the central stories of *both* the *Iliad* and the *Odyssey* are story-descendants, much transmogrified over many centuries and cultural transference, of *The Epic of Gilgamesh* itself. It is even possible that the name *Achilles* is actually a Hellenic derivative, across those centuries and that transference, of the name *Gilgamesh*; but this must be viewed only as a very speculative conjectural possibility.

The point and significance of the causal theory of proper names and its relevance for the divergent ways of thinking about "Homer and history" questions may be seen more fully, and reinforced, by looking at another case. Finding a historical King Arthur has proved rather elusive. One expedient some investigators have come to is to look for archaeological and documentary evidence of an impressive warrior king at approximately the right time and place—the first third of the sixth century, in the Celtic west of Britain—and deciding that if such an individual can be found (and one such candidate has been), that that must have been the real king Arthur, the original for the later tales—even if none of the archaeological or documentary evidence indicates that that individual was *called*

Arthur. These investigators, rather casually, just conclude that this individual (whose real name is known) is the best candidate for the hero, so no doubt *was* called Arthur, the name perhaps having been a *title* or a *nickname*. But this gets things all wrong methodologically. The name is everything. These investigators may have something like an "Arthurian" *world*, in Powell's sense, but they have woefully inadequate evidence that they have Arthur. Methodologically, we need to get from here to there, temporally speaking. Here is present (shared) apparent reference to a named individual, and success would be, if obtainable, showing that apparent reference is real reference, because there is a chain of readings and sayings that go back uninterruptedly to *there* — i.e., to definite reference to a real individual, where each link in the chain involves meaning to refer to the same individual referred to in the context from which one has acquired the name. Finding a material simulacrum, of one degree or other, without a plausible naming chain is irrelevant to *that*.

All of the foregoing affirmed, it is conceivable that Powell, Finley, and others of their views and interests would be impressed, at best only to a point. Even if they came to appreciate the distinction I have drawn, acknowledged the legitimacy of the "Homer and history" question other than *their* "Homer and history" question, they might not unreasonably say that it is possible, even likely, that several of the Homeric characters do go back to once-real people, and even reasonable to believe that some at least of them were involved in or connected with real events — battles and wars and their causes and consequences — at Troy and elsewhere in the Aegean world, in the 13th century B.C. Only — Powell et al. would continue — without contemporaneous Bronze Age texts of some sort, it is not knowable which of the characters may have been real, nor what the events those who were were participant in; and beyond the general fact of some historicity of root one has only idle speculation. We *have* contemporaneous fifth and sixth century texts attesting to the reality of the two Theodorics I referred to earlier; just as we have relevantly chronologically proximate Mesopotamian king lists that attest to the reality of Gilgamesh. What of any of the Homeric characters?

We do enter more speculative territory from this point, but a number of scholars have acknowledged — affirmed, anyway — for some time that surviving Hittite texts do name individuals who *may* be Homeric originals, or figures of early Greek legendary tradition. The Hittite references to a significant country they call Ahhiyawa are now more or less universally agreed to be references to an Achaian kingdom — i.e., *Ahhiyawa* is a Hittite rendering of (Mycenaean) Greek *Achaiwa*. Difference of view continues over whether the referent, more precisely, is a major Achaian state across the Aegean, presumably with Mykenai as its capital, or an Achaian kingdom centred on Rhodes and/or adjacent territory on the Anatolian mainland. The stature Ahhiyawa is accorded by the Hittites, together with the archaeological record, seem to me as well as many others to favour an Argive Achaia — that is, a great kingdom centred at Mykenai. But the case is not yet conclusive, if it ever will be.

Also now more or less universally agreed is that a place the Hittites called Wilusa is the same as the original for Homeric Wilios (Ilios in the later dialectical form, which drops the "w" sound).

Both facts together make it of special interest to see what individuals are represented in the Hittite tablets as having been from these two places. The records concerned, and the individuals they name, have, it hardly needs saying, been subjected to very extensive detailed scholarly scrutiny. There are several such individuals, with names able to be interpreted as Greek (or as plausible names of Greeks, whether or not they have Greek etymologies) in varying degrees. One name *could* represent Greek Etewoklewes, the original form of the classical Eteokles; another *might* be Atresios, which in turn can be argued to be an early patronymic form for Atreios, i.e., son of Atreus — a most interesting possibility of course.[5] But these are speculations, and rather tenuous ones.

The names in the Hittite records that are most promising are, curiously, Trojan ones — or apparently Trojan ones. There is, in fact, rather good reason to believe that a proper name causal chain, of the kind referred to earlier, goes back from the Homeric and other ancient references to Alexandros of Wilios to a king Alaksandus of Wilusa in the Hittite tablets. Alexandros, it will be recalled, is the more common Homeric name for *Paris*, the original cause of the Trojan War by virtue of his fatal lust for Helen, wife of Menelaos of Sparta. There has never been a plausible explanation for why Paris has two names (a few other characters in mythology also do). It has seemed most reasonable to modern scholarship that there were once two characters, in distinct but probably similar or overlapping stories, Paris and Alexandros, who became combined or merged in the period prior to Homer. At any rate, although we now most usually call him Paris, in Homer (and elsewhere in ancient literature) he is far more commonly called Alexandros.

One of the Great Kings of Hatti — the land of the Hittites — in its most glorious period, was king Muwatallis II. (The name is also rendered as Muwat[t]alli.) He evidently reigned from 1295 to 1271 B.C. (following the currently accepted Egyptian chronology). Muwatallis was the Hittite king who fought the famous, and famously inconclusive, battle of Kadesh in 1274 B.C. against the Egyptian Pharaoh Rameses II and his armies. Among the surviving Hittite tablets is one that records a treaty between Muwatallis and King Alaksandus of Wilusa, in which the latter is declared the vassal of the former. The preamble of the treaty asserts that Alaksandus had been adopted as heir by the previous king of Wilusa, a certain Kukunnis, at the insistence, it seems, of the Hittite king.

Now, the name Alexandros is a fairly straightforward Greek name — meaning "repeller of men" — but it is unclear, and debated, whether "Alaksandus" is a Hittite rendering of that name, or whether an originally Asian non-Greek name has been Hellenized in the pre-Homeric period; the former seems the more probable, though the matter remains uncertain. At any rate, there is independent strong indication that Wilusa is located in the vicinity of the Troad, so it seems irresistible—and hardly anyone now resists—that it is Wilios. So we do have here a king Alexandros of Wilios, living sometime in the first quarter of the 13th century B.C. That is rather earlier than the usually accepted date of the Trojan War, which gets placed, standardly, in the 1250–1190 B.C. range.

Some have argued, therefore, that we might think of the Alaksandus of the Muwattilis treaty as a grandfather, or other royal relative, of the individual who is represented in classical epic as awarding a famous apple to Aphrodite and running off with Helen to Troy. Royal names tend to get reused in their bearers' families. However, I would argue that this over-harmonizes the actual realities of the formation of heroic saga, which, we know well from other cases, easily draws the famous from the vicinities, chronological and geographical, of its stories into the expanding vortex of the story, as new names and characters and episodes are needed or desired. The greater likelihood is that Alexandros-Paris *is* Alaksandus himself.

Further evidence for this is the treaty's detail about Alaksandus's unrelated predecessor as king of Wilusa, Kukunnis. Most interestingly, we find in several post-Homeric accounts of the Trojan War the story of a certain *Kyknos*, who is said to have been a son of the god Poseidon and a king in the Troad. A Potiphar's wife story is told about Kyknos and his son, leading to the latter's expulsion with his sister. Subsequently Kyknos is killed by Achilles, at or soon after the Achaian landing at Troy. The story is related in the epic cycle's *Cypria*, which there is good independent reason to regard as preserving a number of old extra-Homeric details of antique heroic saga. The *name* Kyknos means *swan* in Greek. That Zeus transforms himself into a swan to father Helen might invite speculations of the wildest sort. These I won't pursue. In this particular case it seems more plausible to think that *Kyknos* is a Greek version of an originally non-Greek name.

At any rate, I take the facts that Kukunnis and Alaksandus are, in the real world, successive kings of Wilios in the Troad, and Kyknos and Alexandros are associated together in the Trojan War story, a king and the son of a king in the Troad, as evidence that the latter is the case because the former was remembered to be the case at some early stage when a protoform of our Trojan War story was being assembled. It would be perfectly reasonable that Kyknos and Alexandros are brought into the story just because they were remembered as Trojan kings, and not because a historical Trojan War happened in their day.

On the other hand, there have been considerable shifts in the conclusions that archaeology has endorsed or suggested with regard to a siege and destruction of Troy at the hands of Achaian Greeks. According to the *Iliad* itself, Troy falls twice: once in the previous generation, in an assault led by Herakles, with the father of the great Ajax and his brother Teukros, Telamon, as his associate; and then in the war in which the Achaians are led by Agamemnon. Troy VI used to be taken to be the Troy that Herakles conquers, and its feebler successor, Troy VIIa, the one felled by Agamemnon. But Troy VI apparently was destroyed by an earthquake, and Troy VIIa, it now seems, was conquered and burned at the same time as, or even after, the destruction of Mykenai on the Greek mainland.

Much is in confusion in these territories. We do need, it seems, a genuine folk memory of an Achaian seige and conquest of Troy, at some time in a remembered heroic past, ultimately fossilized forever in Homer. How big the expedition was, just what part or parts of the Achaian world it came from, who were its leaders, and what the circumstances of military success were, are all contestable and contested. For my part, I wonder whether a later, perhaps ignoble and more modest, final write-off of Troy — Troy VIIa — in circumstances in which some Greeks may have been involved, has been conflated with an earlier struggle, in the days of kings Muwatallis and Alaksandus, and in which the king of Ahhiyawa — Achaiwa — was involved and present in person. This would be a battle at or with Troy VI. (Herakles, if he came at all, would need to be placed still earlier.)

The preceding ruminations may seem much more speculative and appropriately tenuous than a case ought to be. The case is, in fact still better, that king Alaksandus of Wilusa is prince Alexandros of Wilios, in the sort of causal sequence way I am encouraging and applying. A most remarkable—I will argue, quite astonishing—passage in a text from the sixth century A.D. provides stronger support. It will also have implications for the whole issue of traditional legendary material, and history.

Stephanus of Byzantium was a geographical writer who lived and wrote, apparently, during the reign of Justinian I (527–565 A.D.). Stephanus composed a geographical dictionary called *Ethnika*. We don't have the original, only a lengthy epitome. *Ethnika* consists of a long series of place names, with comments by Stephanus on their locations and occasionally on their history; he provides also lists of various sorts. One of the places enumerated is a town called Samylia, in Caria—i.e., on the southwest Anatolian coast. (In the *Iliad*'s Trojan Catalogue, the Carians are Trojan allies, and the city of Miletus—later a leading centre of Ionian culture—is theirs.)

What Stephanus tells us about Samylia is that in this Carian town an individual named Motylos "received Helen and Paris." The implication for a classical audience or readership will be that Samylia will have been a port of call for Paris and his stolen bride on their voyage from Sparta to Troy. (The lovers, as Homer tells us, had taken a very circuitous route back, with stops in Sidon, in Phoenicia, as well as other places.)

Now: the name Motylos is otherwise unknown in the Greek legendary canon. There are not even minor references or allusions to any such person as this in any other surviving texts. And Motylos, as a number of scholars acquainted with the Hittite records have pointed out, is a reasonable Greek rendering of the name of the Hittite king Muwatallis. Several of these scholars have gone on to connect this interaction, between Motylos and Alexandros, with the treaty of vassalage between Alaksandus and Muwatallis. Some, indeed, have seen an oblique record, echo, or reference to the treaty itself in the datum Stephanus presents. (The distinguished Oxford classicist Martin West is one such scholar.)

But how could such a thing as this even be *possible*? The historical Alaksandus and Muwatallis lived, and compacted their treaty, some time around 1280 B.C. The text in which Stephanus records his brief remark was written, evidently, some time around 530 A.D. A span of about 1,800 years separates them. How *could* a datum like this — a treaty between a great king and a relatively minor local king — be transmitted over that length of time?

Part of an answer, which awakens at least a possibility, is afforded by the fact that Stephanus Byzantius is fairly certainly drawing on earlier geographical treatises, some of them sources — or sources whose sources — are a good thousand years earlier. One of the classes of ancient textual material of which only fragments and references survive are the so-called *periploi*, accounts of coastal navigation, general or specific and practical, intended for navigators or travellers. This literature began, it seems, in the sixth century B.C. and is known sometimes to have included notes and comments about towns and peoples along the coasts described. Contemporaneous with the first periploi, and similar in type though more ambitious, was the *Periegesis* or *Periodos Ges* of Hecataeus, regarded as the first geographer, and whose lost treatise may have included an account of Samylia. It is highly likely that Stephanus will have picked up his datum, about Paris, Helen, and Motylos in the Carian town of Samylia, from a *periplos* or from Hecataeus, very reasonably permitting imagining a written text with the item in a forerunner periplos or comparable document of the mid-sixth century B.C.

Well and good, but that still leaves 700 years or thereabouts between a periplos text and the historical enactment of a treaty of vassalage. How might we even *imagine* the latter coming to the former?

Several classical scholars have discussed and been attracted to the idea that the Stephanus reference goes back — somehow — to Alexandros of Wilios and Muwatallis the Hittite king. Almost nothing I have said so far is novel, or my own bold innovation or speculation. I want now to propose, very tentatively, a skeletal suggestion of a *context* in which the earlier stretch of this chronological journey might have been traversed.

A key part of the suggestions I will make draws on the fact that it is in *Caria* that Stephanus locates the encounter between Paris and Motylos. Caria is a most interesting region of the Anatolian coast and indeed the Aegean world. One needs to distinguish the Carian *people* and the region they historically occupied. The classical authors who discuss both (Herodotus, Thucydides, Strabo, and others) say that the Carian people were a non-Greek-speaking group who had originally lived in the Aegean islands, but were displaced by the Minoans to the Asiatic coasts; including the Troad. The Carians have the special distinction of being evidently the first population group whom the Greeks dubbed *barbarians*; although this claim may just reflect the fact that in the *Iliad*'s Trojan Catalogue the Carians, who provide one of the contingents allied with Troy, are called speakers of an alien tongue. (One might have thought that this would characterize many non-Achaian peoples in Homer, but the Carians are singled out in this way — even the Cyclops in the *Odyssey* speak Greek.)

At any rate, the Carians survived into historic times, and did speak a non-Greek language, leaving a small number of inscriptions in it that have never been deciphered. The Carians were dispossessed from much of Caria by the arrival of the Ionians, from Attica, in the 11th century B.C., several Carian settlements, Miletus among them — a Carian place, in the Trojan Catalogue — becoming major Ionian cities. Southern Caria was, in turn, occupied by Dorian expansionists.

Apparently the Carians themselves in historical times claimed that they had always lived in Caria; they denied Greek claims that they were newcomers in the Minoan period.

At any rate, in classical times the Carians seem mostly or entirely to be found in Caria, which had become as well the domicile of Ionian Greeks; there were also settlements of Dorian Greeks in southern Caria, one of these being Halicarnassus, where Herodotus was from. (Herodotus himself was evidently partly of Carian extraction.) The Ionians were dominant; yet Carians retained some considerable autonomy.

It is with this background that we may take up an interesting section of Herodotus's account of Egypt. He tells us (2.152–154) that Psammetichus, who was king of Egypt 663–609 B.C., came to power partly with the aid of a combined force of Carians and Ionians. They — the Carians and Ionians — had been engaged in piracy together in the eastern Mediterranean, and had come ashore in Egypt, clad in bronze armour, and were ravaging the Egyptian coast. Psammetichus, not yet king but conspiring to achieve the crown, managed to treat with the Carians and Ionians and enlist them on his side, promising them great reward when success came. This duly occurred, and Psammetichus was as good as his word.

> To the Ionians and the Carians, who had taken his side, Psammetichus gave, to dwell in, lands that lie opposite to one another; their name is The Camps, and the Nile runs between the two peoples. These places he gave them and awarded them everything he had promised as well. Furthermore, he turned over to them Egyptian children, to learn the Greek language. It is from these who learned the language that the present interpreters in Egypt come. The Ionians and Carians lived long in these places, which lie near the sea, a little below the city of Bubastis on what is called the Pelusian mouth of the Nile. Afterwards these Greeks were moved away by King Amasis and resettled in Memphis, as his personal guard against the Egyptians. It was because these men were settled in Egypt, and we Greeks were able to have contact with them, that we have such exact knowledge of all that happened in Egypt, beginning from the time of King Psammetichus. For these were the first people of foreign speech to be settled in Egypt (Herodotus, 2.154; Grene translation).

From this account we can infer that Carians and Ionian Greeks, remaining distinct peoples, had extensive cultural interchange, sufficient to form piratical forces together; that the Greeks were the more culturally dominant—for the Egyptians learn Greek from them, not Carian; and that this twin settlement will have been in place in the Nile Delta from about 660 B.C. We reasonably conjecture, I suggest, that it is within this matrix of Helleno-Carian presence in Egypt and the special role that presence played as translators and interpreters for the Egyptians with visitors, especially Hellenic ones, that we should understand the source, grounding, and much of the content of what Egyptians told Herodotus of earlier Greek presence in Egypt, notably including Paris, Helen, and Menelaos's alleged activities in the country during the reign of a king said to be "a man of Memphis whose name, in Greek, was Proteus" (Herodotus, 2.112).

Herodotus tells us that his principal sources in Egypt are priests of Hephaistos in Memphis. They tell him all manner of things about Egyptian and Greek antiquity, among these items, most interestingly, the supposed truth (or a good part of the truth) about the Trojan War. Notably, that Paris and Helen had come to Egypt in their lengthy and roundabout voyage from Sparta to Troy, and that Paris's crewmen had brought action against him, which led to a tribunal before the Egyptian king; the truth coming out, Pharaoh detained Helen until her husband Menelaos came for her. The war at Troy happened anyway, the Achaians not believing that Helen wasn't there. Discovering the truth amid the smouldering ruins of the city, Menelaos duly proceeds to Egypt to fetch Helen. This is, of course, a humanized or secularized version of the well-known Trojan War variant first set out, so far as we know, in the *Palinode* of Stesichorus, the sixth century B.C. Sicilian poet.

What is this tale doing in Egypt, and how and from whom will Herodotus have heard it there? Although he tells us that his informants are priests of Hephaistos, it will be clear that translators will have been involved. It seems reasonable to speculate that the necessary interlocutors will have been Ionians/Carians of the translation-service class, and reasonable also to believe that they may—will—have played a more active interpretive role in rendering Egyptian information to Herodotus than his text would suggest. Egyptians, even of hieratic and annalist class, cannot really have known, unaided, about Menelaos, Paris, Helen, and the Trojan War. But the same impulse that encouraged straightforward Herodotean identifications of Egyptian and Greek gods — which may have come from the same Carian source — may well have caused Carian or Helleno-Carian elements, perhaps after having been domiciled in Egypt some reasonably good while, to have chosen to interpret *something* or other they found or heard in Egyptian accounts as fitting or being graftable onto their own Carian ("Helleno-Carian") records or traditions of the Trojan War story.

Now, Herodotus visited Egypt sometime, it seems, in the middle of the fifth century B.C. The Hellenic world was by then one thoroughly drenched in Homer. The indications are nonetheless, I want to suggest, that a completely Homer-independent account or rendering of "matters Ilian" (and matters "Achaian-and-Ilian") had developed, probably considerably earlier than Homer, in Caria. I speculate that this is the source of many of the features of the Troy-tale as we find it in what survives as the content of the Epic Cycle's *Cypria* — including the story of the "other" Troy, Telephos's Teuthrania, where the Achaians land by mistake before managing to get to Hellespontine Troy eight years later.[6]

I want to conclude by suggesting the following ideas (some of which I have offered, I will be the first to affirm, only scant supportive justification): (1) that there was a totally separate-from-Homer and more nearly contemporaneous account of a Trojan War or Wars; (2) that it may have had some kind of *written* expression in Caria by (say) the 11th century B.C., for it is difficult to see how, otherwise, memory even of something resembling a treaty of vassalage can have survived — people don't sit around campfires, or in noble halls, telling tales of treaties, not even with the aid of oral formulaic poetry; (3) that a filtered version of bits of it, much of its rather garbled — as the most genuinely nearly historical accounts should actually be *expected* to be (the smooth air of seamless verisimilitude is, rather, what one should expect to be fictional) — was encountered by Dorian and Ionian Greeks when they settled in Caria, and fashioned into a "Helleno-Carian" version of a Troy tale, which was then brought by Greeks and Carians to Egypt, Cyprus — where the *Cypria* may have been composed — and, possibly, Sicily — where Stesichorus of Himera encountered it. In the meantime, the spread of Homer was rapid and nearly overwhelming, sufficiently so that if the postulated Helleno-Carian "version" of the Troy tale had ever constituted or been expressed in some single *epic* — and it need not ever have done so — it had disappeared from even local consciousness in (geographical) Caria long before the time of Herodotus. Prior to his period, an official "canonical" version will have sought to unite or harmonize the two versions; where this was impossible, the two — Homer and the extra-Homeric (in some particulars anti-Homeric) but old version, bits of it preserved in Stesichorus and poetry of the Epic Cycle — subsisted alongside each other on into the Classical age as alternatives to be drawn upon as a dramatist, poet, chronicler, or reader may have preferred.

One of the biggest ironies in this skeletal picture, if it has any substance, is that not only could the most authentically "oldest" version of the Troy tale be from sources we think of as post-Homeric, they would also, if Powell's case for a Euboian Homer is accepted, be found in approximately the same area as we had earlier located Homer, in the middle of the western coast of Anatolia: i.e., Caria.

NOTES

1 Barry B. Powell, *Homer* (Blackwell, 2004).
2 H. T. Wade-Gery, *The Poet of the Iliad* (Cambridge, 1952).
3 I will note that while Powell's case for a Euboian Homer, early in the eighth century B.C., is arresting and the arguments offered in its support impressive, there has not been a tide of scholarly consensus in Powell's direction. Most Homeric scholarship continues to favour composition in the Ionian Anatolian area, most likely in the late eighth century. The prominent Nagy "neo-analyst" school of interpretation argues for a successively recomposed sequence of

Homeric poems, culminating in fixed canonical texts only in the sixth century. This view meets with the formidable difficulty of explaining why the surviving versions of *Iliad* and *Odyssey* are as monumentally *intact* as they are, literarily and culturally. The fact that so little of their cultural content is demonstrably of post-700 provenance — even if some of it is — and that there may be discerned so coherent an identification of their "world" for the eighth century (with many surviving "fossil" elements from several centuries earlier) is hard to understand if the poems really had been the "mushrooming" or "snowballing" phenomena that Nagy's and cognate views suppose.

4 Jeffrey H. Tigay, *The Evolution of the Gilgamesh Epic* (University of Pennsylvania Press, 1982), p. 13.

5 The relevant Achaian, in the Hittite texts, is a person named Attarsiyas (who may or may not be a king of Ahhiyawa). In earlier, headier days it was speculated (by Forrer) that this might be Atreus. That option is now generally held to be implausible. I am unaware of any published conjectures of the suggestion I am making here. But the Mycenaean patronymic formed from *Atreus* should be Atreïos (cf. Telamonios). Just as *Taruisha*, or *Truisa*, in the Hittite texts, is taken (by some, not all) to be an Anatolian rendering of what Greeks hear and transmit as *Troia*, so we can speculate that *Atreïos* will present itself as *Atresios*. (The placename Karkisa appears also as Karkija; by analogy then we can have Truisa/ Truija — and Atresios/Atrejios, i.e., Atreïos, "son of 'Atreus.'" That an Achaian might be referred to in Hittite texts by a patronymic might seem unusual. If Atreus had been well-known to Hittites, or if a (mere) brother — Menelaos — of the Ahhiyawan/Achaian king was being referred to, that might make this intelligible. Certainly the Mycenaeans, like Homeric and later Greeks, use patronymic forms for personal reference regularly.

6 The consonance of Stesichorus and Herodotus notwithstanding, it need not have been the case that this postulated earliest record or tradition of the Trojan War to survive into classical times included the Helen-in-Egypt-throughout-the-war item. That item must have come from something, of course, and the goal of restoring the dignity of Helen the goddess — the putative reason for Stesichorus's revising an earlier work to compose the *Palinode* — does not seem adequate or plausible as its sole or primary basis. Helen *was* a goddess, likely before she appears as a human being in Homer. (In which regard, it is worth noting that, in the *Cypria*, Helen is daughter of Zeus and the goddess Nemesis, not the human

Leda; in the standard ancient conception, offspring both of whose parents are divine are themselves divine, whereas children of gods and mortals are, without special divine dispensation, mortal.) Herodotus may simply have been told a euhemerized version of the Stesichorus story, that story having originated with him. Or both may go back to something else, perhaps an idea that an image of the goddess (Helen?) was being held in Troy, and its recovery a primary goal of the siege (West suggests something along these lines); the Palladium story, which first appears in *The Little Iliad*, as far as we know, may point to something like this. At any rate, in the *Cypria* – and Stephanus Byzantius – the flesh-and-blood Helen appears to make it with Paris to Troy.

CHAPTER FIFTEEN

THE OTHER ODYSSEUS, THE FALSE

TROY, AND ORAL TRADITION

The original version of this paper was presented in a classics conference, on myth and genre, at the University of Guelph, in March 2002.

In this chapter, I want to explore some elements of the Trojan War story as it developed in the period subsequent to the composition of the *Iliad* and the *Odyssey*, notably in the *Cypria*. The *Cypria* was the lengthiest of the six post-Homeric epic poems that were later grouped together as the Trojan War part of the so-called Epic Cycle. (The whole Epic Cycle, at least in later times when the sequence was made canonical, comprised 10 works: the *War of the Titans*, three works on the Theban wars, and the six Trojan War poems.) These poems, also composed in dactylic hexameter verse, filled in the chronological gaps between the events depicted in the *Iliad* and the *Odyssey*, and prior and subsequent to the action of both, so that the whole verse structure, Homer plus the six Epic Cycle compositions, comprised for later periods in antiquity a complete recounting of matters Ilian from a first planning of the Trojan War on the part of Zeus to the final fates of the children of Odysseus — perhaps about 50 years of what the classical Greeks conceived as their heroic age of earlier time.[1]

None of the poems of the Epic Cycle survived antiquity, though the whole group seems still to have been extant well into the Roman imperial period. Our most detailed knowledge of their content stems from summaries of the poems that were compiled by a late author named Proclus, who *may* have been the fifth century A.D. Neoplatonist philosopher of that name, and which were in turn set out by the ninth-century Byzantine scholar and Patriarch Photius. We have, in addition, a number of quotations from poems in the cycle, and citations of details of fact or plot in several authors.

The judgment both of antiquity and the modern period, going as it has had to do by surviving fragments and summaries, has been that these poems were composed well after Homer, and were derivative and inferior, their demise accordingly understandable if not merited. A modest case was made by a few scholars in the 20th century that one of the Cycle, notably, the *Aethiopis,* which related events immediately after the *Iliad,* when the Amazons and then the Ethiopians arrived to aid the Trojans, was of Homeric or even possibly earlier date.[2] Certainly the *Odyssey* does seem to presuppose at least much of the detail of story that the *Aethiopis* relates. However, here too the settled assessment of most scholars has been that this poem, like the rest of the Epic Cycle, is to be placed well into the seventh century B.C., or even, in the case of some of the Cycle, the sixth century, and the whole Cycle to be understood as self-consciously echoing, and only feebly aspiring to keep company with, the monumental anchors of the *Iliad* and the *Odyssey.*

It has been noted, for example by Gilbert Murray in a still useful discussion of almost a century ago,[3] that the conception of a Cycle is misleading, suggesting as it may some corporate effort of composition, with a division of labour and a deliberate attempt to cover just so much of what Homer has not covered. We simply do not know just when or where or by whom the poems of the Cycle were composed, or whether there may not have been a plurality of attempts at recounting the events at Troy before and after the *Iliad,* only some surviving. We know from Hesiod's *Works and Days* that from a very early period there were clustered two primary groups of heroic-age tales centred on wars at Thebes and at Troy. There may also have been other independent bodies of oral heroic poetry focused on Perseus, the

Argonauts, a complex of Aitolian and neighboring heroes and stories, Herakles, and possibly others, as well as theogonies and other recountings of gods' activities, but of a Theban *matter* and a Trojan from periods well before (likely several centuries before) Homer there seems little or no doubt.

There is quite a lot, of course, that is simply not known, or knowable, about early stages of Theban and Trojan saga. Quite what degree of fluidity, and invention, and local variation in details of the stories is exceedingly difficult even to conjecture with any confidence. It seems very highly probable that these saga clusters go back to Mycenaean times, specifically to actual battles and wars involving Peloponnesian Greeks on one side and inhabitants of Bronze Age Thebes and Hisarlik respectively on the other side, with continuous transmission of tales of these battles and wars down to the period of composition of the *Iliad* and the *Odyssey* in the later eighth century B.C.; but, obviously, as well, with quite considerable accretion of sheer poetic invention and intrusion of originally quite alien material, legendary and mythological, as the generations subsequent to the actual falls of Thebes and Troy in the 13th century B.C. proceeded. As well as new intrusive material that joined the large aggregation of heroic age story, there must also have been material, whether old and traditional or of later date, that itself did not survive to be transmitted to the formation of the heroic age *canon.* That canon, including what were understood to be inconsistent variant versions of parts of stories (e.g., the real Helen either going to Troy or not doing so) had largely coalesced and settled before Aeschylus achieved his first theatrical victory, in 484 B.C. (interestingly, exactly 700 years after the traditional date of the fall of Troy). Thereafter, the additions are largely matters of detail, or of dramatic or romantic elaboration.

The roles of Homer, and to a lesser extent of Hesiod, not just in the formation but also in the coalescing and jelling of heroic age canonicity, would be difficult to overstate. We appear justified in conceiving of two distinct schools of oral dactylic hexameter poetic composition, the one localized among the Ionian colonies of the midcoast western Anatolian region, the other in mainland Boeotia, from at least the beginning of the eighth century B.C., with individual creative giants, presumably really named Homer and Hesiod respectively, composers of at least the overwhelming cores of the *Iliad* and the *Works and Days* respectively, the two monumental avatars and subsequent iconic anchors of these two schools or traditions, whose productions were soon thereafter a common legacy of the entire Greek world. The mutual relations and antecedents of Homer and Hesiod are themselves a problem that is not addressed here. There are important differences of mythological detail between them; yet the two schools speak essentially the same language: i.e., with largely the same inherited formulaic vocabulary as well as dialect. They must then have stemmed from a common fount, and probably have continued interconnected, though it is difficult to understand how this can have occurred in the relatively Dark Age ninth century B.C. and earlier.

It must be said that there are also a great many uncertainties about our central data fulcrum, the *Cypria*. The work may have been composed at virtually any time in the period 700–575 B.C. (Or even later. J. Wachernagel argued on linguistic grounds for a date of composition not long before 500 B.C.; Malcolm Davies, likewise, dates most of the Epic Cycle, and certainly the *Cypria,* to the second half of the sixth century.)

The classic Homeric question—a single author, or a multiplicity—applies quite unresolved in the case of the *Cypria*. We are told that the work consisted of 11 books—presumably then of about 7,000 verses or so—but even some of the ancient references seem to refer to a plurality of authors. The poem spans so wide a period of heroic age time—from before the marriage of Peleus and Thetis to just before the beginning of the *Iliad*, in the 10th year of the Trojan War—that it was conceived by ancient writers as a string of episodes, without literary or thematic unity. The author was thought to be Homer himself, or his supposed son-in-law Stasinos, or other shadowy early poets, or a group of

Cypriot poets (Stasinos possibly among them)—thus the title, whose exact significance is unclear (reflecting the provenance of an author or the important presence of Aphrodite, the Cyprian goddess, in the poem?).

There seem also to have been distinct versions of the poem, or else different poems of the same name, for our summaries say that Paris and Helen fled Lakedaimon for Phoenicia to avoid pursuit, but Herodotus tells us (2.117) that he has read in the *Cypria* that the lovers made it directly to Troy in three days (and that is why he knows that Homer was not creator of the *Cypria*, since in the *Iliad*, as in our summaries, Paris and Helen go from Lakedaimon to Sidon). The few fragments are not very helpful in these regards. They are in familiar epic dialect, with some novel forms, unsurprising in a seventh-century work.

At any rate, there it is: an interesting, wide-ranging account of the Trojan story before the events of the *Iliad*.

The "other" Odysseus was a Trojan War character who, so far as we can tell, first appears in the *Cypria*. It does seem that he figures also in the Epic Cycle's *Nostoi*, the Returns of the Achaian leaders (other than Odysseus) after the fall of Troy. But otherwise there is no indication of awareness of him anywhere else in the Epic Cycle, so, since he does not appear at all anywhere in the Homeric or Hesiodic corpora, he may really be an innovation of and from the *Cypria*.

The character in question is Palamedes. Though post-Homeric, and indeed, in many respects anti-Homeric, Palamedes came to have a sizeable presence in what we are calling the full and canonical Troy saga. The core of the story is set out in the *Cypria*, where Palamedes is encountered as one of the Argive recruiting team who are seeking to enlist the committed involvement of sundry Achaian kings and chieftains in the projected war against Troy. The original cluster comprises, it seems clear, the Catalogue of Ships regions or states of Mykenai, Lakedaimon, and Argos—the regions led at Troy by Agamemnon, Menelaos, and Diomedes. They have proceeded to involve, it appears, the rest of the Peloponnesus; most importantly, Nestor of Pylos.

Soon thereafter the recruiting team proceed westwards to the island kingdom of Ithaka. Laertes is evidently king, but too advanced in years to lead his people to war (even though he will continue to soldier on, as it were, a good 30 years more in Ithaka). The role should fall then to his son Odysseus. Recently married and now the father of an infant son, Odysseus is reluctant to leave home, and pretends to be mad in order to avoid the summons to war. The *Cypria* may or may not present this as Odyssean cowardice; perhaps the poet, who more or less demonstrably knew the *Iliad* and presumably also the *Odyssey,* conceived this as prefiguring the would-be homebody of the latter work, or reflecting prescience or echoing the prophecy of the Ithakan Halitherses, related in the *Odyssey* (ii.172-176), of how late it would be before the hero made it back home. In the *Odyssey* the prophecy is made at the time the Achaians set sail, but Hyginus, in the *Fabulae,* links it to the feigned madness incident, as the author of the *Cypria* may also have done. The *Odyssey* is aware of Odysseus's reluctance to go to the war, Agamemnon later noting (xxiv.118f.) that "we were a whole month crossing over the wide sea, having hardly persuaded Odysseus." At any rate, evidence of Odysseus's insanity is provided (as Hyginus later tells it) by the hero's yoking a horse and an ox to a plow. It is Palamedes who uncovers the ruse, evidently — this is how it happens in the later retellings — by placing the infant Telemachos in his father's path. When Odysseus turns his plough to avoid injuring or killing his son, his sham madness is uncovered, and he agrees to join the Achaian coalition with the Ithakan forces.

Two elements of the story point to the dominant features of Palamedes' whole presence in the Troy tale. Odysseus is famed for being clever, wily, and inventive. But Palamedes has outsmarted him. Palamedes is represented as the cleverest and most inventive of all the Achaians at Troy — in fact, of all the Achaians of his time. So clever is he that as the story enlarges, a number of inventions and discoveries are assigned to Palamedes. Apparently first in the writings of Stesichorus, he is said to have been an inventor. Among his discoveries were said to be some of the letters of the alphabet, the game of dice, putting military units into formations, structured meal times, arithmetic, and the practice of counting. The latter alleged achievement, in fact, is later lampooned by Plato. In the *Republic* (vii. 523) Plato debunks Palamedes' arithmetical contributions with the remark that if this had been so, we would need to suppose that before Palamedes produced this wonder, Agamemnon would not have been able to know, or to count, how many feet he had.

At any rate, Palamedes comes to figure among the cultural heroes of the Greeks, along with Prometheus and Cadmus, as having discovered or provided humanity with fundamental items of civilized life.

The second notable element of the Palamedes story launched from his first appearance in the Troy saga is the enmity of Odysseus. Because Palamedes has uncovered his ruse, or because he is a rival as a clever counsellor and military organizer, Odysseus forms undying animosity towards Palamedes, which continues relentless and unabated until the accomplishment of Palamedes' death, years afterward, shortly before the opening scenes of the *Iliad*.

The transformation in the post-Homeric story of Odysseus from admirable—one of the bravest and strongest of the heroes, the many-resourced much-enduring warrior and family man of *Iliad* and *Odyssey*—to odious: the deceitful, malicious henchman of the worst schemes of the Atreidai and some fell deeds altogether of his own contrivance, is itself a genre theme of interest, and one that has been studied at some length. (W. B. Stanford's *The Ulysses Theme* gives it particularly detailed attention.[4]) Just as a later classical reader, or audience, will need to be alerted whether a given retelling will have Helen go to Troy or, rather, have been divinely deposited in Egypt for Menelaos to retrieve her there, so too will there be need to know whether Odysseus is hero or villain in someone's later rendering. He can be either. Subsequent to the period of the Epic Cycle, he is more often the villain than the hero. Yet, and not just because of the never-lost power and influence of the great Homeric poems, Odysseus never loses representability in positive mode.

Whether Odysseus' post-Homeric moral descent is a natural and self-contained evolution from his aboriginal wiliness and cleverness—anyone that smart and that tricky (already in the *Odyssey*, a liar several times) can't but use these traits also for ill—or whether the progression critically involves Palamedes, as a rival Wily Lad (or has still other causes), may be difficult to determine. It seems to be an old and regular feature of heroic stories and folktales for the hero celebrated for attribute X to meet one day, in one of his adventures, someone who outdoes him in that attribute. King Arthur and Robin Hood have such encounters. Odysseus is shrewd and clever. Palamedes, contrapuntally, is shrewder and cleverer. In some versions of such story structures, the encounter is a one-off matter, the character who wins out in X just disappearing thereafter; more often, at least in non-Greek cases, the "X-ier" character then joins the band, becomes a friend and ally, usually a subordinate, after the initial rivalry.

This is just one area, however, where Greek cases conform only very imperfectly to the rest of the world's Stith Thompson-type folktale models.[5] In Greek stories, the best usually stays the best, and enmities are reversed only where they have been passionate bursts of anger over perceived wrongs (and usually also where prophecy is thought to have needed them to have occurred). At any rate, clever Odysseus meets someone cleverer than himself, and he can't abide it. He comes, in fact, to enlist his companion in arms Diomedes in his machinations to bring about Palamedes' destruction—in the *Cypria* they cause him to drown while he is fishing; in later versions they stone him at the bottom of a well, or Odysseus plants forged evidence of treason in Palamedes' tent, which leads to his stoning by the whole army.

For all that, Palamedes becomes a figure of significance in the canonical Troy saga—there were tragedies about him by each of the three great Attic tragedians, and his father's attempts to obtain restitution for his death from the Achaians produce important elements of plot in the later versions of the Nostoi, or Returns of the Achaian heroes from Troy—Palamedes remains also shadowy, ephemeral. There can be no doubt that Homer doesn't simply ignore him; he is unknown to him, and almost certainly only comes into the tale, likely into any tale, in the vicinity of the *Cypria*. He is son of Nauplios, who is himself either son of Poseidon or (as he is in Apollonius Rhodius) fifth-generation descendant of an earlier Nauplios who was son of Poseidon. Genealogical variability is not, of course, unknown in the myths; still, this lineage variation seems unusually unanchored. Palamedes does not have his own military contingent, at least none that is identified for us. Moreover, there is no record of anyone whom he kills, at Troy or elsewhere.

He is an Argive; that is, from the Argolid. His father is eponym for the coastal town of Nauplia, a few kilometres from Tiryns. The place is not named in Homer, possibly because its name doesn't scan in epic verse unless the final syllable (in nominative or dative forms) precedes a vowel in the succeeding word, which can shorten it. At any rate it was a Mycenaean site, and prominent in and after the eighth century B.C. At some early stage Nauplios was explicitly said to be from Nauplia — and presumably "baron" or local "basileus" of the place; hence his son likewise. Most likely Nauplios is a fictional creation of oral poetry, the name supplied by an oral context needing an Argive patronymic, and consciousness of Argolic place names in the poet's mind producing this one. That said, Nauplios was to have a life of his own in the heroic age canon, and, indeed, to serve a lynchpin role in connecting the two components of my theme, as will be seen presently.

Just as Nauplios is thought to be named for the port of Nauplia, Palamedes is sometimes said to derive his name from the citadel of Nauplia, which was called the Palamidi. The latter name is only attested, however, from a late date, and it seems possible that the hill is named for the hero rather than the hero for the hill. At any rate, there seems no doubt that Nauplia and environs is from the beginning — likely, that is to say, from the time of composition of the *Cypria* — the domicile in heroic age story of Nauplios and his son Palamedes.

It became standard for the fathers of the Achaians at Troy to be incorporated into the heroic ventures of the previous generation, so it is unsurprising to find Nauplios numbered among the Argonauts. He seems to be first listed in that company by Apollonius Rhodius, but the inclusion might have been made earlier, in a lost tragedian's play. In any case, there is no reason to see him as having any old presence on the Argo. If Nauplios is thought of as an Argonaut, he must also be conceived as extremely long-lived, since he is said to be responsible for serious mayhem visited in revenge upon the Achaian leadership following the sack of Troy.

The early epic has in general a remarkably consistent as well as astonishingly elaborate chronology. This is most manifest in Homer himself. For example, Helen, in the *Iliad,* tells us (xxiv.765f.) that it is the 20th year since she left Lakedaimon with Paris. This seems surprising, given that it is just the 10th year of the Trojan War. But there needs to be have been time since that elopement for the teenage Achilles (whom "Hesiod" tells us [*Catalogues of Women and Eoaie,* fr. 68] was too young to have been among the suitors of Helen) to be recruited for the war, and to manage to get to Skyros, where he fathers Neoptolemos, who will himself be old enough to be brought to Troy to fight and participate in the sack, following his father's death. *Many* features of heroic chronology cohere and work out in the sort of way this cluster of data exhibits. Nauplios had come to Troy, as mentioned, to seek restitution for Palamedes' death. This denied, he is said to have visited Achaian capitals and coaxed chieftains' or kings' wives to adultery, and afterwards planted beacons on the treacherous southern coast of the island of Euboia, which led to the shipwreck and destruction of many Achaians. Although it is not mentioned in our summaries of the poem, this last detail may possibly have figured in the Epic Cycle's *Nostoi*, since we know that Palamedes is referred to in that lost work; or it may be a later addition.

It may seem odd that Palamedes, an Argive, should incur the enmity and abandonment of the Achaian leadership (and not just

Odysseus). According to the geography of the *Iliad's* Catalogue of Ships, Nauplia should lie within the territory whose people are led at Troy by Diomedes, with Sthenelos and Euryalos as his lieutenants. Homer gives no support for the idea that Diomedes is king — wanax — of this territory, and I have argued elsewhere that we should conceive the Argolic region concerned as a province of a great multi-provinced Argive Achaian state, whose capital is Mykenai and whose wanax is Agamemnon.[6] At any rate, it seems odd that Diomedes has it in for Palamedes. The similar formations of their names may suggest that the two are contrapuntally opposed, in story; that just as Palamedes is "the other Odysseus," so is he, in some more obscure fashion, "the other Diomedes."

There are other opaque mysteries in this regard. The *Iliad's* declared sequence of wanaktes "of many islands and over all Argos" (ii. 104–108) is Pelops-to-Atreus-to-Thyestes-to-Agamemnon, which sequence we know, from the *Odyssey*, is continued with Aigisthos-to-Menelaos-to-Orestes. A single dynastic house, but no simple primogenitural succession. The canonical account explains the sequence as due to fratricide, then cousin-murder, and exile. Perhaps these are echoes of real late Bronze Age civil faction and dynastic strife. At any rate, when Orestes kills Aigisthos, a late account — in Pausanias (I.xxii.8) — tells us that Orestes' comrade Pylades despatches "the sons of Nauplius who had come to bring Aegisthus succour." Nauplios had had other sons besides Palamedes, and Pylades will be killing them. But why would they be seeking to aid Aigisthos against his avenging cousin's son? The *Odyssey*, in an oblique passage (iv.517f.), suggests that Aigisthos' own territories had been in the Argolic promontory. If so, this could suggest alliance or connection with folks from Nauplia, nearby. Otherwise, we need to see Naupliadai as supporting Aigisthos as the foe of the Atreidai, who bore some responsibility, at least, for Palamedes' death.

There is one other significant appearance of Nauplios in the canon. Before coming to it, I want to return to the *Cypria*, and its second contribution to my larger myth-genre theme, namely, the "false Troy."

As the *Cypria* tells the story, the Achaians gather in Aulis for their expedition against Troy, set sail, and make a mistaken landfall, not in the Troad, but a few hundred kilometres further south, in Teuthrania, a part of the region known then and later as Mysia. Neither realizing nor, still more oddly, discovering their error, the Achaians assault the town they have come to — the Teuthranian capital – which is stoutly and ably defended by its king, Telephos, a son of Herakles. Telephos kills several Achaians, most prominently Thersandros, son of Polyneikes, the Theban chieftain. The day is saved only by Achilles, who wounds Telephos with his spear (a divine gift from his parents' wedding). At this stage the Achaians finally learn their mistake, and depart, only to have their fleet scattered by unhelpful winds. They then must reassemble the fleet, which, astonishingly, takes a good eight years. The reconvening duly achieved, the fleet once again marshals itself at Aulis, and once again — though this time, only following the putative sacrifice of Agememnon's daughter Iphigeneia (who is first known from this context in the *Cypria*) — they sail, now successfully, to Troy. The *Cypria* adds that Telephos' wound had festered, and he came to Greece — to Aulis? — to be cured of it from its original source, Achilles' spear. This folk magic having been efficacious, Telephos had guided the Achaians to Troy, since, apparently, they still weren't sure how to get there.

All of this is a most odd and peculiar story. It does not seem plausible to account for it as a literary development from, or reaction to, the Homeric account. Moreover, Telephos is not an invention of the *Cypria*. The *Odyssey* knows of him as father of Eurypylos, a late arriving Trojan ally, who brings his warrior Keteioi to the aid of Priam and his people, only to be killed by Neoptolemos, son of Achilles, the most prominent figure Neoptolemos is said to despatch. Priam had bribed Eurypylos's mother to bring this force to Trojan succour at this late hour of the war. Telephos also figures importantly in the Hesiodic corpus, where, in the *Catalogues of Women and Eioae* (composed, M. L. West argues, ca. 540–520 B.C., though incorporating much older material), we find at least a version of the general contours of his story as it was to appear in the full canon.

Telephos was son of Herakles and Auge, daughter of Aleos king of Tegea, in Arkadia. (Both Auge and Aleos are yet further eponymously named characters, Aleos for Alea—either the Arkadian town of that name, or a temple of Athena Alea, in nearby Tegea itself; Auge's name will derive from the town of Augeiai, presumably the one in Lakedaimon.) Herakles had stopped there, and, drunk, had sexually assaulted Auge. The resulting pregnancy had enraged her father, who did not believe or accept his daughter's account of her condition. Full details of just what happens next vary considerably in different ancient sources. They all involve Auge ending up in Teuthrania, where she either marries or is adopted as daughter by Teuthras, the eponymous king there. In the version given in the Hesiodic *Catalogues*, it is even suggested that Auge was already in Teuthrania when Herakles stopped by, en route to Troy, where he was to bring back the horses of Laomedon as one of his labours, and there raped or seduced Auge, with Telephos the result. But more usually, Telephos is born in Arkadia. He then either accompanies his mother across the Aegean Sea, or joins her there only in young adulthood, having grown up in the Peloponnesus and been oracularly advised to seek and find his mother in Mysia. There is a lot of variation, even confusion, then. In due course, though, Telephos is in Teuthrania, and succeeds Teuthras as king, whether as his son-in-law, adoptive son, or adoptive grandson.

The story or stories of Auge, Telephos, and Teuthras are of familiar type—they resemble those of Danae and Perseus, for example—and they figure prominently in classical art, and literature. All three of the great Attic tragedians wrote (entirely lost) trilogies involving Telephos and his family.

What to make of this complex of characters, and this strange, even bizarre double gathering at Aulis, and double assault on Asian kingdoms, both taken to be Troy? In a very fine, entertaining, and scholarly 1946 volume, *Folk Tale, Fiction and Saga in the Homeric Epics*, Rhys Carpenter takes up the issue with energy and imagination. He notes, in fact, a systematic resemblance in details of plot between the Homeric Troy and the Teuthranian "false Troy" and their respective Achaian assaults (in the second case those details coming from a variety of ancient sources). He notes as well the striking fact of double naming of Trojan places in the *Iliad* (most notably of all, of course, Troy and Ilios), and that many of the doubled names are found also as place names in classical Mysia. Thus, Pergamos (or Pergamon), the citadel of Ilios in Homer (where the town is called alternatively Ilios, Troy, and Pergamos), is the name of a rocky ridge above the river Kaikos — the river that runs through Teuthrania from the Aegean. "In addition to Pergamos [Carpenter tells us], the Iliad seems to have borrowed two other place names from the Teuthranian version. Myrina (which in the Iliad is used of a burial mound with an alternate and perhaps correct local name of Batieia) was an actual place name in Teuthrania for an Aeolic town opposite the Kaikos mouth; near by to the south, at Kyme, there flowed an actual river Xanthos" (p. 57) — recall the double-named Trojan river, Skamandros/Xanthos.

Carpenter does not, but we may, note the curious appearance of double personal names of two Trojan figures. Thus, the Trojan prince who has eloped with Helen is both Paris and Alexandros; and Hektor's infant son is both Astyanax and Skamandrios. Only one Achaian in the canonical Trojan War story has two names. Curiously, this is Neoptolemos, also known (though not in Homer) as Pyrrhos. Just as one might suppose that Paris belongs originally at just one of the Troys, and Alexandros originally at the other, so one could view, also, Neoptolemos and Pyrrhos.

Carpenter's speculative suggestion is that Aeolians and Ionans — both of them invading colonizers on the northwestern and western Anatolian coast, from different parts of the Greek mainland — had distinct, though overlapping, traditions of a Trojan War of the heroic past. For the Aeolians, Troy was in

Teuthrania, and for the Ionians it was further north, at Ilios—i.e., at Hisarlik. Carpenter thinks neither tradition very reliable, even if both may go back to Mycenaean oral record of actual wars. Homer, for this view, has become aware of the two traditions, and as an Ionian favours his own, but at the same time seeks to blend and incorporate both. This will correspond, interestingly, to the long-noted minor-key presence of Aeolic linguistic forms in the generally Ionian epic dialect Homer uses.

Carpenter notes, as well, the Homeric account of Achilles' successful raids on 23 towns or places in the general vicinity of Troy, 11 captured on land, 12 by sea, in the period just prior to the action of the *Iliad*. Many of these places are named, and they are about equidistant between Ilios and Teuthrania, hence available—so to speak—as raiding sites for either Troy.

A variant of Carpenter's thesis is encouraged by a number of the inferences that have been drawn from the Hittite tablets of the late Bronze Age. There are oblique indications of a league of western Anatolian states in the 13th century B.C. (some more recent redatings say the 14th century) centred on a kingdom of Assuwa, which is thought likely to be the original of the Greek Aswia—with the earlier "w" sound dropped, Asia. This league or alliance seems plausibly to have stretched from Troy—the "real" Troy; that is, Hisarlik—in the north to Lykia in the south. The declining Hittite empire went to war against this Assuwan league, and subsequent references to the king of Achaiwa operating on the Anatolian mainland in the aftermath of this war have been argued, not unreasonably, to provide a historical setting for the real Trojan War. Assuming, as seems persuasive, that Achaiwa is "Argos Achaiwikon"—the Peloponnesian kingdom centred in Mykenai—we are invited to think of a series of raids or warring forays, some of them of considerable scale, on a number of towns or centres of the weakened Assuwan league, one of them Hisarlik, another Teuthrania, and others places Achilles is said by Homer to have raided. We can easily think of these forays or raids as taking place over a period of several years, even decades, and being perceived in folk memory, and oral heroic poetry, as the wars of the Atreidai on Troy.

G. L. Huxley, A. R. Burn, and others have noted that the *Odyssey's* Keteioi—who are otherwise quite unknown in the canon—are plausibly taken to be Hittites, and that their prince Eurypylos can be a Hittite Urpalla, just as his father Telephos can be Hittite Telepinush, and, for that matter, Teuthras, the eponym of Teuthrania, might derive from the Hittite Tudhaliyas—the third last Hittite emperor was the fourth sovereign of the name (and reigned 1250–1220 B.C., close at least to the presumed date of the fall of Troy). Even if these derivations had substance, they would by no means imply actual Achaian wars with Hittites: Bronze Age lodging of known Hittite names in sources that fed into the expanding oral epos would do.

This is not the place to explore these suggested historical or part-historical roots of the Trojan cycle in any serious or detailed way. It does seem almost certain that that cycle has such roots, along with others—bits of extraneous religious myth, and a very generous portion of sheer poetic invention, most notably. What is almost equally certain is that without concrete historical and archaeological grounding from the original historical period, it is almost impossible to tell what among the scattered array of detail of name and story in the later canon has these roots, or what earlier shape or form those roots might have had. This last is perhaps the point I want most to insist on. It is possible to have a reasonably firm sense that some item is not poetic fiction or elaboration, and probably goes back to *something* that was historical—real people, of those (or resembling) names, doing real things, memory or echo of which was launched on a journey of transmission to a much later time—without having a very good or clear idea of what that something was, or even what it may reasonably be conjectured to have been. This may lead, methodologically, to a result that might be compared to having some pieces of a rather large jigsaw puzzle with no basis from which to hope to assemble even parts of the whole thing.

One indicator, in the oral epic, that something is not poetic invention is that the name for it is metrically problematic. The metrical rules of dactylic hexameter scansion seem to have been stricter originally than they were subsequently allowed to become to accommodate some necessary names. The name of the goddess Aphrodite does not, for example, properly scan, containing as it does a long then a short then a long syllable. But the poets had to be able to refer to Aphrodite. So the first syllable is treated as short, in order to be able to have her appear in epic verse. Similarly, the name Herakles does not scan in its original longer (nominative) form Heraklewes (consisting of two long syllables, then a short, then a long). So, in Homeric verse, the hero appears, usually, in the poetically vivid form *bie Herakleweie* (with four long syllables, two shorts, then two longs) "the Heraklean might." I take this fact to more or less prove that Herakles was not invented for the oral epic, at any stage in its history.

Since his name is *theophoric*—formed from a god's name (Hera, in this case)—he cannot have been originally a god. So the earliest Herakles in stories was a human from outside the oral epic. I infer that it is extremely probable that there was a real historical Herakles, almost certainly a notable person of the late Mycenaen period. Examination of what appear to be the earliest surviving Herakles stories encourages the idea that he was a member of the dynastic family that preceded the Pelopids in Mykenai, and that his activities were localized in the eastern Peloponneus, and also the Cyclades—the island group that includes Rhodes and Kos—as well as the two Troys: the real one and the false one. If sound, these ideas will add him to the complex of jigsaw puzzle pieces that I think we can see in the intersection of legendary data of Homer, Hesiod—and the *Cypria*.

It remains to note that from a reasonably early stage of the formation of the Greek mythological canon, one story item links our two *Cypria*-derived themes. Among the several variant stories of how Auge, mother of Telephos, managed to get to Teuthrania are a number—there are variants of this variant—according to which Auge's father Aleos asked Nauplios of Nauplia (Tegea/ Alea and Nauplia are about 50 kilometres apart) to dispose of his pregnant daughter: either to kill her or sell her into slavery. Either out of compassion or realizing the market value of a princess, Nauplios instead secured Auge's passage to Teuthrania, the rest being, well, not history, but some irrecoverably oblique simulacrum of it.

Still another rather smaller nugget of linkage may be found in a tiny detail of the story of Palamedes as it is set out, fragmentarily and obliquely, in Alcidamas's fourth-century B.C. imaginary case for the prosecution against Palamedes placed in the mouth of Odysseus. Palamedes is on trial before the Achaian host, charged with having sought to betray the army to the Trojans. Odysseus alleges that an arrow has been recovered shot by a Trojan towards Palamedes, and containing details of his duplicitous plan in a written note attached to the arrow. The note purports to be from Paris to Palamedes. Remarkably, it asserts that Palamedes' treachery had been compacted between him and, not Priam, but Telephos.

My purpose in this chapter has been to present and offer reflections on two clusters of Trojan War story that appear first, so far as we know, in the lost *Cypria*, and that further probing show to have still further linkage: the clusters turn out to be intertwined in a curious way. At the same time, one of the clusters appears to be entirely fictional, in a literary sense: invented, so far as we can tell, within the confines of relatively late heroic epic; where the other, by contrast, appears to consist, at least in significant part, of opaque, broken jewels of story of the remotest antiquity, deriving from a tradition importantly distinct from the one that produced the dominant Ionian Trojan War conception. The two *Cypria* clusters may serve to illustrate in a generalizable way central typologies of Greek heroic saga, notably, invention from what appears to be a basis in folk-tale motifs, and a patchwork of several old story elements stitched together in ways that preserve those received elements, even if it is at the cost of narrative implausibility dictated by the towering anchorage of Homer. I am conscious that my own wanderings through these themes manifest a rather unfocused ensemble of speculation, and scattered data brought into uncertain conjunction. They are offered above all as fragmentary commentary on the lost work I have come to find of such interest, the *Cypria*.

NOTES

1 Useful discussions of the Epic Cycle, its circumstances of composition and assembly, and relevant dating and other issues posed by this body of poetry may be found in Martin L. West, ed. and trans., *Greek Epic Fragments* (Loeb Classical Library, 2003); Malcolm Davies, *The Greek Epic Cycle*, 2nd ed. (Bristol Classical Paperbacks, 1989); G. L. Huxley, *Greek Epic Poetry from Eumelos to Panyassis* (Faber and Faber, 1969); and Jonathan S. Burgess, *The Tradition of the Trojan War in Homer and the Epic Cycle* (Johns Hopkins, 2001).

2 Still more recently, Jonathan S. Burgess, *The Tradition of the Trojan War in Homer and the Epic Cycle* (Johns Hopkins, 2001), argues for a much more fluid body of early epic material that will have included versions of several of the poems of the Epic Cycle, independently and in some cases likely prior to the great Homeric epics. I don't myself find Burgess's overall case persuasive. He is an adherent of Gregory Nagy's "neo-analyst" school of Homeric interpretation, whose general stance seems to me problematic in a number of respects.

3 Gilbert Murray, *The Rise of the Greek Epic* (Oxford, 1907).

4 See W. B. Stanford, *The Ulysses Theme* (University of Michigan Press, 1968).

5 Stith Thompson, *Motif-Index of Folk-Literature*, 6 vols. (Indiana University Press, revised and enlarged ed., 1955–1958) remains the essential reference compilation for the recurrent patterns of the world's folk and fabulist literature.

6 See Peter Loptson, "Argos Achaiikon," *L'Antiquité Classique*, vol. 55, 1985.

BIBLIOGRAPHY

Aquinas, Thomas, *Summa Theologiae*. B. Leftow, trans. Cambridge University Press, 2006.

Bacon, Francis, *The Major Works*. B. Vickers, ed. Oxford University Press, 2002.

Bayle, Pierre, *Historical and Critical Dictionary: Selections*. Hackett, 1991.

Beattie, James, *An Essay on the Nature and Immutability of Truth, in Opposition to Sophistry and Scepticism* [1770]. Vol. 2 of J. Fieser, ed., *Scottish Common Sense Philosophy: Sources and Origins*. Thoemmes Press, 2000.

Bernasconi, Robert, ed., *Race*. Blackwell, 2001.

———, and Lott, Tommy L., eds., *The Idea of Race*. Hackett, 2000.

Bradley, F. H., *Appearance and Reality*. Oxford University Press, 1962.

Brandom, Robert, *Making It Explicit: Reasoning, Representing, and Discursive Commitment*. Harvard University Press, 1994.

Burgess, Jonathan S., *The Tradition of the Trojan War in Homer and the Epic Cycle*. Johns Hopkins University Press, 2001.

Butler, Samuel, *The Authoress of the Odyssey*. Ignibus, 2004.

Carnap, Rudolf, *Meaning and Necessity*. Phoenix Books, 1958.

———, *The Logical Structure of the World* and *Pseudoproblems in Philosophy*. R. George, trans. Group West, 2003.

Carpenter, Rhys, *Folk Tale, Fiction and Saga in the Homeric Epics*. University of California Press, 1946.

Caygill, Howard, *A Kant Dictionary*. Blackwell, 1995.

Cicero, *De Natura Deorum* and *Academica*. H. Rackham, trans. Harvard University Press, 1933.

Collingwood, R. G., *Essay on Metaphysics*. Oxford University Press, 1940.

Cornman, James W., and Lehrer, Keith, *Philosophical Problems and Arguments: An Introduction*. 1st ed. Macmillan, 1959.

Dante Alighieri, *The Divine Comedy of Dante Alighieri: Inferno*. Oxford University Press, 1961.

Danto, Arthur C., "Naturalism," *Encyclopedia of Philosophy*. Vol. II. Macmillan, 1967.

Darwin, Charles, *The Descent of Man, and Selection in Relation to Sex*. Princeton University Press, 1981 [1871].

Davidson, Donald, "The Method of Truth in Metaphysics," in Donald Davidson, *Inquiries into Truth and Interpretation*. Clarendon, 1984.

Davies, Malcolm, *The Greek Epic Cycle*, 2nd ed. Bristol Classical Paperbacks, 1989.

Dawkins, Richard, *The Selfish Gene*, 2nd ed. Oxford University Press, 1989.

Dennett, Daniel C., *Elbow Room: The Varieties of Free Will Worth Wanting*. MIT Press, 1984.

Descartes, René, *Principles of Philosophy*. Kluwer, 1982.

———, *Meditations on First Philosophy*. D. A. Cress, trans. Hackett, 1993.

Devitt, Michael, *Realism and Truth*. 2nd ed. Princeton University Press, 1997.

Dummett, Michael, "Can Analytical Philosophy Be Systematic, and Ought It to Be?", in K. Baynes, J. Bohman, T. McCarthy, eds., *After Philosophy*. MIT Press, 1987.

———, *Origins of Analytical Philosophy*. Harvard University Press, 1996.

Engel, Pascal, "Plenitude and Contingency: Modal Concepts in Nineteenth-Century French Philosophy," in Simo Knuuttila, ed., *Modern Modalities*. Kluwer, 1988.

Evelyn-Whyte, H.G., ed. and trans., *Hesiod, the Homeric Hymns and Homerica*. Harvard University Press, 1914.

Eze, Emmanuel Chukwudi, ed., *Race and the Enlightenment: A Reader*. Blackwell, 1997.

Field, Hartry, *Science Without Numbers: A Defence of Nominalism*. Princeton University Press, 1980.

Garber, D., Henry, J., Joy, L., and Gabbey, A., "New Doctrines of Body and its Powers, Place, and Space", in D. Garber and M. Ayers, *The Cambridge History of Seventeenth-Century Philosophy*, 2 vols. Cambridge University Press, 1998.

Graves, Robert, *Homer's Daughter*. Cassell and Company, 1955.

Hacking, Ian, *The Social Construction of What?* Harvard University Press, 1999.

Harris, Marvin, *The Rise of Anthropological Theory*. HarperCollins Publishers, 1968.

———, *Cultural Materialism.* Vintage, 1980.

Heidegger, Martin, *Being and Time.* J. Macquarrie and E. Robinson, trans. Harper & Row, 1962.

Hendel, Charles W., *Studies in the Philosophy of David Hume.* Bobbs Merrill, 1963.

Herodotus, *The History.* D. Grene, trans. University of Chicago Press, 1988.

Hobbes, Thomas, *The English Works of Thomas Hobbes.* Sir W. Molesworth, ed. vol. VII. Longman, 1845.

Homer, *The Iliad.* Richmond Lattimore, trans. University of Chicago Press, 1951.

———, *The Odyssey.* Richmond Lattimore, trans. Harper Collins, 2002.

Hume, David, *Enquiries Concerning the Human Understanding and Concerning the Principles of Morals.* Selby-Bigge, 2nd ed. Clarendon Press, 1902.

———, *A Treatise of Human Nature.* L. A. Selby-Bigge and P. H. Nidditch, eds., 2nd ed. Clarendon Press, 1978.

———, *Essays Moral, Political, and Literary.* Eugene F. Miller, ed. Liberty Fund, 1985.

———, *Dialogues Concerning Natural Religion.* Penguin, 1990.

Huxley, G. L., *Greek Epic Poetry from Eumelos to Panyassis.* Faber and Faber, 1969.

Ibn Khaldûn, *The Muqaddimah: An Introduction to History.* F. Rosenthal, trans. N. J. Dawood, ed. Princeton University Press, 1967.

Kant, Immanuel, *Foundations of the Metaphysics of Morals.* L. W. Beck, trans. Hackett, 1959.

———, *Religion within the Limits of Reason Alone.* H. H. Hudson and T. M. Greene, trans. Harper Collins, 1960.

———, *Critique of Pure Reason.* P. Guyer and A. W. Wood, trans. Cambridge University Press, 1999.

———, *Observations on the Feeling of the Beautiful and Sublime.* J. T. Goldthwait, trans. University of California Press, 2004.

———, *Religion and Rational Theology.* A. W. Wood and G. di Giovanni, trans. Cambridge University Press, 2006.

Knuuttila, Simo, *Modalities in Medieval Philosophy.* Routledge, 1993.

———, ed., *Modern Modalities.* Kluwer, 1988.

Kripke, Saul A., *Naming and Necessity.* Harvard University Press, 2006.

Lamb, Charles, *Essays of Elia.* University of Iowa Press, 2003 [1823].

La Mettrie, Julien Offray de, *Man a Machine* and *Man a Plant.* Hackett, 1994.

Lane Fox, Robin, *Alexander the Great.* E. P. Dutton, 1974.

Lansdowne, Marquis of, ed., *The Petty Papers*, 2 vols. Constable & Co., and Houghton Mifflin, 1927.

La Peyrère, Isaac, *Praeadamitae*. 1655.

Leahey, Thomas Hardy, *A History of Modern Psychology*, 2nd ed. Prentice Hall, 1994.

Linnaeus, Carl, *Systema naturae, sive regna tria naturae, systematice proposita per classes, ordines, genera & species*. Lugduni Batavorum, 1735.

———, *Systema naturae*, 9th ed. 1756.

———, *A General System of Nature Through the Three Grand Kingdoms of Animals, Vegetables, and Minerals Systematically Divided Into Their Several Classes, Orders, Genera, Species and Varieties Etc.*, 7 vols. Lackington (London), 1806.

Loptson, Peter, "Argos Achaiikon," *L'Antiquité Classique*, vol. 55, 1985.

———, "Spinozist Monism," *Philosophia*, vol. 18, no. 1, April 1988.

———, *Reality: Fundamental Topics in Metaphysics*. University of Toronto Press, 2001.

———, *Theories of Human Nature*, 3rd ed. Broadview, 2006.

Mackie, J. L., *Ethics: Inventing Right and Wrong*. Penguin Books, 1977.

McDowell, John, *Mind and World* (With a New Introduction by the Author). Harvard University Press, 1996.

Mineka, F. E., ed., *The Earlier Letters of John Stuart Mill 1812–1848 (The Collected Works of John Stuart Mill*, vol. XII.). University of Toronto Press, 1963.

Moore, G. E., *Philosophical Papers*. Macmillan, 1959.

———, *Principia Ethica*. Cambridge University Press, 1993.

Murray, Gilbert, *The Rise of the Greek Epic*. Oxford University Press, 1907.

The Nibelungenlied. A. T. Hatto, trans. Penguin, 1965.

Palter, Robert, "Hume and Prejudice," *Hume Studies*, vol. xxi, no. 1, April 1995.

Popkin, Richard H., "Hume's Racism," in Richard H. Popkin, *The High Road to Pyrrhonism*. Austin Hill Press, 1980.

———, "Hume's Racism Reconsidered," in Richard H. Popkin, *The Third Force in Seventeenth-Century Thought*. E. J. Brill, 1992.

Powell, Barry B., *Homer and the Origin of the Greek Alphabet*. Cambridge University Press, 1991.

———, *Writing and the Origins of Greek Literature*. Cambridge University Press, 2002.

———, *Homer*. Blackwell, 2004.

Putnam, Hilary, *Realism, Truth and History*. Cambridge University Press, 1981.

——, "Why Reason Can't Be Naturalized," in Hilary Putnam, *Philosophical Papers*, Vol. III. Cambridge University Press, 1983.

——, "Dewey Lectures," *Journal of Philosophy*, vol. xci, no. 9, Sept. 1994; republished (rev.) as *Threefold Cord: Mind, Body, and World.* Columbia University Press, 2001.

Redondi, Pietro, *Galileo Heretic*. Princeton University Press, 1987.

Reichenbach, Hans, *The Rise of Scientific Philosophy*. University of California Press, 1951.

Rorty, Richard, *Philosophy and the Mirror of Nature*. Princeton University Press, 1979.

——, *Truth and Progress*. Cambridge University Press, 1998.

Russell, Bertrand, *Mysticism and Logic*. George Allen and Unwin, 1917.

——, *Our Knowledge of the External World*. New American Library, 1960.

——, *Religion and Science*. Galaxy, 1961.

——, *The Autobiography of Bertrand Russell*. Vol. III. Unwin, 1969.

——, *The Analysis of Matter*. Routledge, 2001.

——, *The Analysis of Mind*. Dover, 2005.

——, *Human Knowledge: Its Scope and Limits*. Routledge, 2005.

Schopenhauer, Arthur, *The World as Will and Representation*, 2 vols. E. F. J. Payne, trans. Dover, 1966.

Sellars, Wilfrid, *Science, Perception and Reality*. Routledge & Kegan Paul, 1963.

Soames, Scott, *Philosophical Analysis in the Twentieth Century*, 2 vols. Princeton University Press, 2005.

Spinoza, Benedict, *Ethics*. S. Hampshire and E. Curley, trans. Penguin Books, 2005.

Stanford, W. B., *The Ulysses Theme*. University of Michigan Press, 1968.

Stephanus of Byzantium, *Ethnika*.

Stich, Stephen, *Deconstructing the Mind*. Oxford University Press, 1996.

Strawson, P. F., *Individuals*. Methuen, 1959.

Stroud, Barry, "The Charm of Naturalism," *Proceedings and Addresses of the American Philosophical Association* 70, 2, Nov. 1996.

Tarski, Alfred, "The Semantic Conception of Truth and the Foundations of Semantics," in H. Feigl and W. Sellars, eds., *Readings in Philosophical Analysis*. Appleton Century Cross, 1949.

Thompson, Stith, *Motif-Index of Folk-Literature*, 6 vols. Indiana University Press, 1955–1958.

Tigay, Jeffrey H., *The Evolution of the Gilgamesh Epic*. University of Pennsylvania Press, 1982.

Vaihinger, Hans, *The Philosophy of As If*. K. Paul, Trench, Teubner & Co., 1925.

Van Fraassen, Bas, "Science, Materialism, and False Consciousness," in J. Kvanvig, ed., *Warrant in Contemporary Epistemology*. Rowman and Littlefield, 1996.

Vico, Giambattista, *The New Science of Giambattista Vico*. Cornell University Press, 1968.

Voegelin, Eric, *The History of the Race Idea from Ray to Carus*. Louisiana State University Press, 1998.

Voltaire, *The Works of Voltaire*. v. XXXIX: *Short Studies in English and American Subjects*. Werner, 1905.

———, *Philosophy of History*. Philosophical Library, 1965.

Wade-Gery, H. T., *The Poet of the Iliad*. Cambridge University Press, 1952.

West, Martin L., ed. and trans., *Greek Epic Fragments*. Loeb Classical Library, 2003.

Whitehead, Alfred North, *Process and Reality*. Macmillan, 1929.

Whyte, Iain, *Scotland and the Abolition of Black Slavery, 1756–1838*. Edinburgh University Press, 2006.

Wilson, Fred, *The Logic and Methodology of Science in Early Modern Thought*. University of Toronto Press, 1999.

Wittgenstein, Ludwig, *Tractatus Logico-Philosophicus*. D. F. Pears and B. McGuinness, trans. Routledge, 2001.

INDEX